About the Authors

Niki Tudge MBA PCBC-A CDBC CDT

Niki Tudge is the founder of The Pet Professional Guild, DogNostics Career Center, The DogSmith and the president of Doggone Safe. She is equipped with a unique combination of business experience, pet training and pet behavior expertise, a background in exceptional customer service, certification as a trainer of trainers, and many years consulting to pet rescue groups. She is also a certified project manager and Six Sigma Black Belt.

Susan Nilson BA (Hons) DipCABT PCBC-A

Susan Nilson began her career with Reuters in London, England, and has over 15 years' editorial experience in print and digital publications across Europe, Asia and the Middle East. She is currently managing editor of *BARKS from the Guild*. She is also a companion animal behavior consultant and trainer (Centre of Applied Pet Ethology) and an accredited professional canine behavior consultant (Pet Professional Accreditation Board).

Debra Millikan PCBC-A AABP-CABT CAP2

Debra Millikan has over 40 years' experience in dog training that has seen her involved in conformation, obedience judging, pet manners classes and puppy pre-school. Currently, she serves on the board of the Pet Professional Guild, Doggone Safe, the Companion Animal Sciences Institute and the Association of Animal Behavior Professionals. She also trains aspiring instructors at Canine Behavioural School in Adelaide, South Australia.

Louise Stapleton-Frappell BA (Hons) PCT- A PCBC-A CAP³ CTDI DN-FSG DN-CPCT CWRI

Louise Stapleton-Frappell is a partner and faculty member of DogNostics Career Center and board member of The Pet Professional Guild. A professional canine trainer and behavior consultant accredited via the Pet Professional Accreditation Board, she is also the regional coordinator of Doggone Safe in Spain and the owner and head trainer of The DogSmith of Estepona, Spain.

Pet Training and Behavior Consulting: A Model for Raising the Bar to Protect Professionals, Pets and Their People

Contents

Foreword 1

Executive Summary 9
    Booming Industry 9
    The Need for Change 11
    Your Role in the Transition 12

Chapter One: What Is Occupational Licensing? 14
    The Process of Licensing 16
    Pets and Their Influence on Our Culture 18
    Industry Certification 18
    Summary 20

Chapter Two: Living Property - The Need for a New Legal Definition 22
    Are Pets Family? 22
    What Do Dogs, Cats, Cars and Chairs Have in Common? 22
    The Issue of Sentience 23
    What Need Does Pet Ownership Fulfil? 24
    Pets as People 25
    Owner vs. Guardian 27
    Legal Times Are Changing 29
    Living Property 30
    Summary 31

Chapter Three: Professionals Should Exemplify and Promote Anti-Cruelty Statutes 37
    Cruelty Cases 37
    Public Policy 38
    Normative Behavior Toward Pets 41
    Truth in Training 42
    Abusive Training Practices 44

Pet Training and Behavior Consulting: A Model for Raising the Bar to Protect Professionals, Pets and Their People

Foreword

In this book, we will present our views on the need for a level and model of oversight in the pet services industry – specifically in the fields of training and behavior consulting – and for those choosing to practice within it. We will discuss the prevalence of individuals who hold no credentials, formal education, knowledge or skills, yet who are today working across the nation with full responsibility for the well-being and welfare of their unknowing clients' precious pets. We will also highlight the lack of consumer protection and transparency across the marketing and operations platforms of many pet services-related businesses, as well as the inherent challenges with how pets are legally classified, and how the lack of reported and enforced animal cruelty laws means there is insufficient protection for pets and their owners when it comes to holding professionals accountable for their methodology, approach and philosophy toward their craft and toward the people and animals they serve.

This body of work is continually being reviewed and revised. Please visit www.PetindustryRegulation.com for the updated text, sectional PDF downloads, and support resources.

Niki J. Tudge
Susan J. Nilson
Debra A. Millikan
Louise A. Stapleton-Frappell
June 2019

> "Until one has loved an animal, a part of one's soul remains unawakened." – Anatole France

This book is dedicated to the millions of pets who share our lives, our homes and our love – You deserve better!

Pet Training and Behavior Consulting: A Model for Raising the Bar to Protect Professionals, Pets and Their People – 1st edn.

DogNostics Career Center Publishing © 2019. All rights reserved.

Front Cover Graphic: © Can Stock Photo/Andreus

Printed in the United States of America

Defining Dominance Theory 45

Professionals and Cruelty 46

Progressive Disengagement 50

Summary 51

Chapter Four: How Pets Learn and the Consequences of Methodology, Equipment and Philosophical Choice 55

Where It Begins 55

Nonassociative Learning 56

Associative Learning 57

Animal Emotions 57

A Review of the Science 58

Applied Behavior Analysis 60

A Behavior or an Emotion? 61

Counterconditioning and Desensitization 62

Corporal Punishment 62

Punishment in Animal Training 63

Outdated Approach 64

Devices Intended to Startle 66

Learned Aggression 66

Nothing Shocking about Shock 67

Escape/Avoid Learning 67

Advocating for Humane Techniques 70

The Fallout 73

Physical Effects 75

Summary 78

Chapter Five: A Call for an Industry Wide, Professionally Acknowledged Best Practice 86

The Humane Hierarchy 87

LIEBI and LIMA 90

Scientific Approach – Tactical Approach and Methodology 90
Key Learning Theory 91
Summary 96

Chapter Six: Canine Communication and Social Behavior 99

Distance Decreasing 100
Distance Increasing 101
Appeasement Signals 102
Specific Signs of Stress or Anxiety 103
Displacement Behaviors 104
Avoidance Behaviors 105
Calming Signals 105
Cutoff Behaviors 106
Tail Carriage 106
General Meeting and Greeting 106
Conflicted Dogs 107
Canine Warnings 110
Dog-Human Interaction 111
Summary 113

Chapter Seven: Competency Is Mission Critical 117

Pet Industry Competence Is Paramount to Industry Professionalism 117
What is Professional Competence? 118
Client Attending Skills 119
Determining Competency 120
Competency Models 122
Assessment of Competencies 123
Competency Standards 125
The Role of Mentoring 128
Mentoring Programs 130
Competency and Continuing Professional Development 132

Determining Continuing Professional Development through Continuing Education Units 134

Summary 135

Chapter Eight: Ethics in Pet Training and Behavior Consulting 139

Defining Ethics, Defining Morals 139

Theories on Ethics 139

Ethics in the Pet Industry 141

Ethics in Medicine 143

Ethical Principles of Psychologists 144

Breed Bias 146

Ethical Standards 148

The Place and Critical Need for Ethical Guidelines and Oversight 149

Ethics Across Professional Associations in an Unregulated Profession 150

Ethics and the Detrimental Effect of Aversives 153

Ethics within the Framework of Competency 155

Informed Consent 156

Summary 157

Chapter Nine: Consumer Protection and Transparency 163

Ethics in Marketing 164

What Is Marketing? 164

Marketing and Conditioning 166

Marketing Ethics 168

Ethics and Law 169

Key Categories of Illegal Marketing Practices: 169

Consumer Protection 170

Key Definitions 171

Misrepresentation 172

The Professional Is the Service! 175

Service Product Clarity 176

Summary 177

Chapter Ten: Pet Industry Oversight Recommended Implementation Model 183

1. Register a 501c6 Not for Profit Corporation 183
2. Develop the Corporate Bylaws 183
3. Apply for Federal IRS Nonprofit Status 184
4. Corporate Structure 184
   a. Board Members 184
   b. Company Officers 184
   c. Executive Director 185
   d. Board Meetings 185
5. Key Operational Policies and Procedures 186
6. Key Policy Advisory Roles 186
7. Membership 187

Appendix A: The Recommended Best Practice Model for Pet Training and Behavior Consulting Professionals 188

Appendix B: The Recommended Model for the Assessment of a Professional's Knowledge and Skill 195

Appendix C: The Recommended Career Stage Mentoring Model 224

Appendix D: The Recommended Consumer Acknowledgement Form for Transparency in Dog Training/Behavior Consulting Services 233

Appendix E: The Recommended Case Study Template for Behavior Consultants 237

Appendix F: The Recommended Corporation Professional Code of Conduct and Ethics Pledge 242

Appendix G: The Recommended Policy for Registration Renewal via Continuing Education 251

Executive Summary

The pet industry is currently experiencing explosive growth. According to the American Pet Products Association (APPA) (2019), 67% of U.S. households now own at least one pet, which equals an estimated 84.9 million homes. Millennials represent the largest segment of pet owners for all pet types owned, especially bird owners, small animal owners, and saltwater fish owners. In addition, more than 80% of Gen Z and Millennial pet owners report owning dogs, while 50% or less own cats. Undoubtedly, these figures represent large numbers of constituents, and if mobilized and called to action, could represent a significant voting bloc.

Many of the changes across the industry have been driven by technology and the ease of online purchases. Kestenbaum (2018) argues that "most of the growth is because of changes in culture. As Millennial and Generation Z consumers have come into adulthood, they have embraced the pet-owning and pet-loving lifestyles to a far greater extent than their elders. While baby boomers account for 32% of pets owned, households headed by younger cohorts account for 62% of pet ownership."

Booming Industry

APPA (2019) reports that pet care spending in 2018 reached a "record-breaking high" of $72.56 billion compared to $69.51 billion in 2017, an increase of 4.3%. In 2019, this booming industry is expected to grow another 4.5%, generating $75.38 billion dollars that are estimated to be spent across several key areas (APPA, 2019):

Food:	$31.6 billion
Supplies/OTC Medication:	$16.4 billion
Veterinary Care:	$18.9 billion
Live Animal Purchases:	$1.9 billion
Other Services:	$6.3 billion

The last category, Other Services, references additional pet industry products such as grooming, boarding, training, pet sitting, behavior consulting, pet exercise, and pet walking and it is these, specifically training and behavior consulting, that will be the focus of this book. Other Services represent a significant growth in pet industry income in the last 20 years, and *Figs. 1* and *2* highlight examples of key statistics and basic analysis, sourced from the APPA's (2019) historical totals.

Fig. 1 shows that Other Services represent around 8% of pet industry total income, or $6.3 billion per year. This has gradually increased as a percentage over the last 20 years from 4%, or $1.2 billion dollars (APPA, 2019).

Fig. 1: Other Services as a % to Total Pet Industry Income

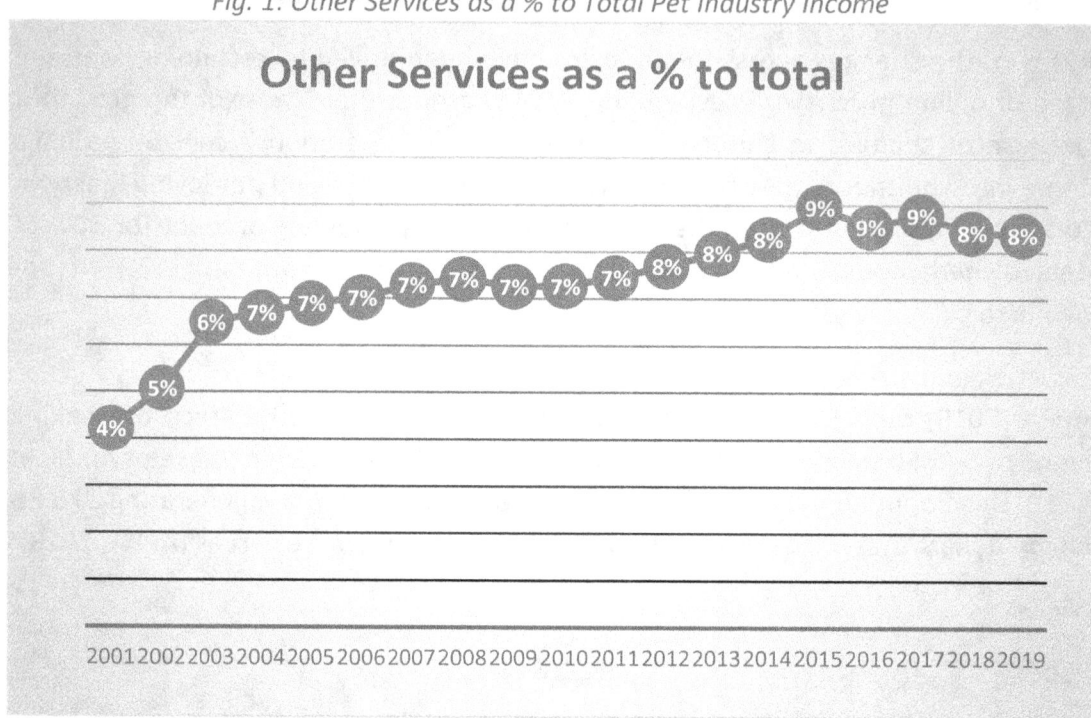

Pet industry income grew from $28.5 billion in 2001 to $72.5 billion in 2018, with, as previously mentioned, 2019 forecast to reach $75.3 billion. *Fig. 2* shows how Other Services, as an income category, have grown as a percentage of total income.

Fig. 2: Pet Industry Total Income vs. Other Services Income for Years 2001 – 2019

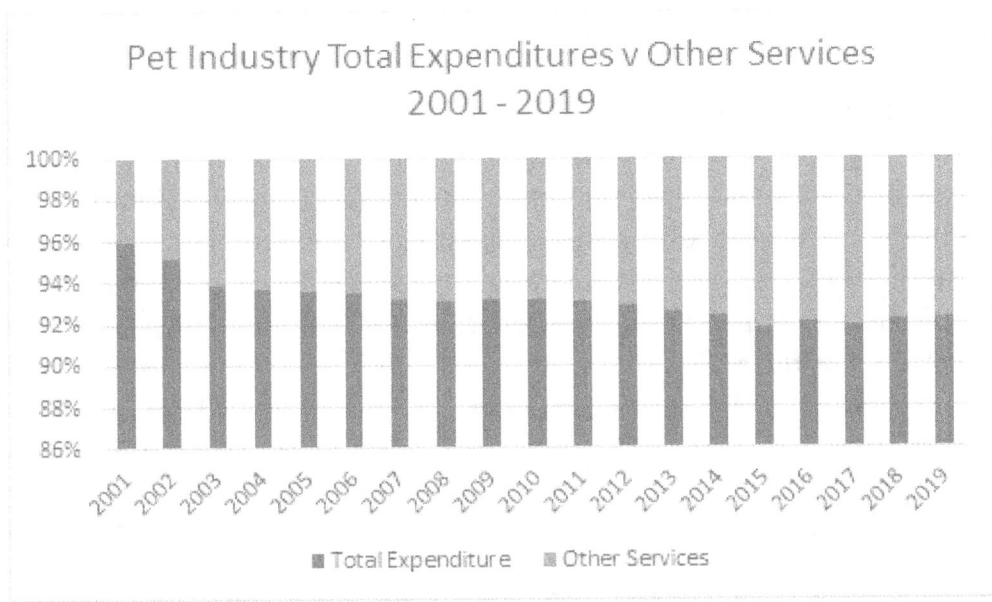

The Need for Change

It is very difficult at present to establish how many individuals are actually working, employed, or contracted to work across the pet industry. As there is no state or federal registration required for pet industry employees (other than veterinarians or board certified veterinary behaviorists), or any requirement to hold relevant qualifications (again, other than veterinarians or board certified veterinary behaviorists), any numbers available are not particularly reliable.

In her article *Working with Animals,* published by the US Bureau of Labor Statistics, Royster (2015) details several pet care job titles, their expected median income, job opening forecast numbers, and qualifying credentials based on data published in 2012. Royster (2015) notes that "[m]ost occupations that involve working with animals have no postsecondary education requirements" and that for positions such as breeders, animal care workers, and animal trainers, the only qualifications required are a high school diploma or equivalent. She points out that any "on-the-job" training required is moderate, a year maximum, "to develop the skills needed to attain competency," with no additional experience required. Royster (2015) also notes that licenses, certifications, or registrations are not required for anyone wanting to fill one of these "Other Services" type positions and join the pet industry.

In this book, the authors will present their views on the need for a level and model of oversight in the pet industry and for those choosing to practice within it. They will discuss the prevalence of individuals who hold no credentials, formal education, knowledge or skills, yet who are today working across the nation with full responsibility for the well-being and welfare of their unknowing clients' treasured pets. They will also highlight the lack of consumer protection and transparency across the marketing and operations platforms of many pet-related businesses, as well as the inherent weakness in how pets are legally classified, and how the lack of reported and enforced animal cruelty laws are insufficient protection when it comes to holding pet professionals accountable for their methods, approach and philosophies toward their craft and the pets they serve. Examples of instances where pets have been injured or died at the hands of so-called pet professionals will be provided.

In terms of any future legislation or oversight geared toward those working in the field of pet care, training, or behavior consulting, it is the authors' opinion that it would do pets and their owners an enormous injustice if any such legislation or industry oversight did not specifically call for practitioners to possess the appropriate skills and knowledge to effectively, efficiently and safely carry out their profession in a way that safeguards pets' physical and emotional welfare. At the same time, any such legislation or industry oversight must also protect the consumer from fraudulent marketing practices, business maleficence and/or outdated training methods and tools that are mispresented by pet professionals as scientific or beneficial

The authors will propose that any implementation of new laws or licensing procedures is not the single blanket solution to the myriad problems associated with the pet training industry as it stands today. Rather, to address current concerns, any new laws or oversight protocols will require a collection of improvements across a number of areas, including required minimum knowledge and skills, competency assessments, best practice models, legalities protecting pets from cruel practices, and an infrastructure of industry experts to provide professional oversight rather than government bodies.

Your Role in the Transition

Throughout the book, the authors will purposefully document multiple key areas that are all interconnected and will be required for the much-needed delivery of a professionalized, ethical and competent, pet professional workforce. As such, the authors will review a full range of topics and subtopics pertaining to the subject at hand and advise on their pertinence in the development of an infrastructure for oversight to support the professional evolution of the pet industry.

In closing, the authors will provide their recommendations on an oversight model for pet professionals that may be applied across individual geographical regions. This model will incorporate the establishment of a nonprofit organizational structure with a recommended board member configuration detailing the relevant roles needed to develop operational and policy guidelines. The key aim for this organization is to act as an intermediary between local industry practitioners and the local government. The model is supported by recommended best practice policies and guidelines to aid implementation and operational success. Each chapter of this work may be used as a standalone educational piece and also forms the backdrop to an educational website, PetIndustryRegulation.com. As a result of this format, key areas of importance may be duplicated, and cross referenced across different chapters.

Bibliography

American Pet Products Association. (2019). 2019-2020 APPA National Pet Owners Survey. Stamford, CT: APPA

American Pet Products Association. (2019). Marketing Research and Data. Retrieved May 3, 2019, from https://www.americanpetproducts.org/Uploads/MarketResearchandData/PetIndustryMarketSize2019.pdf

Kestenbaum, R. (2019). The Biggest Trends in the Pet Industry. *Forbes*. Retrieved May 3, 2019, from https://www.forbes.com/sites/richardkestenbaum/2018/11/27/the-biggest-trends-in-the-pet-industry/#2efa8da5f099

Royster, S. (2015). Working with Animals. The US Bureau of Labor Statistics. Retrieved May 3, 2019, from https://www.bls.gov/careeroutlook/2015/article/working-with-animals.htm

Chapter One: What Is Occupational Licensing?

According to Roth and Ramlow (2016), "Americans have always been rooted in the idea of economic freedom." In other words, Americans tend to be of the belief that hard work and determination will pay off. Children, from a young age, may be told that, rich or poor, if they have the right attitude, a good work ethic and are honest, then success will be attainable. We might, then, wonder why the practice of licensing has become so prevalent. Why does the government, through occupational licensing, place obstacles such as complex rules and barriers to the so-called American dream, especially since some of the current research we will looked at here suggests a failure to meet these goals?

More specifically, and for the purposes of this book, is there a role to play and a suitable occupational license for trainers and behavior consultants within the pet industry? We will attempt to answer this important question and, from there, provide a recommended model of best practice for the oversight of pet industry trainers.

In the United States, more than one-quarter, or 25-30% of workers, are now required to hold a license to perform their jobs. Many of these licenses are controlled and administered at a state level (Roth & Ramlow, 2016). In fact, there has been a five-fold growth in state level licensing since the early 1950s. In states such as Wisconsin, the growth of licenses and licensees has actually outpaced the population growth. Much of this change and growth can be attributed to a change in the workforce configuration toward personal and professional white collar services and away from more supervised, less empowered blue collar, low-skilled jobs.

According to the Treasury Office of Economic Policy, the Council of Economic Advisors and the Department of Labor (2015), "1,100 occupations are licensed in at least one state but fewer than 60 are licensed in all 50 states." This reflects the priorities and motivations of individual states and their given preferences over licensing trades. South Carolina, for example, has a 12% licensed workforce whereas Iowa, at the higher end, licenses 33% of its labor force. Such differences in licensing regulations across states are not only down to differences in the types of occupations that require a license, but also to an individual state's specific policies and licensing philosophy.

Licensing requirements across individual states and occupations also vary in terms of educational requirements and professional experience. For example, to become a security guard in Michigan, one would need to undertake three years of education and training whereas, in other states, just 11 days will suffice. Numerous examples of this type of disparity are available across many job types making it very difficult for a transient labor force to enter and compete within their given profession.

Roth and Ramlow (2016) show that there has also been a steady pace of occupational licensing reform as a result of bipartisan interest across numerous states. The reforms have fallen across two categories, those that serve no state interest and those that have little impact on health and safety. In 2015, Attorney General and Governor of Texas, Gregg Abbott, signed a bill eliminating a $200 annual licensing fee from various professions, thus impacting 600,000 workers. In 2016, Governor of Arizona Doug Doucy signed a bill eliminating licensing for citrus packers, yoga instructors and noncommercial driving instructors. And, in 2015, Governor of Rhode Island, Gina Raimondo, eliminated 27 licenses for a selection of occupations, music therapists, barbers, cosmetologists and estheticians. Overall, reforms have taken place across 12 states from 2014 to 2016.

In economics, there are two competing propositions in favor of occupational licensure: rent-seeking and public interest (Maurizi, 1974). The rent-seeking theory presents that occupational licensing limits access to certain occupations, which increases wages for those practicing and costs for those consuming (Friedman, 1962). The public interest theory argues that licensure is needed to the extent that it protects the general public from unlicensed professionals and that the end user (the client or customer) may lack the necessary knowledge or information to make an informed decision, which can, in turn, poorly impact local communities (Arrow, 1963).

Those in favor of licensing argue that its key purpose and function, when designed and implemented correctly, is to provide consumers with two main benefits: high quality services, and more structured health and safety standards. Other opinions suggest that governments license for three primary purposes:

1. To generate income for the state.
2. To protect public safety.
3. To raise the standards of the profession.

According to Roth and Ramlow (2016), licensing also serves a fourth and often understated function: to protect members of a profession from competition and hiking up consumer prices. This speaks to the process of "grandfathering," a system whereby all existing practitioners in an industry are automatically granted a license when new licenses are developed and rolled out. This, in some cases, occurs without a need for them to meet even the basic minimum of standards.

A report prepared by the Department of the Treasury Office of Economic Policy, the Council of Economic Advisers, and the Department of Labor (2015) suggests that occupational licensing encourages individuals to professionalize and creates career pathways incorporating education and skill training requirements. However, a review of the literature and research in the same report shows, in fact, that the opposite may occur, and that occupational licensing may:

- Increase barriers for entry into an industry.
- Increase small business overheads through licensing fees.
- Reduce employment opportunities.
- Increase service pricing for consumers, varying from 3-16%.
- Not significantly improve the level of service quality.
- Create a 10-15% disparity in earnings between licensed and unlicensed workers with similar education, experience, and training.
- Accelerate a decline in innovation and research.
- Restrict worker mobility across states.

The Process of Licensing

As already stated, occupational licensing is a form of government regulation that requires individuals wanting to practice their trade to obtain permission from a government body. According to Kleiner (2017), it is "the process by which governments establish qualifications required to practice a trade or profession, so that only licensed practitioners are allowed by law to receive pay for doing work in the occupation." However, all too often, licensing is converged with or misrepresented as credentialing when, in reality, the two are very different. The argument also exists that it is not the role of an individual or institute to provide oversight for an industry or specific areas of an occupation where one is not an expert. For dog trainers, who form part of those Other Services we discussed in the Executive Summary, one way of taking control of their destiny would be to establish a standard level of education. Dunbar (qtd. in Hubbard Sorlie, 2018) suggests "a degree-level course that is more practical than any other type of training course being offered, and everyone has to have it...It needs to be offered worldwide, translated into Spanish, Japanese and other languages. This would be the gold standard in education...otherwise another profession will do it, or heaven forbid, the government."

The process of licensing whereby one is granted permission by state or federal governments to practice a particular occupation or profession legitimizes all practitioners who are either grandfathered into a new licensing tenure or meet the minimal requirement guidelines by the government oversight body. This is, more often than not, a body of individuals who are versed in government policy, but not necessarily in the required competencies of the skilled licensed holder. In Maryland alone, the Division of Occupational and Professional Licensing oversees 21 licensing boards, commissions and programs appointed by the Governor. The Division is responsible for regulating the activities of more than 246,000 individuals and businesses across 25 professions (Maryland Government, 2018).

> "Public policies have created conflict across many spectrums ranging from animal cruelty laws to breed specific legislation, cat colony management, pet hoarding and kennel licensing. These policies all affect both animal welfare and the human-animal relationship, a relationship that has become more humanized and has developed a large and politically powerful voting bloc."
> - Hunter & Brisbin (2016)

As the licensing process involves the power of the state, should a practitioner violate the licensing terms, they can be held legally accountable under civil or criminal law of the governing body. In few industries, however, do the minimal educational and or skill requirements really speak to competency of the practitioner and fewer, in reality, protect the consumer from unethical or dangerous practices. Recent political trends are seeing a bipartisan interest in licensing reform, with real efforts being made to remove licensing requirements from occupations where it is deemed unnecessary. As Roth and Ramlow (2016) state, it is licensing that serves no state interest, has little impact on health and safety and only serves to fence out opportunity, that is in need of reform.

Meanwhile, politics and pets seem to be irrevocably connected. The lives of our pets are significantly impacted by politics through ownership regulation, public policy, and criminal and regulatory law enforcement.

Pets and Their Influence on Our Culture

In the United States, pets are an important part of the culture and play key roles in many facets of people's lives. Given the number of studies reflecting that ownership of pets increases the amount of exercise undertaken by their owners, reduces stress and blood pressure, and produces hormones that positively impact pleasure, there is an economic and social value to pets in our societies (Centers for Disease Control and Prevention, 2019). In children, pet ownership has been shown to reduce allergies and assist with development. And let us not forget or underestimate the many functions pets serve and perform for the sick, disabled, and those in need of assistance (Hunter & Brisbin, 2016).

Thus, with increasing numbers of animal welfare organizations and groups now demanding political action to protect the physical, emotional and environmental well-being of pets, coupled with the fact that pets can generate costs to public health and welfare through rescue, sheltering, cleanup and care, we are beginning to see movements at a state level regarding the licensing of professionals who work with pets.

> "In the United States, pets are an important part of the culture and play key roles in many facets of our lives. Given that numerous studies reflect that ownership of pets increases the amount of exercise undertaken by their owners, reduces stress and blood pressure and produces hormones that positively impact pleasure, there is an economic and social value to pets in our societies." - Centers for Disease Control and Prevention (2019)

Industry Certification

The process to become certified in any given field can be more rigorous than becoming licensed. However, certifications are generally nongovernmental. They are usually earned from academic or professional societies or institutions and often have renewal terms and conditions attached to them.

> *Along with a number of other industries...including the pet industry, there is currently no legal requirement to be certified and no legal mechanism in place to protect the consumer from negative or injurious consequence that transpires as the result of an individual's lack of certification.*

Certifications recognize individuals for meeting specific criteria of skills and knowledge. They are a way for practitioners to seek self-promotion and differentiate themselves from their competitive set. Certifying organizations set standards of competency and their certification programs are designed to use these predetermined competencies as benchmarks for pass or failure performances. Consumers draw inference from certifications that a professional has met a specific standard of competency and/or carries a particular body or depth of pertinent knowledge. Along with a number of other industries, however, including the pet industry, there is currently no legal requirement to be certified and no legal mechanism in place to protect the consumer from negative or injurious consequence that transpires as the result of an individual's lack of certification.

In such cases, the only line of recourse a consumer may take regarding a professional who advertises a specific credential is through the credential provider and the possibility of a credential recall or removal from the credentialing organization. Remember, credentialing is a declaration that the individual has successfully completed the course of study, passed an examination, or in some other manner displayed that they can meet the credentialing criteria.

It is not uncommon for a government body to decree that licensed professionals must be certified to a minimum standard to retain their licensing status, but this, in turn, begs questions about what types of credential are available and what the ethics and integrity of the approved credentialing body are.

Wilson (2016) summarizes the difference between licensing and certification thus: licensing presumes the activity is forbidden whereas certification presumes the activity is permitted by right. Licensing increases the power of government whereas certification empowers the consumer and not the government.

To delve deeper, there are certificates and there are certifications. Certificates are often issued from a narrow scope of subject matter. There are fewer tangible criteria for achieving a certificate and sometimes just participating in an educational program will deem an individual to be eligible. With industry certifications, some are administered and issued in the best interest of the credentialing organization while others take into consideration the interests of the professional, the consumer, and the industry as a whole.

It is all too common for credentials to be issued based on little objectivity and less ethical guidelines. This, as opposed to development by teams of subject matter experts who determine Job Task Analysis and a review of relevant literature to determine the required minimum standards of competency and what constitutes the required job task skills and knowledge. When the latter occurs, it is often by professional credentialing bodies who are guided by strong professional ethics and a recourse and accountability system for professionals who stray from agreed and approved operating standards. (*See also* Chapter Seven: Competency Is Mission Critical / Assessment of Competencies.)

Summary

Licensing as a regulation may be best suited to industries and trades where there is a need to protect the physical and emotional interests of an individual or sentient being and where practitioners can impact the safety and health of the consumer and their best interests. No sound minded individual would entertain medical advice or surgery from an unlicensed doctor. The licensing discussed here speaks to a level of competency and guarantees a minimum level of education and skills supported by ethical guidelines.

In industries such as the pet industry, where quality impacts public safety and protects against dangerous practitioners, there may be room for a model that provides the necessary competency and operational guidelines as well as a level of oversight and ethical supervision for trainers and behavior consultants while protecting the needs of pets and their owners and providing for transparency and consumer protection.

Bibliography

Arrow, K. (1963). Uncertainty and the Welfare Economics of Medical Care. *American Economic Review 53:* 941-9. Retrieved December 29, 2018, from https://web.stanford.edu/~jay/health_class/Readings/Lecture01/arrow.pdf

Centers for Disease Control and Prevention. (2019). About Pets and People. Retrieved December 29, 2018, from https://www.cdc.gov/healthypets/health-benefits/index.html

Friedman, M. (1962). Capitalism and Freedom. Chicago, IL: University of Chicago Press

Hubbard Sorlie, D. (2018, Fall). APDT Founder urges trainers to take control of their profession. *APDT Chronicle of the Dog* 27-31

Hunter, S., & Brisbin, R.A. (2016). Pet Politics. West Lafayette, IN: Purdue University Press

Kleiner, M.M. (2017). The influence of occupational licensing and regulation. IZA World of Labor 2017: 392. Retrieved December 29, 2018, from https://wol.iza.org/uploads/articles/392/pdfs/the-influence-of-occupational-licensing-and-regulation.pdf

Maryland Government. (2018). Department of Labor, Licensing and Regulation. Retrieved November 6, 2018, from https://www.dllr.state.md.us/license

Maurizi, A. (1974). Occupational Licensing and the Public Interest. *Journal of Political Economy 82*: 399-413. Retrieved December 28, 2018, from https://www.jstor.org/stable/pdf/1831186.pdf

Roth, C., & Ramlow, E. (2016). Fencing out opportunity: Occupational licensing in the Badger State. Milwaukee, WI: Wisconsin Institute for Law and Liberty. Retrieved December 28, 2018, from http://www.will-law.org/wp-content/uploads/2016/11/Licensure-FINAL.pdf

Treasury Office of Economic Policy, the Council of Economic Advisors and the Department of Labor. (2015). Occupational Licensing – A framework for policy makers. Retrieved December 28, 2018, from https://obamawhitehouse.archives.gov/sites/default/files/docs/licensing_report_final_nonembargo.pdf

Wilson, L. (2016). Legal Guidelines for Unlicensed Practitioners. (n.p.): L.D. Wilson Consultants, Inc.

Chapter Two: Living Property - The Need for a New Legal Definition

In the preface of his book, *Animal Law*, Favre (2011) speaks of a picture of his cat: "Moppet is a being, a being who lives with me. She is alive. Look into her eyes; she is aware, aware of me but perhaps not self-aware...To touch her is to feel like you are touching a cloud...Her Spirit is positive and engaging." Moppet, apparently, likes human companionship and knows "who the members are of our multi-species family."

Are Pets Family?

According to The Harris Poll (2015), "nearly all pet owners (95%)...consider their pets to be members of the family." Yet, legally, pets are still considered property or chattel. "Technically in the eyes of the law, [cats and dogs] are no different from a couch or a car." (Grimm, 2014).

The terms "property" and "chattel" may be defined as follows:

Property: Anything that is owned by a person or entity. Property is divided into two types: "real property," which is any interest in land, real estate, growing plants or the improvements on it, and "personal property," sometimes called "personality," which encompasses everything else. (The Free Dictionary, 2018).

Chattel: An item of personal property which is movable, as distinguished from real property (land and improvements). (The Free Dictionary, 2018).

What Do Dogs, Cats, Cars and Chairs Have in Common?

Favre (2011) believes people need to reflect more on where pets fall in the world of moral and legal obligations, as well as how they deal with pets as family members in terms of their legal status and our own legal responsibility toward them. Historically, in common law, personal pets were considered separately from the domestic versus wild classification of animals, giving them a "peculiar status." (Noall, 1985). "Pets were considered to be kept for the 'pleasure, curiosity or whim' of the owner and of little or no value. Therefore, pets were not considered 'property' in the traditional sense. They were also deemed to have no economic value so were not considered property." (Noall, 1985, citing Blackstone, 1765-1769). In 1897, in *Sentell v. New Orleans & Carrolton R.R. Co* 166 U.S. 698, 701 at the Supreme Court of Louisiana, it was said of dogs that "they are useful neither as beasts of burden for draught nor for food." (Favre, 2011, p, 32). The trend of courts since the 1930s has been to remove this special status given to pets and treat them like other domestic animals, viewing them as property after all (Favre, 2011). Meanwhile, between 1977 and 2000, there was no organized effort to institutionalize the teaching of animal law at American law schools.

In any legal system, the concept of property is fundamental. When something is considered property, it means the owner has the right to control and direct. Across the Unites States, individual state governments control ownership under property law concepts. As such, "either the state courts or the state legislatures are fully empowered to deal with the issue of ownership of animals." (Favre, 2011, p.30).

The Issue of Sentience

What, then, do dogs, cats, cars and chairs have in common? In states or provinces where pets are still considered movable property, it means that, according to Kinnard (2014), "from a legal standpoint, animals have no more rights than a pair of shoes, and this opens the door to inhumane practices ranging from abandonment to cock fighting." However, The Civil Code of Québec states that: "Animals are not things. They are sentient beings and have biological needs." (Légis Québec, 2016). The European Union also recognizes animals as "sentient beings," stating that "Union and the Member States shall...pay full regard to the welfare requirements of animals." (Official Journal of the European Union, 2012). According to Moss (2016), "[i]n 2014, French Parliament reclassified animals as 'living beings' instead of simply property. [In 2015], New Zealand passed the Animal Welfare Amendment Bill, acknowledging that animals are "sentient" beings just like humans (New Zealand Legislation, 2013). Under amendments to animal welfare legislation in the Australian Capital Territory in May 2019, all pets were to be recognized as "sentient beings with intrinsic value." (Brewer, 2019). And, in December [2016], the Civil Code of Québec granted animals the same rights as children under its laws." But the Code also states that: "In addition to the provisions of special Acts which protect animals, the provisions of

> *What, then, do dogs, cats, cars and chairs have in common? In states or provinces where pets are still considered movable property, it means that, according to Kinnard (2014), "from a legal standpoint, animals have no more rights than a pair of shoes."*

this Code and of any other Act concerning property nonetheless apply to animals." (Légis Québec, 2016).

What Need Does Pet Ownership Fulfil?

Crowell-Davis (2008, p.423) states that people choose to own animals "for a variety of reasons." At its deepest and most profound, however, the relationship between a human and an animal can be deeply emotional.

In its 2019-2020 National Pet Owners Survey, the American Pet Products Association (APPA) reported that 67% of U.S. households own a pet (an estimated 84.9 million homes). As outlined in the *Executive Summary*, pet care spending in 2018 reached a "record-breaking high" of $72.56 billion compared to $69.51 billion in 2017, an increase of 4.3%. In 2019, this booming industry is expected to grow another 4.5%, generating $75.38 billion (APPA, 2019).

Areas of expenditure across pet food, supplies and services reflect how pets are increasingly being treated like family members. Pets often sleep in their owner's bed, eat gourmet food, have their birthdays celebrated, receive seasonal gifts, drink bottled water, receive monthly toy and treat subscriptions, watch pet television and hold club memberships. The Harris Poll (2015) references that "...growing percentages of pet owners are frequently or occasionally buying birthday presents for their pets (45%) and cooking for them (31%), majorities of pet owners frequently or occasionally let their pets sleep in bed with them (71%) and buy them holiday presents (64%). Just over two in ten at least occasionally dress their pet in some type of clothing (22%), while just over one in ten at least occasionally bring their pets to work (12%)." In a similar vein, Saint Leo University, Florida, reporting on the results of a 2018 poll conducted to find out how much Americans planned to spend on their pets in the forthcoming holiday season, quote Waddell, a professor of social work at the university who teaches an interdisciplinary course about therapy and service animals: "We as a nation are embracing more than ever our pets as family members...Many people have

> According to Antolec (2018), the Federal Bureau of Investigation (FBI) "takes animal abuse so seriously it began tracking the crime in 2014 and uses the data to help identify serial killers." In 2016, the Bureau added animal cruelty to its list of Class A felonies, alongside homicide and arson.

substituted their animals for the choice to have children, and thus they lavish their pets as they normally would their own children."

Some pet owners are also electing to be buried with their pets. In 2016, 56th Governor of New York Andrew M. Cuomo signed a bill permitting the interment of pet cremated remains in not-for-profit cemeteries, meaning owners can have their pets buried with them if they so desire. The law allows for a variety of animals to be buried with their owners, including cats and dogs (New York State Department of State Division of Cemeteries, 2016).

Pets as People

Grimm (2014) observes that: "Pets aren't just becoming more like people in our laws and homes. They're also becoming more like people in our society. Every year, they take on more roles and more responsibilities, providing critical services in our increasingly dangerous and fractured world."

> *In the aftermath of Hurricane Katrina in New Orleans, Louisiana in 2005, the findings of a poll by The Fritz Institute (2006) found that 44% of New Orleans residents chose not to evacuate because they refused to abandon their pets.*

In addition, when pets' lives risk being negatively impacted for any reason, humans often step in to prevent them from coming to any harm. For example, in the aftermath of Hurricane Katrina in New Orleans, Louisiana in 2005, the findings of a poll by The Fritz Institute (2006) found that 44% of New Orleans residents chose not to evacuate because they refused to abandon their pets. When Hurricane Harvey moved into the Houston, Texas area in 2017, laws were enacted quickly to allow pets to accompany residents into shelters. A dozen years later, Katrina is viewed as a watershed moment in planning for pets during natural disasters. It changed federal and state policies and, as a result, the Federal Government started to encourage the rescue and protection of family pets during natural disasters. Additionally, animal advocates and experts say, it made it clear that Americans have widely embraced the idea of dogs and cats as family members (Brulliard, 2017).

In 2015, the *Huffington Post* published a piece by Hodgson, *Re-Classifying Dogs as Sentient Beings: It's Time, America, It's Time*. The author also references the aforementioned Civil Code of Québec, stating that it has "welcomed pets into the circle of 'sentient' beings by granting them many of the same rights as children in the eyes of the law" and "lifts the legal status of specific animals from mere property, i.e. inanimate objects like toaster ovens and iPhones that can be manipulated any which way, to sensitive, emotional beings that require nurturing and respect."

> "...by using the MRI to push away the limitations of behaviorism, we can no longer hide from the evidence. Dogs, and probably many other animals (especially our closest primate relatives), seem to have emotions just like us." – Berns (2013)

States Berns (2013), a professor of neuroeconomics who completed the first fMRI scans of dogs' brains: "Dogs have long been considered property. Though the Animal Welfare Act of 1966 and state laws raised the bar for the treatment of animals, they solidified the view that animals are things — objects that can be disposed of as long as reasonable care is taken to minimize their suffering. But now, by using the MRI to push away the limitations of behaviorism, we can no longer hide from the evidence. Dogs, and probably many other animals (especially our closest primate relatives), seem to have emotions just like us. And this means we must reconsider their treatment as property." McDonald (2014) agrees: "If Canis lupus familiaris can be shown to have emotions, and a level of sentience comparable to that of a human child, there is a moral imperative to reassess how they are treated under law."

The solution to a moral imperative such as this is not an easy one, however. Crowell-Davis (2008) references the *Journal of Consumer Research* and cites Hirschman, who "groups the reasons for pet ownership into six categories":

1. Some people have pets so that they can perceive and relate to them as humans (i.e., the animal is a companion, friend, or family member). This is the most common reason for pet ownership.
2. Some people have pets as pieces of equipment. These animals serve a function, such as protecting, herding, or hunting.
3. Some people have pets as avocations, exhibiting or showing them. These animals are perceived as property to be bought and sold.
4. Some people have animals as status symbols.
5. Some people have animals as ornaments (e.g., koi, birds with colorful plumage). These animals are kept specifically for their esthetic value.

6. Some people consider animals to be objects in their environment that function as extensions of themselves. This relationship may be a subconscious one.

Owner vs. Guardian

Blouin (2013) studied the variations in dog owners' attitudes toward their pets in terms of interactions and their treatment. He concludes that the relationship pet owners have with their pets is one of three orientations:

1. A dominionistic relationship where owners have a relatively low regard for their pets seeing them only for the value they provide; a function such as protection work.
2. A humanistic orientation whereby owners elevate their pets to a status, such as surrogate human. The pets are valued for the benefits they provide to their owners resulting from a close relationship and attachment.
3. A protectionist orientation where owners have a very high regard for their pets and, in fact, all animals in general. Pets are viewed as highly valuable companions and are creatures with their own interests.

Blouin's study reflects a wide variation in how owners consider and value their pets, ranging from having functional value to being seen as a companion who deserves to have his or her own interests protected. Indeed, if one were to ask pet owners how they would like their pets to be classified, there would most likely be a vast array of opinions varying from one end of a continuum to another.

Owner, guardian, and parent are the most commonly used terms to describe the relationship between pets and their humans and there have been some efforts to redefine the relationship between the two parties by taking on board the term "guardian" as a replacement for the word "owner." Pet owners "in 17 cities, one state, and two counties in California can legally refer to themselves as animal guardians." (Nolen, 2011). Yet, according to Favre (2010) as documented by Nolen (2011), "[y]ou can't just change a word and expect the whole legal system to change." According to Nolen (2011), citing Dennis, "the appeal of guardianship is the suggestion it will somehow result in less animal abuse and neglect." Dennis also identifies problematic legal implications: "To lawyers, 'guardian' has a considerable amount of legal significance. Ownership and guardianship are not matters of semantics; they're not interchangeable terms." (Nolen, 2011).

States Berns (2013): "One alternative is a sort of limited personhood for animals that show neurobiological evidence of positive emotions. Many rescue groups already use the label of 'guardian' to describe human caregivers, binding the human to his ward with an implicit responsibility to care for her...If we went a step further and granted dogs rights of personhood, they would be afforded additional protection against exploitation. Puppy mills, laboratory dogs and dog racing would be banned for violating the basic right of self-determination of a person." However, Berns (2013) suspects society is "many years away from considering dogs as persons."

Crowell-Davis (2008, p.428) determines that a pet owner's reasons for having a pet are also likely to "significantly affect his or her tolerance of various behavior problems." If this is the case, then surely the legal determination for a pet needs to take into consideration not just the factor of ownership, but also a degree of responsibility to their mental, physical and environmental well-being.

For owners, the concern regarding the legal classification of pets may stem largely from some, or all, of the following:

- When pets are considered property, it does not take into consideration that they are not inanimate objects, but sentient beings.
- With one's own property, one has full rights to do with it as one pleases. This will not always be in the best interest of a pet and is entirely dependent on the decisions of the individual owner.
- If the legal status were to change and pets were universally given rights in the same way children are, then this could impact the liability issues of pet "ownership" insurance and/or pet medical insurance and may bring with it an overbearing ability for authorities to more easily remove a pet from a home or take custody of a pet without perceived due process.
- As pets are legally considered property, responsible and caring pet owners can make important and unchallenged decisions on behalf of their pets such as medical care, behavior modification and euthanasia, should it be necessary.
- As property, irresponsible pet owners may neglect the needs of a pet up to and including taking his life in what some would deem an inhumane manner.

Pet Training and Behavior Consulting: A Model for Raising the Bar to Protect Professionals, Pets and Their People

Legal Times Are Changing

In 2000, the city of Boulder, Colorado "made history" when it added the word "guardian" to the "section of its municipal code addressing animal ownership. It was the first instance of a city referring to the legal relationship between a person and a pet as something other than owner and property." (Nolen, 2011). The reasoning behind this change was the belief that, if residents believed they were pet guardians, it would positively impact how they treat their pets.

In the case *Rego v. Madalinski* (2016-Ohio-7339), where a dog was attacked by another dog, the Ohio Sixth District Court of Appeals held that, while it is "undisputed that Ohio classifies dogs as personal property…pets do not have the same characteristics as other forms of personal property, such as a table or sofa which is disposable and replaceable at our convenience." The Court also highlighted the fact that "various courts and law review articles have discussed the plausibility of reclassifying companion animals under a 'semi-property' classification suggesting such terms as companion property, or sentient property."

> McLain (2009) presents that "because pets are becoming such a big part of our lives, some courts are beginning to change this analysis, and are willing to treat pets more like children. To date, this has primarily occurred only with dogs. Courts are now taking into consideration the best interest of the pets in determining who gets custody of them."

For families that are going through any kind of separation, legal disputes may erupt over pet ownership. As a result, pets are sometimes now detailed in divorce settlements with both parties keen to remain the sole guardian of their four-legged family member, or, at least agreeing to joint custody. Given that pets are legally personal property and capable of human ownership and control, divorce courts used to always rule in favor of the human. But McLain (2009) presents that "because pets are becoming such a big part of our lives, some courts are beginning to change this analysis, and are willing to treat pets more like children. To date, this has primarily occurred only with dogs. Courts are now taking into consideration the best interest of the pets in determining who gets custody of them." There are also cases where pet guardians are awarded shared custody and/or visitation rights, with alimony payments being made from one partner to another (McLain, 2009).

In 2017, the Illinois State House "passed a law that would force divorce courts not just to divvy pets up between their 'parents' in a custody battle, but to think about their well-being, too...Illinois is only the second state to adopt a law that would consider the well-being of animals in custody battles. [In 2016], Alaska became the first to amend its divorce statutes so that judges are now required to consider it in their judgments. They can also assign joint custody over an animal." (Monyak, 2018). In California, on January 1, 2019, a law went into effect requiring judges to "consider an animal's interests in divorce proceedings and allow joint ownership of a companion animal." (Quirk, 2018). Says Assembly Member Bill Quirk, who introduced the bill: "The signing of AB 2274 makes clear that courts must view pet ownership differently than the ownership of a car, for example. By providing clearer direction, courts will award custody on what is best for the animal. I am proud that [California] Governor Brown, as a fellow pet owner, agrees that we need to alter our view of pet safety and animal welfare." Says Favre (2018) of the new law: "Before it was an issue of who owns the dog and how you distribute the property. But pets aren't quite the same thing as china and sofas. They're more like children, in that they're living beings who have their own preferences." The California law defines a pet as "any animal that is community property and kept as a household pet." (Gregorian, 2018).

> "...pets aren't quite the same thing as china and sofas. They're more like children, in that they're living beings who have their own preferences." - Favre (2018)

Living Property

Conventional price theory and standard economic accounts of tort and contract law assume that property rights are fixed. Merrill (2002, p.331), in his paper on the evolution of property rights, explains that "property regimes are not static but change over time." Given the assumption of fixed property that otherwise prevails in economic literature, this makes it very challenging to explain property rights or set new meanings to existing law around the context of property rights.

McLain (2009) suggests that, "[i]f the law is expanded in the future, questions such as which relationships and species should qualify for greater protection under the law will need to be answered. One good starting point for discussing a solution is Michigan State University College of Law's animal law professor David Favre's concept of 'living property,' which he defines as 'physical, movable living objects –

not human – that have an inherent self-interest in their continued well-being and existence.'" According to Favre (2010) himself, "our legal system already accommodates a number of animal interests within the criminal anti-cruelty laws and civil trust laws. To make a more coherent package of all animal-related public policy issues, it is useful to acknowledge the existence of a fourth category of property, living property."

Tischler (2012) also cites Favre, referencing his advancement of "the idea that property in an animal can be divided between legal and equitable title and the equitable title can be transferred to the animal." Indeed, Favre (2010) asks: "What if some of the objects, some of the property, have interests independent of the humans who own them? This raises a conflict that is different from the usual individual human versus individual human or individual human versus human society conflicts with which the law most often struggles. However, this is not a universal problem with property; it arises only in the case of a special category of property, living property."

Summary

In the past, the concept of the Five Freedoms (see *Chapter Four: How Pets Learn and the Consequences of Methodology, Equipment and Philosophical Choice / Escape/Avoid Learning*) has been considered the gold standard of animal welfare that falls under human control and has since been adopted by a number of related groups and organizations. The concept originated in Brambell's (1965) report looking into the welfare of animals kept under intensive livestock husbandry systems in the United Kingdom, which stated that farm animals should have the freedom to stand up, lie down, turn around, groom themselves and stretch their limbs (Brambell, 1965). These Five Freedoms were modified in July 1979 under the direction of the Farm Animal Welfare Council to include animal behavior.

The Five Freedoms propose the following for the adequate welfare of agricultural animals:

1. Freedom from hunger or thirst by ready access to fresh water and a diet to maintain full health and vigor.
2. Freedom from discomfort by providing an appropriate environment including shelter and a comfortable resting area.

3. Freedom from pain, injury or disease by prevention or rapid diagnosis and treatment.
4. Freedom to express (most) normal behavior by providing sufficient space, proper facilities and company of the animal's own kind.
5. Freedom from fear and distress by ensuring conditions and treatment which avoid mental suffering. (Brambell, 1965).

Building on the Five Freedoms, Favre (2011) developed a list, which he referred to as his own "ponderings," to help initiate discussions regarding the rights of pets. These state that pets should:

1. Not to be held for or put to prohibited uses.
2. Not to be harmed.
3. To be cared for.
4. To have living space.
5. To be properly owned.
6. To own property.
7. To enter into contracts.
8. To file tort claims.

For the purposes of this work, we have expanded on each point and fleshed out what we believe to be its context and purpose:

1. Prohibited Uses: Pets should not to be held for or put to prohibited uses, such as blood sports, research, captivity.
2. Not to Be Harmed: Pets should not have pain or suffering inflicted on them.
3. To Be Cared for: A pet's emotional, environmental and physical well-being is a priority and requires a minimum level of care to constitute being "cared for."
4. To Have Living Space: Pets should be provided with adequate space to ensure sufficient and appropriate physical and mental enrichment.
5. To Be Properly Owned: If a pet is not living under the conditions of the first four points, then he may be removed from the owner.
6. To Own Property: The rights for a pet to be legally gifted assets to protect his current or future well-being.

7. To Enter into Contracts: Should a pet be included in a contract for breeding, sale or some other scenario, then that contract represents the best interests of the pet.
8. To File Tort Claims: A pet can sue a human if they violate one of the pet's primary interests. This would cover a pet's legal rights, e.g. if their guardian bequeaths them property or cash to look after them.

Nonhuman animals have "interests of their own that deserve to be nurtured and protected from human harm, both in the consideration of ethical acts and the laws that we humans implement on their behalf." (Favre, 2010, p.1070). Further, "…those of us at the heart of the animal law movement envision a world in which the lives and interests of all sentient beings are respected within the legal system, a world in which animals are not exploited, terrorized, tortured, or controlled to serve human whims or purposes." (Tischler, 2012).

Bibliography

American Pet Products Association. (2019). 2019-2020 APPA National Pet Owners Survey. Stamford, CT: APPA

Berns, G. (2013, October 5). Dogs Are People Too. *New York Times*. Retrieved February 2, 2019, from https://www.nytimes.com/2013/10/06/opinion/sunday/dogs-are-people-too.html

Blouin, D.D. (2013). Are Dogs Children, Companions, or Just Animals? Understanding Variations in People's Orientations toward Animals. *Anthrozoös 26* (2) 279-294. Retrieved January 1, 2019, from https://www.tandfonline.com/doi/abs/10.2752/175303713X13636846944402?journalCode=rfan20

Brambell, R. (1965). Report of the technical committee to enquire into the welfare of animals kept under intensive livestock husbandry systems. London, UK: Her Majesty's Stationery Office

Brewer, P. (2019). Do let the dogs out: Huge fines for pet confinement part of ACT animal welfare overhaul. Retrieved May 22, 2019, from https://www.canberratimes.com.au/story/6124428/do-let-the-dogs-out-huge-fines-for-pet-confinement-part-of-act-animal-welfare-overhaul/

Brulliard, K. (2017). How the chaos of Hurricane Katrina helped save pets from flooding in Texas. *The Washington Post*. Retrieved February 2, 2019, from https://www.washingtonpost.com/news/animalia/wp/2017/08/31/how-the-chaos-of-hurricane-katrina-helped-save-pets-from-flooding-in-texas/?noredirect=on&utm_term=.911f9711212d

Chattel [Def]. (2018). In The Free Dictionary. Retrieved January 1, 2019, from https://www.thefreedictionary.com/chattel

Crowell-Davis, S. (2008, August). Motivation for Pet Ownership and Its Relevance to Behavior Problems. *Compendium (30)* 423-8

Favre, D. (2010). Living Property: A New Status for Animals Within the Legal System. 93 Marquette Law Review 1021. Retrieved January 1, 2019, from http://scholarship.law.marquette.edu/mulr/vol93/iss3/3

Favre, D. (2011). Animal Law, Welfare, Interests, And Rights. New York, NY: Wolters Kluwer Law and Business

Favre, D. (2018, December 29). New California divorce law: Treat pets like people — not property to be divided up. (Dareh Gregorian, Interviewer). NBC News. Retrieved February 2, 2019, from https://www.nbcnews.com/politics/politics-news/new-california-divorce-law-treat-pets-people-not-property-be-n952096

Fritz Institute. (2006). Hurricane Katrina: Perceptions of the Affected. Retrieved January 1, 2019, from http://www.fritzinstitute.org/PDFs/findings/HurricaneKatrina_Perceptions.pdf

Gregorian, D. (2018, December 29). New California divorce law: Treat pets like people — not property to be divided up. NBC News. Retrieved February 2, 2019, from https://www.nbcnews.com/politics/politics-news/new-california-divorce-law-treat-pets-people-not-property-be-n952096

Grimm, D. (2014, April 7). Q&A: Pets Are Becoming People, Legally Speaking (Rachel Hartigan Shea, Interviewer). *National Geographic*. Retrieved January 1, 2019, from https://news.nationalgeographic.com/news/2014/04/140406-pets-cats-dogs-animal-rights-citizen-canine/

Hodgson, S. (2015, December 4). Re-Classifying Dogs as Sentient Beings: It's Time, America, It's Time. *Huffington Post*. Retrieved January 1, 2019, from https://www.huffingtonpost.com/sarah-hodgson/reclassifying-dogs-as-sen_b_8717888.html

Kinnard, N. (2014, September 3). Animals are not objects. University Affairs. Retrieved January 1, 2019, from https://www.universityaffairs.ca/news/news-article/animals-are-not-objects/

Légis Québec. (2016). Civil Code of Québec. Book Four: Property, General Provision 898.1. Retrieved January 1, 2019, from http://legisquebec.gouv.qc.ca/en/ShowDoc/cs/CCQ-1991

McDonald, S. (2014, March 17). Dogs love us, says science – so we have to love them back. *The Guardian*. Retrieved February 2, 2019, from https://www.theguardian.com/commentisfree/2014/mar/17/dogs-rights-canine-sentience-research

McLain, T. (2009). Brief Summary of Pets in Divorce/Custody Issues. Michigan State University College of Law. Animal Legal and Historical Center. Retrieved January 1, 2019, from https://www.animallaw.info/intro/custody-pets-divorce

Merrill, T.W. (2002). Introduction: The Demsetz Thesis and the Evolution of Property Rights. *The Journal of Legal Studies (31)* S2 S331-S338. Retrieved January 1, 2019, from https://www.jstor.org/stable/10.1086/374348?seq=1#page_scan_tab_contents

Monyak, S. (2018, February 2). When the Law Recognizes Animals as People. *The New Republic*. Retrieved February 2, 2019, from https://newrepublic.com/article/146870/law-recognizes-animals-people

Moss, L. (2016, June 23). Should Dogs Have Legal Rights? Mother Nature Network. Retrieved January 1, 2019, from https://www.mnn.com/family/pets/stories/should-dogs-have-legal-rights

New York State Department of State Division of Cemeteries. (2016). Pet Cremated Remains FAQ. Retrieved Jun 14, 2019, from https://www.dos.ny.gov/cmty/pet-cremation.html

New Zealand Legislation. (2013). Animal Welfare Amendment Bill. Retrieved January 1, 2019, from http://www.legislation.govt.nz/bill/government/2013/0107/latest/DLM5174807.html

Noall, W. M. (1985). Animal Law in California. 12 Pepperdine Law Review 2. Retrieved February 2, 2019, from https://www.animallaw.info/article/animal-law-california

Nolen, R.S. (2011, April 1). After More Than A Decade, Has Pet Guardianship Changed Anything? *Journal of the American Veterinary Medical Association News*. Retrieved February 2, 2019, from https://admin.avma.org/News/JAVMANews/Pages/110401a.aspx?mode=mobile

Official Journal of the European Union. (2012). Consolidated Version Of The Treaty On The Functioning of the European Union: Part I Principles, Title II Provisions Having General Application, Article 13. Retrieved February 2, 2019, from https://eur-lex.europa.eu/resource.html?uri=cellar:2bf140bf-a3f8-4ab2-b506-fd71826e6da6.0023.02/DOC_2&format=PDF

Property [Def]. (2018). In The Free Dictionary. Retrieved January 1, 2019, from https://www.thefreedictionary.com/property

Quirk, B. (2018). Judges Will Now Consider the Care of Pets in Divorce Proceedings. Retrieved February 2, 2019, from https://a20.asmdc.org/press-releases/20180927-judges-will-now-consider-care-pets-divorce-proceedings

Rego v. Madalinski. (2016-Ohio-7339). Court of Appeals No. L-16-1030, Trial Court No. CVF-15-04492. Retrieved February 2, 2019, from https://www.courtlistener.com/opinion/4312864/rego-v-madalinski

Saint Leo University Polling Institute. (2018). Americans to Spend Big on Pets for Holidays, New Saint Leo U Poll Shows. Retrieved February 2, 2019, from http://polls.saintleo.edu/americans-to-spend-big-on-pets-for-holidays-new-saint-leo-u-poll-shows/

The Harris Poll. (2015). More Than Ever, Pets are Members of the Family. Retrieved February 2, 2019, from https://theharrispoll.com/whether-furry-feathered-or-flippers-a-flapping-americans-continue-to-display-close-relationships-with-their-pets-2015-is-expected-to-continue-the-pet-industrys-more-than-two-decades-strong/

Tischler, J. (2012, July 1). A Brief History of Animal Law Part II (1985-2011). Stanford Journal of Animal Law and Policy (5) 27. Retrieved January 1, 2019, from https://www-cdn.law.stanford.edu/wp-content/uploads/2018/05/tischler.pdf

Chapter Three: Professionals Should Exemplify and Promote Anti-Cruelty Statutes

As a population, human beings are all unique. Each one of us is a combination of our own individual genetics and environment. We are shaped by how we filter stimuli and how we think. Our behavior is an output of our own individual experiences, assumptions and perceptions, which are affected and distorted by our own personal values, beliefs, attitudes and expectations within a given location, setting or context. As individuals, we develop our own concepts, ethics and opinions, and this includes animal welfare (Tudge, 2015).

While we are now well into the 21st century, forceful restraint, startling, invoking fear, pain, and punishment are still commonly practiced in the pet care industry, including in day care, boarding, groomers and training facilities, and by owners themselves. However, opinions as to what constitutes cruelty differ vastly depending on who you ask. For some, any behavior or attitude toward an animal that is not deemed productive, helpful or in any way constructional to their physical and mental well-being is cruel or inhumane. For others, there are very specific lines drawn between the animals we nurture in our homes, the animals we farm for food production, and the exotic and wild animals some admire and protect from afar, but that others yearn to hunt.

> *According to Shelley-Grielen (2019), when cruelty cases appear across social media or in local news outlets, "it is not the everyday but the horrendous incidents that get media attention, e.g. the death of a dog by strangling during a nail trim in San Mateo, California (CBS SF Bay Area, 2016)."*

Cruelty Cases

According to Shelley-Grielen (2019), when cruelty cases appear across social media or in local news outlets, "it is not the everyday but the horrendous incidents that get media attention, e.g. the death of a dog by strangling during a nail trim in San Mateo, California (CBS SF Bay Area, 2016), a dog fatally mauled at a dog day care in Florida (Newby, 2017), multiple summer time deaths from heat stroke in a Florida grooming van (Birch, 2016), 23 dogs dying after being left overnight without cooling or ventilation in an Arizona boarding facility (Mitchell, 2016), abuses such as placing shock collars on dogs without owner knowledge at a Chicago day care to stop barking (Ludwig, 2017), or baked to death at a day care after falling unnoticed under a kiddie pool in South Carolina (Jacobs, 2016). After a covert video exposed a trainer at a Long Island, New York day care repeatedly jabbing a rod into a crated dog to stop him from growling was publicized (among other abusive practices at the site), New York State Senator Todd Kaminsky introduced a bill in late 2016 for licensing requirements for dog trainers." (*At the time of publishing, Kaminsky's bill had not passed. Meanwhile, in June 2019, a bill sponsored by New Jersey Assembly Members Carol Murphy and Valerie Huttle requiring the licensure of dog trainers was introduced. At the time of publishing, that had not passed either.*) (*See also* Chapter Three: Professionals Should Exemplify and Promote Anti-Cruelty Statutes / Truth in Training *and* Chapter Nine: Consumer Protection and Transparency / Misrepresentation.)

When cases such as these are reported, they are often met with outrage from both local and wider communities. Often, rescue organizations seek donations for help and support in high profile cruelty cases and, in many cases, the outpouring of financial support far surpasses the monetary needs for the individual case. Ultimately, this public outrage for high profile cases often helps fund multiple scenarios and provide much needed resources for rescue groups to support the "less offensive" cases. In the court of public opinion, some may get angry and demand severe punishment for the offenders. Others may take an opposing view, voicing sentiments such as, "it's just a dog," or "there are bigger problems in the world," or simply dismiss the event with no response at all.

According to Arluke (2002, p.421), "...humorous slants on cruelty are plentiful and can be seen in children's cartoons and comics, as well as in adult advertising and movies and even occasional talk-radio programs." Examples of cruelty such as blowing up pets, dragging them behind vehicles, or threatening them with weapons such as a baseball bat are commonplace and, in turn, become reflected in real instances of real cruelty in everyday life. It is, or should be, of enormous concern that "[o]ver a million websites offer jokes about animal abuse or cruelty." (Arluke & Sanders, 1996, p.40).

Public Policy

According to Tudge and Nilson (2019), "[a]s anyone who has ever shared their life with an animal knows, humans and their pets have a special bond. When we look at dogs in particular, the relationship is unique in that, across generations over tens of thousands of years, we have purposefully adapted this one species through natural selection to be more collaborative, more reliant and more functional to support our human needs. This selection process has resulted in hundreds of canine breeds working across multiple functions to support and collaborate with humans (Overall, 2013). Indeed, there are 'fingerprints in dogs' DNA that suggest convergence or coevolution with humans in neurochemical patterns.' (Overall, 2016)."

Hunter and Brisbin (2016, p.17) define cruelty as the "infliction of suffering or pain by a perpetrator on an undeserving subject." In the companion animal relationship, humans are the perpetrators. How each of us chooses to treat pets is a voluntary decision but does vary due to our political and cultural diversity. Arluke (2006) discusses how the term cruelty may be minimized and glossed over as well as the school of thought that "abuse is done deliberately, while neglect is unintentional or even accidental." Arluke (2006) also discuss opinions such as those maintaining that abuse results in tragic injury to animals, while neglect "only" creates hardship for them. Rowan (1993) suggests that the term cruelty should only be used in cases where the offender is in some way satisfied from the harm they cause. Regardless of where one stands on this point, however, and irrespective of the motives of the perpetrator and whether the cruelty be sadistic or negligent, no pet intentionally seeks to be punished and no pet deserves to be the victim of cruelty (Hunter & Brisbin, 2016).

> "When we look at dogs in particular, the relationship is unique in that, across generations over tens of thousands of years, we have purposefully adapted this one species through natural selection to be more collaborative, more reliant and more functional to support our human needs." - Tudge & Nilson (2019)

As a result of political pressure applied by constituents to local governments, fueled by the general growth of the Animal Welfare Movement from the early 20th century onwards, where, "[b]y the end of the 1980s, membership in animal advocacy organizations had reached 10 million people in the United States," (Encyclopedia.com, 2019), anticruelty laws have become more commonplace and fines increased. Nevertheless, "in many countries, states and counties, laws are woefully inadequate to protect the lives of dogs…Where such laws do exist, they are often weak, poorly written and/or not well-enforced, leaving gaping loopholes for perpetrators of animal crimes." (Steinker, 2018).

According to the Humane Society of the United States (2019), a majority of anticruelty laws are "limited to cases involving aggravated cruelty, torture or cruelty to companion animals." All in all, 48 states, the District of Columbia, Puerto Rico and the Virgin Islands have laws making certain types of animal cruelty a felony offense. (*Note: North Dakota classifies it a Class A misdemeanor and South Dakota as a Class 1 misdemeanor.*) While 46 of 50 states' felony provisions are first-offense provisions, some state laws allow felony charges "only if the perpetrator has a previous animal cruelty conviction…Four states (Pennsylvania, Ohio, Iowa and Mississippi) have laws that apply felony charges only to subsequent offenses." However, "only a fraction of animal cruelty acts are ever reported or successfully prosecuted." (Humane Society of the United States, 2019).

In recent developments, in April 2019, Indiana State Senator Jon Ford authored Senate Bill 474, which moves to "establish a mandatory condition of probation and parole that would not allow any person convicted of animal abuse to own, harbor, or train a 'companion animal.'" The bill was passed in the Indiana House by a unanimous vote and has since moved to Indiana Governor Eric Holcomb (Essex, 2019). Also in 2019, a bill signed by Virginia Governor Ralph Northam was set to ensure anyone found guilty of abusing dogs and cats would face stiffer punishments than previously: "Dubbed 'Tommie's Law,' after a pit bull who was tied to a fence and intentionally set on fire…the bill elevates cruel and unnecessary 'beating, maiming, mutilating, or killing a dog or cat' to a Class 6 felony charge. Earlier legislation had stipulated an animal had to die because of abuse to be considered a felony offense in the state." (Mosbergen, 2019). (*Note: Information correct at the time of publication.*)

According to Antolec (2018), the Federal Bureau of Investigation (FBI) "takes animal abuse so seriously it began tracking the crime in 2014 and uses the data to help identify serial killers." In 2016, the Bureau added animal cruelty to its list of Class A felonies, alongside homicide and arson. According to Ferry (2016), of the FBI's Criminal Statistics Management Unit, "[s]ome studies say that cruelty to animals is a precursor to larger crime." (qtd. in FBI, 2016). The National Sheriffs' Association, meanwhile, has for a number of years cited studies linking animal abuse and other types of crimes, highlighting the "overlap animal abuse has with domestic violence and child abuse." (FBI, 2016). States Thompson (2016), deputy executive director of the National Sheriffs' Association: "If somebody is harming an animal, there is a good chance they also are hurting a human…[animal cruelty] is a crime against society." (qtd. in FBI, 2016).

Normative Behavior Toward Pets

Hunter and Brisbin (2016) present a scale of normative behavior toward pets commencing with sadistic behavior and ending with empathy. The scale addresses whether cruelty is defined by motivation or hardship suffered and can be summarized as follows:

1. Sadistic Behavior: This includes acts of intentional murder and the pleasurable sense of excitement perpetrators experience when inflicting pain. Displays are exhibited by audiences at dog fights and individuals who inflict torture on pets motivated by a sick sense of curiosity.
2. Passive Cruelty: This speaks to ignorance, apathy and a generally immature sense of empathy as the perpetrator has feelings of disgust for or an ambivalence toward a pet, perhaps viewing them as a commodity only. The moral consequence is that persons displaying passive cruelty "unsee" the suffering of animals (Hunter & Brisbin, 2016, p.17). Passively cruel behaviors are not always considered illegal or pathological like sadistic behavior. Examples include chaining a dog for 24 hours, social isolation, mental and physical deprivation, harsh and unyielding punishment, and/or mental intimidation of the family pet.
3. Neglectful Behavior: Although far from ideal, this can sometimes be remedied through local laws. It differs from passive cruelty as it is an involuntary lack of due care and may not be aimed at causing the pet to suffer. This encompasses owners who overlook necessary and important veterinarian treatment.
4. Empathy: This is shown by people who consider it their moral duty to protect animals from cruelty. They have emotional intelligence and the ability to understand and share the feelings of the pet and expect society to treat pets as they themselves would like to be treated.

As stated earlier, examples of extreme incidents of dogs being killed or sustaining serious injuries at the hands of pet professionals have been, and continue to be, reported in the media. Such incidents have occurred at the hands of professional groomers, dog trainers and/or boarding kennels, the very professionals engaged and compensated by pet owners to care for their pets. It is important to note here that in the United States (and elsewhere) the pet training industry is "entirely unregulated, meaning that anyone can say they are a trainer or behavior consultant," regardless of education, experience, skill, or knowledge – or lack thereof (Pet Professional Guild, 2016). Of the European Union, Masson et al. (2018) note that dog training is also "largely unregulated...so there is a risk that many trainers do not have a proper education in canine ethology and learning theory, both dense, complicated fields." We will come back to these issues in later chapters. (See *Chapter Seven: Competency Is Mission Critical / What is Professional Competence?, Chapter Eight: Ethics in Pet Training and Behavior Consulting / Ethics Across Professional Associations in an Unregulated Profession* and *Chapter Ten: Pet Industry Oversight Recommended Implementation Model*.)

Truth in Training

In November 2017, Hillsborough County Commissioners in Tampa, Florida, voted five to two in favor of a groundbreaking ordinance that regulates the dog training industry in their county. It was the first of its kind in the nation. The bill was named Truth in Training but is commonly known as Sarge's Law. It came about when puppy Sarge, who weighed just 8 pounds, died after a physical altercation with a dog trainer that took place in full view of his owner. As reported by the *Dogington Post* (2017): "Sarge was a happy, healthy Shih Tzu/Pekingese puppy whose loving parents sent him to doggy day care each day as part of their efforts to give him the best life possible. Sarge's owner, Lorie Childers, opted to use the day care's training services to teach her little dog to walk nicely on a leash."

> "Sarge was so happy to see me and just wanted to play. That's when the trainer grabbed him – clamped his hand over his mouth and held it closed, and grabbed his neck with his other hand. Sarge thrashed and collapsed." – Lori Childers

Says Childers: "I picked Sarge up from day care on the day he died. We began to work with the trainer on teaching him how to heel next to me. Sarge was so happy to see me and just wanted to play. That's when the trainer grabbed him – clamped his hand over his mouth and held it closed, and grabbed his neck with his other hand. Sarge thrashed and collapsed. His eyes were glazed over and his tongue was hanging out. It was stiff, and it had turned white. I knew something was horribly wrong...I picked Sarge up and rushed him to the nearest animal hospital...As I was driving, Sarge was crying, struggling to breathe, and was unable to hold his head up. As I picked him up to carry him into the vet, I saw there was blood both on me and on the car seat. Just as we approached the door of the hospital, I felt Sarge's heartbeat starting to fade. He died in my arms as I crossed through the doorway. Our puppy, Sarge, died on May 1, 2015 at just 3½ months old." (Steinker, 2018).

Steinker (2018) reports on further cases of abuse, negligence and death of dogs in training, day care or boarding in Hillsborough County, including Blue (taken off property from a boarding kennel without his owner's consent, slipped his leash and was hit by a car – his owner later found out kennel staff had used a frayed slip leash); Finn (died in a board and train facility – he had bruising around his neck and blood in his nostrils, leading the vet who conducted the necropsy to suspect he had been strangled); Gunner (died two days after his stay at a board and train facility – he had open sores on his legs, fluid coming from his mouth and appeared to have difficulty moving when his owners collected him); and Max (helicoptered four times and punched by a trainer). (See also Chapter Nine: Consumer Protection and Transparency / Misrepresentation.)

> Hippocrates (400 B.C.) wrote: "The physician must be able to tell the antecedents, know the present, and foretell the future—must mediate these things, and have two special objects in view with regard to disease, namely, to do good or to do no harm." Working with animals, whether in the veterinary field or any other capacity, the moral and ethical obligation to do no harm is surely just as meaningful.

Crucially, however, the Truth in Training bill does not provide any oversight on the methods or tools employed in the training, management and/or care of pets. It simply states that professional trainers must inform their clients how they intend to train a dog by way of a written training plan and a transparency document that must be signed by both parties.

Dog trainers who use punishment based approaches and equipment designed to work by causing fear and/or pain commonly market themselves under a variety of verbiage and marketing slogans such as "balanced," "positive relationship," "natural methods," "relationship building," "positive only," and "no food necessary." These are all taglines that are bandied around but mislead unsuspecting owners who are looking for humane ways to train their pets. Meanwhile, the terminology used may be carefully crafted to appeal to pet guardians who may not always understand the various training methods available, or the fallout and unintended consequences of making the wrong choice. Such trainers are thus not providing consumers the necessary autonomy to make ethical decisions on behalf of their pets, nor do they provide any kind of consumer protection. This, compounded with the inability of a pet to offer informed consent, further questions the ethics of such training practices given that the foundation for anyone working in behavioral sciences must surely be to do no harm (Pet Professional Guild, 2016).

> Dog trainers who use punishment based approaches and equipment designed to work by causing fear and/or pain commonly market themselves under a variety of verbiage and marketing slogans such as "balanced," "positive relationship," "natural methods," "relationship building," "positive only," and "no food necessary."

Over 2,000 years ago, referring to the medical profession, Hippocrates (400 B.C.) wrote: "The physician must be able to tell the antecedents, know the present, and foretell the future—must mediate these things, and have two special objects in view with regard to disease, namely, to do good or to do no harm." Working with animals, whether in the veterinary field or any other capacity, the moral and ethical obligation to do no harm is surely just as meaningful. (*See also Chapter Five: A Call for an Industry Wide, Professionally Acknowledged Best Practice / Key Learning Theory*).

Abusive Training Practices

Listed below are just some of the abusive practices still seen across the dog training industry:

- Hanging – the dog is raised off the floor by his collar or a leash, in some cases until he loses consciousness.
- Swinging – the dog is swung around with his feet off the floor by his collar or leash.
- Slamming – the dog is lifted up and slammed into the floor or wall
- Shocking – electric shock is administered through a collar around the dog's neck, stomach or genital area.
- Multiple shocking – more than one electric shock collar is attached to a dog around the neck, stomach and/or genitalia.

- Alpha roll – the dog is purposefully rolled onto his back as a means to control and intimidate, often paired with harsh, loud, and offensive verbiage.
- Kicking, hitting, prodding – the dog is physically assaulted with a human body part or a prod-type instrument.

> *We are now in a position to know better. In fact, in most professions that involve counseling, mental health, education, or training, there is a professional expectation and, indeed, a legal mandate that, no matter what the field, a professional must practice according to the best, most reliable and up-to-date scientific research available.*

In recent years, much creditable scientific study has been given to dog training and behavior modification methods and their respective efficacy and consequences (*see Chapter Four: How Pets Learn and the Consequences of Methodology, Equipment and Philosophical Choice / A Review of the Science*). The preponderance of the evidence shown by current research indicates that the implementation of training and/or behavior modification protocols predicated upon "dominance theory" and social structures ("alpha," or "pack leader"), and/or the implementation of physical or psychological intimidation, threats, coercion, or fear are empirically less effective and risk creating problematic consequences, including "fallout" behaviors that may be dangerous to the human and animal involved such as growling, snapping and biting.

Defining Dominance Theory

According to DogNostics Career Center (2018), dominance theory is used within the same species to predict the winner of a conflict when fighting over a specific, context-oriented resource. Scientifically, dominance only applies to two beings of the same species, thus a human cannot be dominant over a pet nor can a pet be dominant over a human. In a wolf pack the dominant beings are the wolf pups; however, wolf researchers have moved away from alpha terminology and are now using terms that correspond with the role of the particular pet in the family unit.

Using dominance theory to train dogs is today considered to be outdated and obsolete, with current scientific knowledge recanting the findings of previous studies that promote the implementation of alpha rolls and so-called dominance training. Leading expert and board certified veterinary behaviorist, Dr. Karen Overall (2016) states: "Dominance theory has shut off scientific research and has crept into medicine to the point where we think we can do things to animals whereby we are asking them to 'submit.' In pop psychology, dominance theory is insidious and has crept into everything we do with dogs and it's wrong. It has gotten in the way of modern science and I've just about had it. Every single thing we do with dogs hurts them because we don't see them as individuals or cognitive partners...Unfortunately, the dominance, discipline and coercion approach has affected every aspect of how we interact with dogs from basic training to treating troubled dogs. We *must* abandon these cruel, scientifically unsupported labels and approaches and replace them with a humane, scientifically-based approach that is dog-centric and attempts to understand situations from the viewpoint of the dog." We will continue our examination of dominance theory in *Chapter Four: How Pets Learn and the Consequences / Outdated Approach*.

> Using dominance theory to train dogs is today considered to be outdated and obsolete, with current scientific knowledge recanting the findings of previous studies that promote the implementation of alpha rolls and so-called dominance training.

People may think that to work in the pet industry one must love animals, yet, in reality, how can this be possible given the varied topography of pet care? In addition to the examples of cruelty, abuse and neglect highlighted earlier, we must also consider pet professionals who still rely on outdated training practices and cultural myths while ignoring the growing body of science that proposes specific, humane methods and approaches. Is this really so different to a public policy that accepts the use by a medical professional of alcohol as an anesthetic, or leather arm cuffs as restraints as standard operating procedures? We are now in a position to know better. In fact, in most professions that involve counseling, mental health, education, or training, there is a professional expectation and, indeed, a legal mandate that, no matter what the field, a professional must practice according to the best, most reliable and up-to-date scientific research available. We will talk more about the medical and counseling professions in *Chapter Eight: Ethics in Pet Training and Behavior Consulting*.

Professionals and Cruelty

There are two important questions we can ask here:

1. What causes people and, in particular, pet professionals, to be cruel to the pets in their care?

2. How do said professionals accommodate the consequences of their behavior?

While there is no complete or consistent explanation as to why people are sadistic or cruel to pets, in those who choose to work with pets as an occupation a commonality would appear to exist in a tendency to view the animals as "other," or significantly different to people. Hunter and Brisbin (2016) explain that the person may feel in some way threatened by the existence of the pet, whether it be emotionally, egotistically, or physically. Under such circumstances, any cruel behavior is seen to be "justified" as "teaching the pet a lesson," and/or there may be a motivation to nullify the "other" by inflicting suffering. Hunter and Brisbin (2016, p.19) conclude that cruelty "in its various forms is thus a human emotional and cognitive response to perceptions or predictions of unpleasant contacts with companion animals." Meanwhile, from an animal's perspective, it is in no way in his best interests to intentionally set out to be what a human may perceive to be "annoying" or "frustrating," or to inflict pain on his caregivers, yet how many times do we hear a pet owner or professional say a dog is being "stubborn" or "naughty?"

> *Patel (2019) figure 1emphasizes the importance of getting a measure on what is observable when analyzing behavior, which "allows us to put numbers on what we actually see occur rather than create a story in our heads."*

In reality, applying labels to behavior that have nothing to do with the animal's actual emotional state or motivation is anthropomorphic at best and, at worst, runs the risk of complete misinterpretation. While anthropomorphism has its uses, Patel (2019) emphasizes the importance of getting a measure on what is observable when analyzing behavior, which "allows us to put numbers on what we actually see occur rather than create a story in our heads." All behavior "has a function and can produce a number of functional outcomes: The organism is always correct; they are just functioning on the conditions available to them." (Patel, 2019). Frightening or aversive environmental stimuli, including punitive pet training methods and scary techniques, are, more often than not, the cause of aggression from pets directed to people. But, states Patel (2019): "If you listen to the whispers, your dog has no reason to shout or scream."

One might argue that passive cruelty or neglect tend to manifest from convenience or function. For example, professional groomers or dog trainers may be motivated by a need or desire to get results at whatever cost to the pet. Economically, they may be motivated by profit and the need for expeditious business transactions. These practices may include pinning down a dog to trim his nails or applying physical punishment, such as a leash jerk, to prevent a dog from pulling on the leash.

> "The organism is always correct, they are just functioning on the conditions available to them." (Patel, 2019). Frightening or aversive environmental stimuli, including punitive pet training methods and scary techniques, are, more often than not, the cause of aggression from pets directed to people. But, states Patel (2019): "If you listen to the whispers, your dog has no reason to shout or scream."

Returning to our second question, for those who elect to inflict cruelty on the animals in their care, how do they accommodate the consequences of their behavior? How does a dog trainer justify to themselves that hanging a dog until he almost chokes, shocking a dog to the point where he is so fearful he loses control of his bowels, or physically hitting a dog, is acceptable on any scale?

We might ask the same of the groomer who physically pins a dog on the grooming table if he does not immediately comply and stand in the required position for the perfect haircut. Bear in mind in a situation such as this, no time may have been taken to train the dog to stand in said position or create a positive association for him, as opposed to presenting an aversive situation that he would now prefer to escape from or avoid altogether. States Martiya (2016): "If you have ever worked in a grooming salon, this scenario is probably familiar to you: The dog is on the table with a noose around his neck attached to the grooming arm above. He is moving about while the groomer is trying to scissor some part of his body. Frustrated by his movement, the groomer raises the grooming arm. The dog struggles, so the groomer raises the grooming arm some more. Now the dog stops struggling, but it is not because he has 'learned to behave.' He has stopped struggling because he is effectively being hung from the grooming arm and must devote all of his energy just to breathing."

Adds Shelley-Grielen (2019): "Dog trainers, groomers and pet sitters often learn handling techniques by trial, error and guesswork with no guarantee that their intuition is correct or welfare focused...Individuals wanting to learn dog grooming at an actual brick and mortar school can complete a two- or three-month private school training course. However, due to the brevity of the training and lack of instruction on stress free restraint methodologies or handling protocols there is a resulting over-reliance on restraint such as muzzles, ties and aversive handling. Stress of this sort may cause a dog to submit to a grooming session but will cause more defensive resistance on successive grooming sessions."

We may also ask the question of the dog walker who drags and chokes a dog to mandate that he walks at a specific and very unnatural pace. States Chamings (2018): "Training in this way gives a dog no choice at all; he is complying because he is avoiding discomfort." Yet these are all examples of practices that some individuals – who have *chosen* to make their living training and caring for pets – find completely acceptable.

Arluke's (2006) ethnographic study of animal control officers, animal hoarders and shelter workers "illustrated how an individual's identification of animals interacts with emotions, professional standards and practices, willingness to obey authority and personal identity." (Hunter & Brisbin, 2016, p.19). These components along with early childhood socialization and experiences can create a social confusion regarding the ethical treatment of animals (Hunter & Brisbin, 2016).

Hunter and Brisbin (2016) also reference other studies that indicate a desire for power, social background, or other demographic factors may have an influence on individuals in terms of whether they may display passive cruelty or neglect toward animals. Alternatively, it may just be that cruelty is influenced by the direct visibility of the act or differing interpretations of cruelty toward different species. As noted by Hunter and Brisbin (2016), O'Sullivan argues that animal cruelty is impacted by the visibility of the harm to the animal versus the normative assessments of cruelty and the current legislation to protect the animal.

When sadistic behavior, passive cruelty or neglect have taken place, pet owners may resort to moral disengagement to justify this. As such, the offender may be able to reconstruct or reframe their behavior as acceptable without feeling the need to change either their moral standards or their behavior: "Moral disengagement is behavior designed to avoid censure for injurious conduct." (Hunter and Brisbin, 2016, p.20).

Vollum, Buffington-Vollum and Longmire (2004) surveyed Texas residents to gauge the perceived severity of numerous violent acts against nonhuman animals as well as the preferred criminal justice response and indicated their surprise as the "findings lend some (albeit limited) support for an important theory of animal abuse (Agnew, 1998), as well as Bandura's (1990, 1999) compelling theory of moral disengagement."

According to Bandura (2002), however, disengagement does not instantly transform an individual from being kind and considerate to being cruel, but is a more gradual process as said individual is exposed to more and more, for them, uncomfortable situations. In the case of a dog trainer or pet groomer, the individual may have started out by using aversive practices on pets and found that they paid off, thus making them able to tolerate the acts because of the benefit associated with them. These might involve saving a groomer time thanks to the ease of working with a dog who is pinned to the table, or, in the case of a dog trainer, expediting compliance via the use of electric shock while suppressing potentially irritating but normal canine behaviors such as wandering, sniffing, or lack of focus. Situations such as these may apply in pet care or training environment for the professional who is on a time schedule, lacks knowledge, or has little empathy for the pet in their care.

Progressive Disengagement

Over time, "progressive disengagement of self-censure" occurs and "the level of ruthlessness increases, until eventually acts originally regarded as abhorrent can be performed with little anguish or self-censure. Inhumane practices become thoughtlessly routinized." (Bandura, 2002, p.110). It should, then, and, indeed, must be of great concern to public policy makers that when a person inflicts cruel actions on a pet and undertakes moral disengagement such as this, "the continuing interplay between moral thought, affect, action and its social reception is personally transformative. People may not even recognize the changes they have undergone as a moral self." (Bandura, 2002, p 110). Consequently, this should also be enormously concerning to pet owners given that pet professionals, more often than not, avoid being held accountable for any cruelty toward the pets in their care, pets who have little or no say in their own well-being and welfare.

Ultimately, all parties involved need to exercise moral agency. This has the dual purpose of being both inhibitive and proactive. The inhibitive form embodies the power to refrain from behaving inhumanely whereas the proactive form is expressed in the power to behave humanely. Therefore, people who practice higher order morality do good things, as well as refrain from doing bad things (Bandura, 1999).

Summary

The findings by Vollum et al. (2004) showed that people are "concerned about the social problem of animal cruelty and believe that it should be taken seriously by the criminal justice system." In 2019, the Animal League Defense Fund, the United States' leading legal advocacy group for animals, released its 12th annual year-end report and ranked the animal protection laws of all 50 states under a three-tier system. According to the report, the five top states for animals are:

1. Illinois
2. Oregon
3. Maine
4. Colorado
5. Massachusetts

While the five worst states are:

1. New Mexico
2. Wyoming
3. Iowa
4. Mississippi
5. Kentucky

States the Animal League Defense Fund (2019): "The disparity in various jurisdictions' animal protection laws demonstrates the unfortunate reality that, in many places, the law significantly underrepresents animals' interests." On a brighter note, the Rankings Report "also presents an opportunity to improve laws everywhere." (Animal League Defense Fund, 2019).

Bibliography

Animal League Defense Fund. (2019). 2018 U.S. Animal Protection Laws State Rankings. Retrieved December 31, 2018, from https://aldf.org/wp-content/uploads/2019/01/Animal-Protection-Laws-of-the-United-States-2018-full-report.pdf

Antolec, D. (2018, July). Living in Fear. *BARKS from the Guild (31)* 54-66. Retrieved February 2, 2019, from https://issuu.com/petprofessionalguild/docs/bftg_july_2018_online_edition_opt 1/54

Arluke, A. (2002). Animal Abuse as Dirty Play. *Symbolic Interaction (25)* 4 405–430. Retrieved December 31, 2018, from https://onlinelibrary.wiley.com/doi/pdf/10.1525/si.2002.25.4.405

Arluke, A. (2006). Just a Dog: Understanding Animal Cruelty and Ourselves. Philadelphia, PA: Temple University Press

Arluke, A., & Sanders, C. (1996). Regarding animals. Philadelphia, PA: Temple University Press

Arnold, B. (2017, November 15). Tampa Becomes First-in-Nation to Pass Groundbreaking Dog Training Ordinance. *The Dogington Post*. Retrieved December 31, 2018, from https://www.dogingtonpost.com/tampa-becomes-first-nation-pass-groundbreaking-dog-training-ordinance

Bandura, A. (1999). Moral disengagement in the perpetration of inhumanities. *Personality and Social Psychology Review* [Special Issue on Evil and Violence] 3 193–209. Retrieved December 31, 2018, from http://www.uky.edu/~eushe2/Bandura/Bandura1999PSPR.pdf

Bandura, A. (2002). Selective Moral Disengagement in the Exercise of Moral Agency. *Journal of Moral Education (31)* 2. Retrieved December 31, 2018, from https://web.stanford.edu/~kcarmel/CC_BehavChange_Course/readings/Additional%20Resources/Bandura/bandura_moraldisengagement.pdf

Birch, J. (2016, May 11). 3 dogs die at Miramar groomer, pet owner demands answers. Local 10 ABC News. Retrieved May 14, 2019, from https://www.local10.com/pets/3-dogs-die-at-miramar-groomer-pet-owner-demands-answers

CBS SF Bay Area. (2016, November 22). Pet Dachshund Owners Sue PetSmart After Dog Dies During Grooming. Retrieved May 14, 2019, from http://sanfrancisco.cbslocal.com/2016/11/22/pet-dachshund-owners-sue-petsmart-after-dog-dies-during-grooming

Chamings, S.R. (2018, January). But Does It Work? *BARKS from the Guild (28)* 28-30. Retrieved May 15, 2019, from https://issuu.com/petprofessionalguild/docs/bftg_january_2018_online_edition_op/28

DogNostics Career Center. (2018). A Practical Lexicon for Pet Trainers & Behavior Consultants! The Language You Need to Know. (n.p.): Authors

Encyclopedia.com. (2019). Animal Rights. Retrieved February 2, 2019, from https://www.encyclopedia.com/social-sciences-and-law/sociology-and-social-reform/social-reform/animal-rights-movement

Essex, C. (2019). Indiana Animal Abuse Bill Set To Head To Governor's Desk. WTHI-TV10. Retrieved June 14, 2019, from https://www.wthitv.com/content/news/Indiana-animal-abuse-bill-set-to-head-to-governors-desk-508065991.html

FBI. (2016). Tracking Animal Cruelty. Retrieved June 14, 2019, from
https://www.fbi.gov/news/stories/-tracking-animal-cruelty

Hippocrates. (400 B.C.). Of the Epidemics (Book 1, Section II). Retrieved May 14, 2019, from
http://classics.mit.edu/Hippocrates/epidemics.1.i.html

Humane Society of the United States. (2019). Animal cruelty facts and stats. Retrieved June 14, 2019, from https://www.humanesociety.org/resources/animal-cruelty-facts-and-stats

Humane Society of the United States. (2019). State Animal Cruelty Chart. Retrieved June 14, 2019, from https://www.humanesociety.org/sites/default/files/docs/state-animal-cruelty-chart.pdf

Hunter, S., & Brisbin, R.A. (2016). Pet Politics. West Lafayette, IN: Purdue University Press

Jacobs, H. (2016, May 3). Owner claims pet 'baked' at doggy daycare, no laws regulating S.C. facilities. Live5News. Retrieved May 14, 2019, from
http://www.live5news.com/story/31877881/owner-claims-pet-baked-at-doggy-daycare-no-laws-regulating-sc-facilities

Ludwig, H. (2017, March 23). Dog Day Care Put A Shock Collar on My Dog Without Permission, Owner Says. DNA Info Chicago. Retrieved May 14, 2019, from
https://www.dnainfo.com/chicago/20170323/mt-greenwood/posh-pet-day-spa-shock-collar-doggie-daycare-luke-mullaney

Masson, S., La Vega, S., Gazzano, A., Mariti, C., Da Graça Pereira, G., Halsberghe, C.,…Schoening, B. (2018). Electronic training devices: Discussion on the pros and cons of their use in dogs as a basis for the position statement of the European Society of Veterinary Clinical Ethology. *Journal of Veterinary Behavior 25* 71-75. Retrieved May 28, from
https://www.sciencedirect.com/science/article/pii/S1558787818300108?fbclid=IwAR0rsVM-689ZbE2CFDUuMAmatkmEKiIk9id15xbJrTiLac9Nj5UGtPZW9ho

Martiya, M. (2016, July). Grooming Restraints. *BARKS from the Guild (19)* 38-39. Retrieved May 15, 2019, from https://issuu.com/petprofessionalguild/docs/bftg_july_2016_opt/38

Mitchell, G. (2016, July 1). Green Acre kennel owners accept plea deal in deaths of 23 dogs in Gilbert area. AZ Central. Retrieved May 14, 2019, from
http://www.azcentral.com/story/news/local/gilbert-breaking/2016/06/30/green-acre-kennel-owners-accept-plea-deal-deaths-more-than-20-dogs-gilbert/86563596

Mosbergen, D. (2019). Animal Cruelty Now A Felony Offense In Virginia. Huff Post. Retrieved June 14, 2019, from https://www.huffpost.com/entry/tommies-law-animal-cruelty-virginia-felony_n_5ca30956e4b0a453fb74f5aa

Newby, J. (2017, November 30). Woman wants justice after dog mauled at Gulf Breeze boarder. Pensacola News Journal. Retrieved May 14, 2019, from
https://eu.pnj.com/story/news/local/2017/11/30/dog-dies-mauling-gulf-breeze-groomer-april-showers/910265001

Patel, C. (2019, April). Functionally Analyzing Aggression! Paper presented at Pet Professional Guild Canine Aggression and Bite Prevention Seminar, Portland, OR

Pet Professional Guild. (2016). Open Letter to Veterinarians on Referrals to Training and Behavior Professionals. Retrieved December 31, 2018, from https://petprofessionalguild.com/Open-letter-to-veterinarians-on-referrals-to-training-and-behavior-professionals

Rowan, A. (1992). The Dark Side of the "Force". *Anthrozoös (5)* 1 4–5. Retrieved December 31, 2018, from https://www.researchgate.net/publication/287864914_The_Dark_Side_of_the_Force

Shelley-Grielen, F. (2019, January). Room for Improvement. *BARKS from the Guild (34)* 40-43. Retrieved December 31, 2018, from https://issuu.com/petprofessionalguild/docs/bftg_january_2019_online_edition_op/40

Shelley-Grielen, F. (2019). Understanding and Accomplishing Animal Welfare. Retrieved May 29, 2019, from https://www.animalbehaviorist.us/AccomplishingWelfare.html

State of New Jersey 218th Legislature. (2018). Assembly Bill 4066: Requires licensure of dog trainers. Retrieved May 29, from https://legiscan.com/NJ/text/A4066/id/1805579

Steinker, A. (2018, March). The Dark Side of Dog Training and Pet Care. *BARKS from the Guild (29)* 14-21. Retrieved December 31, 2018, from https://issuu.com/petprofessionalguild/docs/bftg_mar_2018_online_edition_opt/14

The New York State Senate. (2016). Senate Bill S8219: An act to amend the agriculture and markets law, in relation to requiring the commissioner of agriculture and markets to establish licensing and educational standards for individuals providing canine training for non-service and non-police dogs. Retrieved May 29, from https://www.nysenate.gov/legislation/bills/2015/s8219

Tudge, N.J. (2015). People Training Skills for Pet Professionals. Tampa, FL: The DogSmith
Tudge, N.J. & Nilson, S.J. (2019, January). The Case for Scientifically-Informed, Kind Practices. *BARKS from the Guild (34)* 18-26. Retrieved December 31, 2018, from https://issuu.com/petprofessionalguild/docs/bftg_january_2019_online_edition_op/18

Vollum, S., Buffington-Vollum, J., & Longmire, D. (2004). Moral Disengagement and Attitudes about Violence toward Animals. *Society and Animals 12* 209-235. Retrieved December 31, 2018, from https://www.researchgate.net/publication/233638450_Moral_Disengagement_and_Attitudes_about_Violence_toward_Animals

Chapter Four: How Pets Learn and the Consequences of Methodology, Equipment and Philosophical Choice

Before we enter into the science of learning and behavior, it is important to point out that on July 7, 2012, a prominent international group of cognitive neuroscientists, neuropharmacologists, neurophysiologists, neuroanatomists and computational neuroscientists gathered for the for the Francis Crick Memorial Conference at the University of Cambridge in England to reassess the neurobiological substrates of conscious experience and related behaviors in human and non-human animals. This resulted in the Cambridge Declaration on Consciousness (Low, 2012). While comparative research on this topic is naturally hampered by the inability of nonhuman animals, and often humans, to clearly and readily communicate, "the declaration concludes that 'nonhuman animals have the neuroanatomical, neurochemical, and neurophysiological substrates of conscious states along with the capacity to exhibit intentional behaviors. Consequently, the weight of evidence indicates that humans are not unique in possessing the neurological substrates that generate consciousness. Nonhuman animals, including all mammals and birds, and many other creatures, including octopuses, also possess these neurological substrates.'" (Bekoff, 2012).

> In cases of high emotional arousal ("emotional hijacking"), the emotional brain inhibits the rational brain and an animal will go into fight or flight mode. In biological terms, this means it is difficult, if not impossible, for them to learn productively when in a fearful or anxious state, other than to fear or distrust the person (or other, corresponding stimulus) causing the negative emotional response.

Where It Begins

While natural selection helps pets adapt to changes across generations, it is not so effective in helping them cope with rapid changes in their immediate environment, for example, when they are adopted into a new home. McKeon (2017) states, specifically of racing greyhounds but just as applicable to any dog who finds himself the product of an impoverished early environment: "They have not generally seen or encountered microwave ovens, televisions, stairs, other breeds of dogs, small animals or children…Coming into a domestic environment must feel rather like landing on an alien planet. One day you are living in the familiar, and the next you are transported to a place where you do not speak the language, know the customs, or understand what is expected of you, and where everything appears alien."

This is undoubtedly a tough ask, and one that is perhaps not always appreciated or fully realized by new pet owners, however good their intentions. In order to adapt to new and changing environments, pets must be able to learn, which we can define as a measurable change in behavior that takes place through experiences to events, i.e. stimuli, and is essential for survival. Chance (2008, p.24) states that "learning takes up where reflexes, modal action patterns and general behavior leave off."

Like humans, animals can learn in a healthy, humane and safe manner, or, conversely, through pain, force and fear. In cases of high emotional arousal ("emotional hijacking"), the emotional brain inhibits the rational brain and an animal will go into fight or flight mode. In biological terms, this means it is difficult, if not impossible, for them to learn productively when in a fearful or anxious state, other than to fear or distrust the person (or other, corresponding stimulus) causing the negative emotional response.

> According to Bekoff (2008), it is simply "bad biology to argue against the existence of animal emotions. Scientific research in evolutionary biology, cognitive ethology (the study of animal minds) and social neuroscience support the view that numerous and diverse animals have rich and deep emotional lives."

We now know, as if there were ever any doubt among those who share their lives with animals, that pets are sentient beings with central nervous systems and brain functions. It is thus time to lay to rest disagreements and propositions about these differences in terms of learning and emotions because, as mammals, we all share many of the same biological systems and functions, and we each learn through nonassociative and associative means.

Nonassociative Learning

Nonassociative learning is defined by how animals change their response to a stimulus without associating it with a positive or negative reinforcer. This occurs in the form of habituation or sensitization.

Habituation occurs when an animal is frequently subjected to a stimulus and thus starts to show a reduction in, or complete elimination of, response to the stimulus. This can happen, for example, if you live near an airport or a train track. You

> *Scientific laws imply a cause and effect between observed elements and must always apply under the same conditions. In order to be considered a scientific law, a statement must describe some aspect of the universe and be based on repeated experimental evidence.*

habituate to the continuous noise. Sensitization, meanwhile, occurs when there is an increased response after first being presented with a strong or novel stimulus. Thus, the key difference between the two is that habituation denotes a decreased response to a repeated stimulus, whereas sensitization denotes an increased response.

Associative Learning

Associative learning is defined as a form of conditioning, a theory that states behavior can be modified or learned based on a stimulus and a response. Associative learning processes include respondent and operant conditioning. We'll discuss these in greater detail later in this chapter.

One way to look at the mammalian nervous system is to separate it into two functioning areas: the voluntary, or somatic, nervous system and the involuntary, or autonomic, nervous system. The somatic system carries out the pet's operant behaviors such as walking, eating, sitting etc. while the autonomic system is responsible for functions that do not require conscious thought, such as breathing, blood pressure and heart rate (Bone, 1999).

Animal Emotions

According to Bekoff (2008), it is simply "bad biology to argue against the existence of animal emotions. Scientific research in evolutionary biology, cognitive ethology (the study of animal minds) and social neuroscience support the view that numerous and diverse animals have rich and deep emotional lives." Panksepp (2012) defined seven fundamental emotions in mammals: SEEKING, RAGE, FEAR, LUST, CARE, PANIC/GRIEF, and PLAY, which he called "the emotional primes, the primary-process emotional systems associated with specific brain networks and specifically designated in the brain-stimulation studies of emotions." He capitalized them "because the evidence supports a category of evolutionarily homologous experiences, equivalent across different species of mammals."

With such rich emotional lives, then, there can be no doubt that all pets deserve to live in a safe, nurturing, stable, enriched environment where they are treated humanely, are free from force, pain and fear, and have each of their individual needs met. This, in turn, can go a long way toward preventing future behavioral issues. Even then, depending on an individual dog's genetics, environment and/or early learning experiences, behavioral issues can still occur and owners need to be aware that, having ruled out any medical cause, such issues can be consistently, reliably and effectively resolved – or at the very least successfully managed – with the implementation of humane, modern, science-based training methods based on positive reinforcement. An important part of this is increased access to better pet care education via competent and qualified specialist organizations and associations to help owners understand that significant physical and emotional damage can occur from the use of aversive tools or techniques, including so-called electronic stimulation. In our cyber-driven world, where information is not always accurate or scientifically sound, however, it can be difficult for pet owners to make the best decisions.

A Review of the Science

As Friedman (2005) states, "It's not that science can be relied on to always provide the Truth. We've all been jerked and pulled by the capricious findings of science too many times to be so naïve. I mean, until they make up their minds about chocolate, coffee and red wine, count me in. Scientists themselves concede that a fact is only a fact until it's replaced by a better one. However, what science does offer, far better than common sense, conventional wisdom and other ways of knowing, is a process of self-correction over time that is achieved by two fundamental activities – public, peer-review and verification of findings across independent groups of researchers. Thus, although what is known today may indeed change tomorrow, it is the very best, most reliable information available at this moment."

Indeed, there is a law to science. Scientific laws imply a cause and effect between observed elements and must always apply under the same conditions. In order to be considered a scientific law, a statement must describe some aspect of the universe and be based on repeated experimental evidence. A scientific law is "a statement of fact meant to explain an action or set of actions such as the law of gravity. Laws are generally accepted as valid because they have been repeatedly observed to be true. The most fundamental law of behavior is the Law of Effect that states behavior is a function of its consequences." (Friedman, 2005).

The approach to pet training is gradually shifting away from more traditional practices that rely on aversive strategies. Today, achieving a desired goal by inflicting pain, force or fear is increasingly considered to be less acceptable than it was in the past: "In the last twenty years the pendulum swing has been toward methods that use minimal pain, fear or intimidation – or none at all." Donaldson (2017).

Abuse such as deprivation, restricting a pet's access to food, water, play, freedom and reduction of choice protocols, and executing maximum control over a pet, are also increasingly being considered as inhumane, and the growing body of evidence as presented by Ziv (2017) argues for efficient, humane training that empowers the pet and offers choices.

> States Patel (2018): "Training is no longer something we do to animals but something we do with animals. It is a conversation. We want participation rather than compliance. Let dogs choose the behaviors they are most comfortable with rather than tell them what to do."

Empowerment training provides an environment where the pet feels safe to be creative, persistent, and industrious, and helps promote behavioral well-being. Choice in dog training means providing "more than one scenario for a pet to choose from. Giving pets and humans choices empowers them to choose to comply rather than forcing them to comply which sets them up for more ideal learning that is less stressful and more fun. Empowerment training keeps the emphasis on the emotional state of the pet, reinforcing behaviors consistent with fun, joy and play (O'Heare, 2011).

States Ramirez (2016): "The end goal of training should be animal welfare. The primary goal of training is something that directly benefits the individual animal such as physical exercise, mental stimulation and cooperative behavior. We put the animal's needs first. Choice is a huge reinforcer for animals. If you use force, then choice is pretty much off the table."

Via the use of the appropriate philosophical approach, training methodology, recommended equipment, and applied behavior analysis, a pet can learn in a fun and family friendly manner. States Patel (2018): "Training is no longer something we do to animals but something we do with animals. It is a conversation. We want participation rather than compliance. Let dogs choose the behaviors they are most comfortable with rather than tell them what to do."

Applied Behavior Analysis

In pet industry training and behavior counseling, the practitioner must observe, apply and understand the science of applied behavior analysis (ABA). There is no place for an uneducated but so-called commonsense approach; common sense is not grounded in science and is often "little more than a social record of folk wisdom, clichés and homilies about behavior. Common sense maintains the status quo so we continue to do what we know best rather than seeking out the best we can do." (Friedman, 2004).

States Patel (2016): "Science looks at seeking nature's truths and a specific effort is taken to gather and evaluate information in a deliberate and systematic manner. We should always be thinking about what is the function of the behavior. We need to understand behavior not just from how it looks, but why animals do what they do."

ABA is the scientific approach to behavior change used by training and behavior practitioners. According to Cooper, Heron and Heward (1987): "Applied behavior analysis is the science in which the principles of the analysis of behavior are applied systematically to improve socially significant behavior and experimentation is used to identify the variables responsible for behavior change." Autism Speaks (2019) defines ABA as a therapy "based on the science of learning and behavior" that helps us understand how behavior works, how behavior is affected by the environment, and how learning takes place, stating that "ABA therapy applies our understanding of how behavior works to real situations. The goal is to increase behaviors that are helpful and decrease behaviors that are harmful or affect learning." While the principles of ABA are typically used with human patients, they are equally relevant in the field of animal behavior (Applied Behavior Analysis Programs Guide, n.d.). Further, according to Wikipedia (2019):

- **Applied**: Means that the behavior being studied must be socially important. Socially important behavior is behavior that happens in everyday life.
- **Behavior**: A behavior is anything that a person or animal does. Feelings are not studied because they are internal so they cannot be measured. ABA treatments measure rates of behavior.

- **Analysis**: The process of breaking a complex topic or substance into smaller parts to gain a better understanding of it.

(See also *Appendix E: The Recommended Case Study Template for Behavior Consultants*.)

A Behavior or an Emotion?

An animal's behavior can be overt or covert. Overt behavior is anything an animal does that we can observe or measure. In other words, any behavior we can see and directly impact through our management, care and training. Covert behaviors, on the other hand, are hidden and unobservable. They include actions like thinking and imagining. As pet owners, we can probably all agree that our pets do both, even if we cannot directly see them (Tudge, 2017).

Behaviors are also considered to be voluntary or involuntary. They are either shaped by their environmental consequences or through an association with environmental stimuli. Voluntary behaviors are known as operants and are strengthened or weakened by their consequences, a process known as operant conditioning (Tudge, 2009). Operant conditioning occurs when a voluntary behavior is changed. Involuntary, or respondent, behaviors, meanwhile, are elicited from an emotional reaction to a situation. In a process known as respondent (or classical or Pavlovian) conditioning, the presence of one stimulus begins to reliably predict the presence of a second stimulus (Tudge, 2017). This is not a consciously learned process; it happens automatically and without thought. The significant concept here is that in respondent conditioning, we are managing and changing emotions; in operant conditioning we are managing and changing behaviors. (*Note: A more detailed description of operant and respondent conditioning can be found in Chapter Five: A Call for an Industry Wide, Professionally Acknowledged Best Practice / Key Learning Theory*).

Because of how pets learn, it is important for those working with behavior issues, and specifically cases involving fear, anxiety, or aggression, to have a thorough understanding of the scientific elements of behavior modification. So-called positive trainers focus on building relationships with pets by using positive reinforcement to train new skills, and to build new behaviors as replacements for problematic ones.

Counterconditioning and Desensitization

The application of counterconditioning and desensitization protocols are employed to change or "counter" problematic emotions to more healthy, appropriate ones. Counterconditioning is a training process that "modifies undesired associations (fear) by replacing them with desired associations (joy). This is the procedure used to change a problematic emotional response to a relaxed or happy response. Counterconditioning works alongside a graded desensitization plan. During the counterconditioning component of the systematic desensitization protocol, there must be a contrast between the 'open bar' process of the systematic desensitization and the 'closed bar.' When the fear eliciting stimulus is presented, all great things happen, and they are quickly removed with the exit of the fear eliciting stimulus. There must be both a temporal relationship and a contingency between the conditioned stimulus and the unconditioned stimulus for conditioning to occur and for the problematic emotional response to be replaced with a new, more appropriate response." (Tudge, 2017).

Corporal Punishment

The United Nations (UN) Committee on the Rights of the Child (2006), defines corporal or physical punishment as "any punishment in which physical force is used and intended to cause some degree of pain or discomfort, however light…Physical punishment may involve hitting…children with the hand or with an implement…but it can also involve, for example, kicking, shaking or throwing children, scratching, pinching, biting, pulling hair or boxing ears, forcing children to stay in uncomfortable positions, burning, scalding or forced ingestion (for example, washing children's mouths out with soap or forcing them to swallow hot spices). Nonphysical forms of punishment that are cruel and degrading and thus incompatible with the Convention include, for example, punishment which belittles, humiliates, denigrates, scapegoats, threatens, scares or ridicules the child." The Committee views corporal punishment as "invariably degrading." (United Nations Committee on the Rights of the Child, 2006).

Corporal punishment is now banned from schools in 66 percent of all countries (131 out of 198) worldwide and 54 countries have prohibited the practice in all settings (e.g. day care, penal institutions), including the home. (Global Initiative to End All Corporal Punishment of Children, 2018). According to Gershoff and Font (2016), in the United States, "corporal punishment is currently legal in 19 states," although the "prevalence of school corporal punishment has been on a steady decline since the late 1970s." They state that, according to research, corporal punishment is "not effective" at teaching children how to behave and that, "the more children receive corporal punishment, the more likely they are to be aggressive and to misbehave over time." They also cite research by Gershoff and Grogan-Kaylor (2016) that has found corporal punishment is "associated with unintended negative consequences" for children.

> States Overall (2017): "Consider the universe told you that everything you did was wrong. That's what punishment does. Take the individual responses and then punish the dog until he gets the right answer. Consider, instead, telling dogs what's right and when their decision is taking them away from the right answer. To change behavior, you must script a detailed path to success."

The American Academy of Pediatrics (AAP) recommends that "adults caring for children use healthy forms of discipline, such as positive reinforcement of appropriate behaviors, setting limits, redirecting, and setting future expectations. The AAP recommends that parents do not use spanking, hitting, slapping, threatening, insulting, humiliating, or shaming." (Sege & Siegel, 2018).

Punishment in Animal Training

Increasingly, research in the field of animal behavior reflects this. Herron, Shofer and Reisner (2009) state that "reward-based training is less stressful or painful for the dog, and, hence, safer for the owner." Rooney and Cowan (2011) suggest high levels of punishment may have "adverse effects upon a dog's behaviour whilst reward based training may improve a dog's subsequent ability to learn." Deldalle and Gaunet (2014) found that "using a negative reinforcement–based method demonstrated lowered body postures and signals of stress, whereas dogs from the school using a positive reinforcement–based method showed increased attentiveness toward their owner."

Ziv (2017) conducted a review of the scientific literature on the effects of various canine training methods and summarized that methods using punishment, fear and pain jeopardize both the physical and mental health of the pet. He concludes that "there is no evidence to suggest that aversive training methods are more effective than reward-based training methods. At least three studies in this review suggest that the opposite might be true in both pets and working dogs (Blackwell, Bolster,

Richards, Loftus & Casey, 2012; Haverbeke, Laporte, Depiereux, Giffroy & Diederich, 2008; Hiby, Rooney & Bradshaw, 2004). Because this appears to be the case, it is recommended that the dog training community embrace reward-based training and avoid, as much as possible, training methods that include aversion."

States Overall (2017): "Consider the universe told you that everything you did was wrong. That's what punishment does. Take the individual responses and then punish the dog until he gets the right answer. Consider, instead, telling dogs what's right and when their decision is taking them away from the right answer. To change behavior, you must script a detailed path to success. Telling someone what will not work or is not desired is of minimal utility in a world of a million choices, and 999,999 of them will be wrong...Remember, fear is an individual response and what's punishing or a punisher must be considered in terms of the recipient, so while 'fear' is not in the definition of punishment, it may be one of the effects of punishment. How many of you have never asked a question in your life? That is what we expect dogs to do."

Outdated Approach

Despite the growing body of scientific research to the contrary, the "dominance" approach is one that some still elect to use in animal training and behavior modification, specifically with regards to dogs and horses. The underlying philosophy of so-called dominance theory in its application to pet dogs is, at best, outdated, at worst, impacts negatively the entire approach educated pet professionals should be taking. (*See also* Chapter Three: Professionals Should Exemplify and Promote Anti-Cruelty Statutes / Defining Dominance Theory.)

The theory of dominance in dogs "originated from work conducted several decades ago. According to Miller (2018), '[t]he erroneous approach to canine social behavior known as dominance theory is based on a study of captive zoo wolves conducted in the 1930s and 1940s by Swiss animal behaviorist Rudolph Schenkel (1947), in which the scientist concluded that wolves in a pack fight to gain dominance, and the winner is the alpha wolf. Schenkel's observations of captive wolf behavior were erroneously extrapolated to wild wolf behavior, and then to domestic dogs.'" (Bradley, 2019).

The idea that humans should be exerting physical control over animals was first widely popularized in the 1970s in the book, *How to Be Your Dog's Best Friend,* by the Monks of New Skete, which recommended the infamous alpha roll to deal with undesired behaviors. The alpha roll, in which, as mentioned in <u>Chapter Three: Professionals Should Exemplify and Promote Anti-Cruelty Statutes / Professionals and Cruelty</u>, a human flips a dog onto his back and pins him until he shows "submissive" behaviors, was founded on 1960s studies of captive wolves kept in an area too small for their numbers and composed of members that would not naturally be found together in a pack in the wild. These conditions resulted in increased numbers of conflicts in which one wolf would appear to pin another wolf. However, current scientific knowledge has recanted the findings of these studies, acknowledging that this behavior is not typical of wolves living in the wild (Mech, 1999). Despite these findings and the great disparity in behavior between wolves and dogs, dominance theory became applied to pet dogs, popularized, and remains a widely-propagated training style today, even though it is an "obsolete and aversive method of interacting with animals that has at its foundation incorrect and misinterpreted data which can result in damage to the animal-human relationship and cause behavioral problems in the animal." (Pet Professional Guild, 2018).

> *Despite these findings and the great disparity in behavior between wolves and dogs, dominance theory became applied to pet dogs, popularized, and remains a widely-propagated training style today, even though it is an "obsolete and aversive method of interacting with animals that has at its foundation incorrect and misinterpreted data which can result in damage to the animal-human relationship and cause behavioral problems in the animal." - Pet Professional Guild (2018)*

But in the 21st century, can there really still be any debate over the issue of using pain and fear as "methods" of animal training? Research has already given us the good news that, no, we do not need to use any training or behavior modification protocols that utilize escape or avoidance behavior, or that cause fear or pain. Instead, we can reference the growing body of knowledge and findings from the scientific community which advocate for humane, positive reinforcement-based protocols. Such protocols are known to promote a positive emotional state and therefore improve an animal's ability to learn new things. In addition, they set an animal up for success, build his confidence, allow him to think for himself, and empower him to make good choices (O'Heare, 2011).

Devices Intended to Startle

Unfortunately, the concept of dominance and the perceived need to have total control over one's pets has evolved into a range of commercially available tools and equipment designed to stop, prevent, or punish pets for behaviors their owners deem unnecessary, unacceptable or simply annoying. As an example, in the marketplace, one can find so-called pet correction devices. These are simply aversive stimuli intended for pet care, management, or training by eliciting a "startle response," and/or an alarm reaction. Ramirez-Moreno and Sejnowski (2012) define the startle response as a "largely unconscious defensive response to sudden or threatening stimuli, such as sudden noise or sharp movement" that is "associated with negative affect." This equipment, through its design and intended application, operates using fear as motivation. (Pet Professional Guild, 2018). It is promoted and sold to prevent barking, jumping up, growling, or any other problematic behavior. This approach is not, however, advisable because using the startle response to correct behavior can be perceived as highly threatening by a pet and quickly create fear. A fearful response may then not only be directed toward the specific piece of equipment, but also to the operator or any other stimulus that happens to be present at that time, e.g. another person or animal. Fear, if left unchecked, can progress to all out aggression, a problematic behavior for all concerned. The startle response (or aversive reflex) is "enhanced during a fear state and is diminished in a pleasant emotional context." (Lang, Bradley & Cuthbert, 1990).

Learned Aggression

Fear-based aggression is a case of "learned aggression that happens when an animal…experiences intense fear combined with an inability to escape it with fight-or-flight-style behavior…The first time a dog growls, snaps, or bites out of fear, it is often a last-ditch resort. But man, does it work. The scary animal or person backs off, and this serves as a reward, making aggressive responses more likely when the

> *The key difference between escape and avoidance learning is this: In escape learning, the dog's behavior allows him to escape the electric shock, whereas in avoidance learning, his behavior avoids the onset of the shock altogether. In both instances, the learning is based on fear.*

dog feels fear in the future. The real problem is fear aggression is so self-reinforcing—it almost always makes the scary thing go away—that dogs...start to use it in instrumental, preventative ways rather than as reactions to truly threatening stimuli." (Wood, 2016).

As an example, using an aversive sound such as an air horn to interrupt barking risks pairing the owner or trainer with the unpleasant stimulus and, in particular, the hand or arm that is in motion while using the tool. Repeated instances may generalize to the pet attempting to flee. But if the pet believes that flight is not possible and/or not a safe or reliable course of action, he may instead conclude that he has no other alternative to protect himself than to exhibit aggressive behaviors toward the arm or hand movement, the individual making the movement, any other stimulus present in the environment at the time, or any approach behavior.

Nothing Shocking about Shock

Some owners or trainers elect to subject their pets to learning via the application of electric shock, which works through escape and avoidance learning. Let's think about that for a moment. A pet is placed in a situation where he learns to exhibit an "acceptable" behavior by the presentation and removal of a scary or painful stimulus, i.e. an electric shock. This uses both positive punishment and negative reinforcement, principles of operant conditioning that work at opposite ends of a continuum. To break it down further, the pet is punished through the application of positive punishment (i.e. the addition of an aversive stimulus), and as soon as he offers a more acceptable behavior in order to escape or avoid the scary or painful stimulus, the stimulus is then removed by the trainer (negative reinforcement, i.e. the removal of the aversive stimulus).

Escape/Avoid Learning

Let's look at an example of escape learning. Say a dog is running in a different direction to his owner and the owner/trainer applies the shock stimulus while shouting, "Come." The dog will be startled and may stop or begin to move back toward the owner/trainer. When the dog does this, the owner/trainer stops applying the shock so the dog learns that by running back toward the owner, the pain can be removed (i.e. the shock is removed). In other words, the dog learns that he can escape the aversive stimulus by engaging in a different behavior. In the case of avoidance behavior, it is exactly as it sounds: a dog learns how to avoid a painful or scary stimulus.

With a shock containment system, such as an electric, or "invisible" fence, the dog learns to stop moving forward toward the boundary when he hears the warning beep. If he proceeds, then he will receive an electric shock. As in the previous example, the goal of his behavior is to avoid the fear and pain this will cause. His learning has taken place from being shocked and, therefore, getting hurt, while his new behavior is reinforced by fear as he works to avoid the beeping. The result of this is a dog who has been contained in his own area, his supposed safe haven, through fear and/or pain. (Tudge, 2009).

> *Increasingly, peer reviewed, scientific studies show, whether discussing dogs, humans, dolphins or elephants, that shock as a form of training to teach or correct a behavior is ineffective at best and physically and psychologically damaging at worst (Schilder & van der Borg, 2004; Schalke, Stichnoth, Ott, & Jones-Baade, 2007; Polsky, 2000; Cooper, Cracknell, Hardiman, Wright & Mills, 2014).*

The key difference between escape and avoidance learning is this: In escape learning, the dog's behavior allows him to escape the electric shock, whereas in avoidance learning, his behavior avoids the onset of the shock altogether. In both instances, the learning is based on fear. In the case of the "invisible" fence, the beep on the boundary system comes before the shock is delivered. Due to his conditioning history (i.e. learning and experience), the dog has learned that the beep predicts a painful electric shock if his current behavior continues. He will aim to avoid this at all costs. (Tudge, 2009).

This is the science behind why a dog, when shown a newspaper or spray bottle, will cease to exhibit the problem behavior. It is why we hear unsuspecting pet owners, in defense of positive punishment, make statements like, "My dog never gets shocked, or sprayed or hit any more. As soon as he sees me grab the antibark, shock or spray collar, bottle or newspaper, he stops what he's doing." They do not realize that fear is now preventing the behavior, because the piece of equipment has been paired with pain in the past. As a result, the behavior has been suppressed due to fear and or anxiety, but no preferable replacement behavior has been taught. As such, the pet is not being trained, just punished. Fear or anxiety then result in the expression "of a range of adaptive or defensive behaviors, which are aimed at escaping from the source of danger or motivational conflict. These behaviors depend on the context and the repertoire of the species." (Steimer, 2002, p.28).

Increasingly, peer reviewed, scientific studies show, whether discussing dogs, humans, dolphins or elephants, that shock as a form of training to teach or correct a behavior is ineffective at best and physically and psychologically damaging at worst (Schilder & van der Borg, 2004; Schalke, Stichnoth, Ott, & Jones-Baade, 2007; Polsky, 2000; Cooper, Cracknell, Hardiman, Wright & Mills, 2014). Overall (2013) states that shock collars, aka e-collars, "violate the principles of three of five freedoms that define adequate welfare for animals: Freedom from pain, injury, and disease, freedom to express normal behavior and freedom from fear and distress."

> Several countries, including England, Wales, Austria, Germany, Switzerland, Slovenia, Denmark, Sweden, Norway and Finland, the province of Québec in Canada, and the states of New South Wales, Australian Capital Territory and South Australia in Australia, have already banned electronic stimulation devices.

The freedoms Overall refers to are Brambell's (1965) Five Freedoms, which have been a standard for assessing animal welfare since 1965, which we referred to in _Chapter Two: Living Property - The Need for a New Legal Definition / Living Property_.) Applying an electric shock to an animal via any system or any other pain inflicting device provides no effective strategy for him to learn a new or alternative behavior; it simply inflicts pain and risks making him fearful, anxious and/or aggressive. Evidence indicates that, rather than speeding up the learning process, electronic stimulation devices slow it down, place great stress on the animal, can result in both short- and long-term psychological damage, and lead to fearful, anxious and/or aggressive behavior.

State Masson et al. (2018): "E-collars are not recommended for the treatment of behavior problems because they do not take into consideration the root cause of the problems. Such lack of redress can result in problems worsening, being masked or expressed in other ways (e.g., in the case of e-collar use to stop barking in separation-related problems, if barking is suppressed, dogs can develop other behaviors such as destructiveness or compulsive/obsessive-compulsive disorders)...Pain directly triggers aggression (Polsky, 1994), but additionally, the use of aversive techniques can worsen any negative associations (e.g., the trainer) by which a dog already feels threatened. Finally, using shocks to punish warning signals of aggression, such as growling or baring teeth, can lead to a suppression of these, so the dog in the future may attack without overt warning, resulting in apparent unpredictability and increasing the risk of injury (Overall, 2013)."

Advocating for Humane Techniques

The current scientific data, in addition to the moral and ethical concerns about mental and physical damage to animals subjected to methods using force, fear and/or pain have moved a number of representing professional organizations to advocate for the use of humane training techniques founded on evidence-based learning theories and avoid training methods or devices which employ coercion and force (Tudge & Nilson, 2016). Examples include, but are not limited to:

- "Misinformation about pet behavior is rampant...The AAHA guidelines oppose aversive training techniques, such as prong (pinch) or choke collars, cattle prods, alpha rolls (forcibly rolling a pet on his or her back), electronic shock collars, entrapment, and physically punishing a pet. The guidelines note that aversive training techniques can harm or even destroy an animal's trust in his or her owner, negatively impact the pet's problem-solving ability, and cause increased anxiety in the animal. Aversive techniques are especially a concern if pets are already fearful or aggressive, rendering any aggressive dog more dangerous. According to the AAHA guidelines, the only acceptable training techniques are non-aversive, positive techniques that rely on the identification of, and reward for, desirable behaviors. Positive reinforcement is the most humane and effective approach." - American Animal Hospital Association (2019).

- "The Canadian Veterinary Medical Association (CVMA) supports the use of humane training methods for dogs that are based on current scientific knowledge of learning theory. Reward-based methods are highly recommended. Aversive methods are strongly discouraged as they may cause fear, distress, anxiety, pain or physical injury to the dog." - Canadian Veterinary Medical Association (2015).

- "Aversive, punishment-based techniques may alter behaviour, but the methods fail to address the underlying cause and, in the case of unwanted behaviour, can lead to undue anxiety, fear, distress, pain or injury." - British Columbia Society for the Prevention of Cruelty to Animals (2019).
- The British Small Animal Veterinary Association (BSAVA) recommends against the use of electronic shock collars and other aversive methods for the training and containment of animals. Shocks and other aversive stimuli received during training may not only be acutely stressful, painful and frightening for the animals, but may also produce long term adverse effects on behavioural and emotional responses…The BSAVA strongly recommends the use of positive reinforcement training methods that could replace those using aversive stimuli." - British Small Animal Veterinary Association (2019).
- "The British Veterinary Association (BVA) has concerns about the use of aversive training devices to control, train or punish dogs. The use of devices such as electronic collars, as a means of punishing or controlling behaviour of companion animals is open to potential abuse and incorrect use of such training aids has the potential to cause welfare and training problems…Electric pulse devices are sometimes used in dog training as a form of punishment to prevent a dog from repeating bad behaviour. Although training a dog is important for their well-being, research shows that electric pulse collars are no more effective than positive reinforcement methods. BVA has consulted with experts and examined the evidence. Research by Schalke, Stichnoth and Jones-Baade (2005) showed that the application of electric stimulus, even at a low level, can cause physiological and behavioral responses associated with stress, pain and fear. In light of the evidence, BVA has concluded that electric pulse collars raise a number of welfare issues, such as the difficulty in accurately judging the level of electric pulse to apply to a dog without causing unnecessary suffering." - British Veterinary Association (2018).
- "An incorrect training regime can have negative effects on your dog's welfare. Reward based training which includes the use of things that dogs like or want (e.g. toys, food and praise) is enjoyable for your dog and is widely regarded as the preferred form of training dogs. Training which includes physical punishment may cause pain, suffering and distress. These techniques can compromise dog welfare, lead to aggressive responses and

worsen the problems they aim to address." - Department for Environment, Food and Rural Affairs (United Kingdom) (2017).

- "The New Zealand Veterinary Association (NZVA) does not support the use of electronic behaviour modifying collars (e-collars) that deliver aversive stimuli for the training or containment of dogs. E-collars have the potential to harm both the physical and mental health of dogs. They are an aversive training method that have in some studies been associated with significant negative animal welfare outcomes. Positive reinforcement training methods are an effective and humane alternative to e-collars for dog training…The use of pain to train dogs is no more acceptable or humane when it is administered by remote control, than if it was delivered as a physical blow such as a punch or kick." - New Zealand Veterinary Association (2018).

- "E-collar training is associated with numerous well documented risks concerning dog health, behavior and welfare. Any existing behaviour problem is likely to deteriorate or an additional problem is likely to emerge, when such a collar is used. This becomes an even greater risk when this aversive tool is used by an unqualified trainer (as training is largely unregulated throughout the EU, it appears that a large number of trainers are unqualified). Additionally, the efficacy of these collars has not been proven to be more effective than other alternatives such as positive training. Hence, European Society of Veterinary Clinical Ethology (ESVCE) encourages education programmes which employ positive reinforcement methods (while avoiding positive punishment and negative reinforcement) thereby promoting positive dog welfare and a humane, ethical and moral approach to dog training at all times." - European Society of Veterinary Clinical Ethology (2017).

Several countries, including England, Wales, Austria, Germany, Switzerland, Slovenia, Denmark, Sweden, Norway and Finland, the province of Québec in Canada, and the states of New South Wales, South Australia and the Australian Capital Territory (ACT) in Australia, have already banned electronic stimulation devices. Under recent amendments to ACT animal welfare legislation, anyone who places an electric shock device, such as a shock collar, on an animal, will attract a maximum penalty of AU$16,000 [$11,000] and a year's imprisonment (Brewer, 2019). In Scotland, "strict guidance" has been published by the Scottish Parliament which provides "advice on training methods and training aids for dogs, with particular focus on the welfare issues that may arise from the use of aversive methods including e-collars. It highlights the potential consequences of the misuse of aversive training aids, including possible legal consequences." (The Kennel Club, 2018). In the United States and elsewhere, meanwhile, a significant number of respected and credentialed canine behavior and training professionals are supporting an initiative spearheaded by the Shock-Free Coalition to "build a strong and broad movement committed to eliminating shock devices from the supply and demand chain. This goal will be reached when shock tools and equipment are universally unavailable and not permitted for the training, management and care of pets." (Shock-Free Coalition, 2018).

> O'Heare (2005) explains that the stress caused in such situations [whereby pets become habituated to the sense of fear or anxiety] can have a significant effect on a pet's well-being due to increasing cortisol levels and heart rate, not to mention the psychological impact.

The Fallout

There are significant and common problems resulting from the use of electronic stimulation devices or any other device designed to inflict pain or fear. As already explained, in the case of an electric shock collar, the shock is applied and then stopped when the dog discontinues his current behavior, which is whatever the person administering the shock deems to be inappropriate. There is no actual, constructive teaching involved, and the dog is given no opportunity to learn a specific and more appropriate new behavior. If the aversive device is absent at any time, there is no guarantee the dog will do what is expected of him because he has never actually been taught a new behavior within that context.

Any environmental stimulus not paired with a positive stimulus is, at best, neutral and, at worst, frightening and/or painful to the pet. Pets who learn to exhibit behaviors to escape or avoid fear or pain are, by definition, subjected to an aversive, unpleasant or frightening stimulus, as opposed to a pleasant stimulus that they seek out voluntarily and which can be used as a powerful and effective training aid.

In addition, when punishment is applied to a pet's behavior and a change in behavior is not seen immediately, trainers/owners may elect to increase the frequency, duration or intensity of the punishment. The punishment may thus be applied more harshly, applied for a longer period of time, or applied more frequently (or any combination of the three). This results in the pet making more deliberate or desperate attempts to escape or avoid the punishment, so a counterproductive paradigm develops whereby he simply learns to fear the stimulus, the context, and/or the person delivering it. Alternatively, some pets tend to be more "stoic" and may fail to show any kind of fear response, irrespective of increased levels of anxiety, fear or frustration.

In some cases, pets become habituated to the sense of fear or anxiety and, again, this perpetuates the owner/trainer in using increased levels, duration or frequency of the punishing stimulus. O'Heare (2005) explains that the stress caused in such situations can have a significant effect on a pet's well-being due to increasing cortisol levels and heart rate, not to mention the psychological impact. Just as concerning is the fact that pets who are punished can generalize the anticipation of fear and pain to the presence of the owner/trainer, impacting the level of trust and safety they feel around people. Further, a pet repeatedly subjected to aversive stimulation may also go into a state of "shutdown," or a global suppression of behavior. This is frequently mistaken for a "trained" pet, as the pet remains subdued and offers few or no behaviors. In extreme cases, pets may refuse to perform any behavior at all, known as "learned helplessness." In such cases, pets may try to isolate themselves to avoid incurring the aversive stimulation. This is evidently counterproductive to training new, more acceptable behaviors. (O'Heare, 2011).

> *In extreme cases, pets may refuse to perform any behavior at all, known as "learned helplessness." In such cases, pets may try to isolate themselves to avoid incurring the aversive stimulation. This is evidently counterproductive to training new, more acceptable behaviors. (O'Heare, 2011).*

Masson et al. (2018) note there are many parameters to consider when modulating the intensity of shock delivered and highlight all of the following as concerns: "...the level of pain felt by the dog...shock intensity (Schilder and van der Borg, 2007, Lindsay, 2005), shock duration (Schilder and van der Borg, 2007), electrode size (Lindsay, 2005), beep warning and response time (Schalke et al. 2007), degree of humidity, and the morphology of the dog itself [hair length, moisture level of skin, subcutaneous fat level (Jacques and Myers, 2007)]. Together, these data render it nearly impossible to determine the appropriate intensity of shock for a particular dog in any given situation (Lindsay, 2005)."

There also appears to be a significant individual difference among dogs in terms of sensitivity to the pain caused by an electric shock. This is unrelated to the thickness of the dog's coat (Masson et al., 2018). Masson et al. (2018) address reports by individuals who have tested an electric shock collar on themselves and stated that it does not hurt by pointing out that dog skin is "more sensitive to shock" than human skin. Indeed, the canine epidermis is 3-5 cells thick; however, in humans, it is at least 10-15 cells thick." (Vet West Animal Hospitals, 2019).

Prins, a patrol-dog handler who worked on a program for the Canine Department of the Netherlands National Police Agency which involved training dogs in tracking, explosive and narcotics detection, climbing, rappelling, traveling by helicopter and boat, working with cameras, and to follow radio or laser guidance at long distances, and also teaching new trainers to train dogs in these skills, used methods "heavily weighted toward positive reinforcement" *except* "where a dog exhibits behavior that puts himself, humans or the operation at risk," in which case, an electronic collar may be used (qtd. in Yin, 2012). Yin explains that, under Prins' teaching model, before his police dog training students use an electronic collar on one of the dogs, "they must wear the collar around their own necks and see what it's like to be trained this way. They find out what it feels like when a correction is given, and even worse, given at the wrong moment as commonly happens even with the most skilled trainers. 'Then they understand how difficult it is, and they do not like to use it,' says Prins. Overall, aversive methods comprise less than 1/1000 of the training." (Yin, 2012).

Physical Effects

In addition to the potential psychological effects of using training devices that cause pain or evoke fear, there is also the issue of possible physical damage to consider. We present here a variety of perspectives offered by veterinarians, canine research scientists, a professional dog trainer, and an engineer:

- "The thyroid gland is a butterfly-shaped organ just in front of the larynx and trachea, and the mandibular salivary glands are found on the side of the face just below the ears. Thus, they can be easily injured by trauma and sudden pressure forces (like could occur from the slip ring and chain of metal collar, and a metal prong or hard braided leather collar)." - Dr. Jean Dodds (2013).
- "The all-important laryngeal nerve is *trivia alert* the longest nerve in the body, and it travels down the left-hand side of the neck near the windpipe.

Anything that severely compresses this nerve can damage the way the larynx works. This is why choke collars are not recommended." - Dr. Pippa Elliott (2017).

- "A sudden jerk to the neck as part of inappropriate behavior training is another too common reason for laryngeal paralysis. It's the fear-based, old school and 'you must be dominant over your dog' training, where neck pops with the leash, or prong or choke collars are used. When the trachea cartilage is popped repeatedly during this type of 'training,' the dog can wind up with tracheal damage. This type of handling puts a tremendous amount of pressure on the larynx because the collar sits right on top of it." - Dr. Karen Becker (2017).

- "I see many dogs who have been previously corrected with shock collars. Each and every one of these patients has become behaviorally worse than they were prior to the shock collars (more fearful, more aggressive). The emotional damage caused by shock collars is often beyond repair and requires a lifetime of treatment. The wounds I see are beyond skin-deep, they are soul deep." - Dr. Lynn Honeckman (2018) (qtd. in Shock-Free Coalition).

- Shock collars carry a risk of physical damage to the skin of the neck (Polsky, 1994): "To ensure that the metal pins are in close contact with the skin of the neck, an e-collar must be fitted tightly. Aside from being uncomfortable, the points where the metal pins make contact with the skin can become irritated, and this can result in the development of pressure necrosis or wounds. Antibarking collars and electronic fence collars must be worn for long periods, so these risks are especially high in these contexts. Furthermore, there is a risk of device malfunction, which can lead to damage caused by electricity." - Masson et al. (2018).

- "Blogs written by well-respected trainers such as Grisha Stewart describe and provide photographic evidence of 'burns' on a dog's neck, the result of a shock collar. Don Hanson, past president of the APDT and also a respected trainer, writes of personally witnessing burns on a dog's neck. There are letters from veterinarians claiming to have treated burns created by shock collars." - Jan Casey (2012).

- "Assume a typical big dog: 80 pounds, 20-inch neck size. The dog can pull with more than his own weight because his weight is low and forward compared to the distance between his front and back feet, and he won't lift his front feet by pulling until he's pulling a lot more than he weighs. 80-pound dog: 120 pounds of pulling force is easily possible. Much more if he gets a running start before he gets to the end of his leash. Newton taught us that every action (force) has an equal and opposite reaction. So take the 1.5-inch web collar. The bottom of the collar supplies all the force to the dog's neck. If he pulls with his own weight, the contact force is around 5⅓ pounds per square inch. (80 pounds/(10 inches of collar x 1.5 inches wide). Now consider a choke collar made of 0.25-inch nylon cord. A chain choke would be similar as the links make a nearly continuous contact band. Even if it does not slide tight, in the same configuration as the web collar the contact force will be 32 pounds per square inch – 6 times as much, before one even considers the drawstring effect. This is far more likely to cause injury to the larynx or restriction of blood flow in the neck. A prong collar has a pair of prongs approximately every inch. The prongs are made of wire, approximately 0.09 inches in diameter. Still ignoring the drawstring effect – each prong contacts the neck with an area of only about 0.007 square inches. 20 prongs, 80 pounds, generate about 579 psi at each prong tip, assuming they are blunt and not pointy. If the prongs are located atop the larynx it is hard to imagine injury (at least bruising) NOT occurring. This pressure will easily collapse any blood vessel that suffers the fate of being beneath a prong. So: contact force is over 6 times greater for a simple choke, and over 100 times greater for prongs FOR THE SAME PULL." - Jim Casey (2015) (qtd. in Garrod).

Summary

According to Ha and Campion (2019), training with reinforcement and training with punishment use two different neural pathways. They reference a study by Wächter, Lungu, Liu, Willingham and Ashe (2009), in which the researchers were able to "correlate the neural substrates of reward and punishment with qualitatively different behavior outcomes suggesting that these modulators might indeed operate through different motivational systems." State Ha and Campion (2019): "Animals can learn through both positive and negative learning, which operate on different brain pathways and use unique dopamine receptors…the DR1 receptors are generally viewed as 'positive' receptors, while the DR2 receptors are 'negative' receptors. Across multiple species, studies have shown that individuals will prefer to stimulate their DR1 receptors over their DR2. While punishment, which stimulates the DR2 receptors, might appear to have an immediate result, stimulating the DR1 receptors is more effective for learning in the longer term. Combining positive and negative with one another neurologically and psychologically confuses the learning process."

Fig. 3: What Is Positive Punishment?

Positive Punishment is the application of a stimulus that a pet would choose to avoid or escape from. It is a stimulus they find scary or frightening.

Shouting, physical pressure, and/or the use of a corrective device can all function as Positive Punishers.

It is important for those who live and work with dogs to have an understanding of basic behavioral science such as this as it makes "all the difference between effective and ineffective interactions…including training." (Ha & Campion, 2019). Bearing this in mind, here are just a few examples of positive reinforcement training protocols that may be used in place of aversive methods:

- Rather than waiting for a dog to make a mistake so you can punish him, reinforce behavior you like to help the dog learn and so both parties feel more positive about the relationship.
- Rather than using a choke chain or prong collar which rely on punishing undesirable behavior, use targeting and a harness to train and reinforce

good behavior while, at the same time, ensuring less trauma to the dog's neck.
- Rather than positively punishing a dog for jumping on visitors at the door, train him to "go to mat," "sit," or "four on the floor" and reinforce nonjumping behavior. (*Note: in technical terms, when adding an aversive to weaken or decrease a behavior, it is known as positive punishment – see Fig. 3. See also* [Chapter Five: A Call for an Industry Wide, Professionally Acknowledged Best Practice / Key Learning Theory](#)).
- Rather than using an electric fence or punishing a dog for crossing boundaries, e.g. on your property, teach him about boundaries and reinforce him for staying within the boundary.
- Rather than positively punishing a growl, learn to read a dog's body language and evaluate the situation to better understand what he is trying to say.
- Rather than positively punishing a dog for stealing something such as a shoe or something from the trash, teach him to exchange or swap and reinforce the exchange.
- Rather than positively punishing a dog for being on the furniture (if you do not want him there – this is a personal preference), target or lure him down and reinforce him for being on his bed next to you.
- Rather than positively punishing a dog for what you consider poor behavior, reconsider your expectations of him and whether they are realistic. Consider what alternative behaviors you can train instead. If you are not sure, seek more information from an appropriate source.
- Rather than positively punishing a dog for not returning to you when called (i.e., in his eyes, giving up his freedom), teach him that it is valuable and worthwhile to come back to you and that it may not mean his freedom is restricted at all.
- Rather than put all the responsibility for the dog's behavior on the dog, take it upon yourself to teach him alternative behaviors that can be reinforced and benefit the mutual relationship.

Foubert (2016) notes that: "Even a simple exercise of teaching a dog to sit on cue requires the trainer to have skills in timing and reinforcement in order for effective and lasting learning to occur. Timing is a mechanical skill that requires practice. A dog's behavior will respond to reinforcement that is given within a limited timeframe. The reinforcer is required to inform the dog exactly what behavior the trainer liked. Reinforcement that comes too early or too late will not result in a dog learning the desired behavior."

Because the use of aversives in training can suppress behaviors, it is contraindicated in pets given that the suppression removes any natural communication system of fear or pain. This makes any aggression more difficult to monitor, predict, or anticipate. Without ritualized aggressive behaviors, people and other pets risk receiving no warning before the pet subjected to punishment feels forced to resort to biting. Pets who experience repeated aversive stimulation may also be respondently conditioned to associate the fear and/or pain with certain contextual cues in their environment, which can promote redirected aggression toward the stimulus associated with fear and or pain.

Bibliography

American Animal Hospital Association. (2019). AAHA behavior guidelines offer solutions to managing behavior problems with your pet. Retrieved May 25, 2019, from
https://www.aaha.org/pet_owner/lifestyle/aaha-behavior-guidelines-offer-solutions-to-managing-behavior-problems-with-your-pet.aspx

Applied Behavior Analysis [Def]. (2019). In Wikipedia. Retrieved March 25, 2019, from
https://simple.wikipedia.org/wiki/Applied_behavior_analysis

Applied Behavior Analysis Programs Guide. (n.d.). Applied Behavior Analysis in Animal Behavior Training. Retrieved June 12, 2019, from
https://www.appliedbehavioranalysisprograms.com/specialties/aba-in-animal-behavior-training/

Autism Speaks. (2019). What is Applied Behavior Analysis? Retrieved June 12, 2019, from
https://www.autismspeaks.org/applied-behavior-analysis-aba-0

Becker, K. (2017). A Vet's Dire Warning: This Favorite Product Can Cause a Life-Threatening Emergency Down the Road. Retrieved May 28, 2019, from
https://healthypets.mercola.com/sites/healthypets/archive/2017/02/12/laryngeal-paralysis.aspx

Bekoff, M. (2008). Do Animals Have Emotions? Of course they do. Retrieved January 4, 2019, from
https://thebark.com/content/do-animals-have-emotions

Bekoff, M. (2012). Animals are conscious and should be treated as such. The New Scientist. Retrieved January 4, 2019, from https://www.newscientist.com/article/mg21528836-200-animals-are-conscious-and-should-be-treated-as-such/

Bone, J.F. (1999). Animal Anatomy and Physiology (Vol. 2). Englewood Cliffs, NJ: Prentice Hall

Bradley, A. (2019, January). The Durability of "Dominance." *BARKS from the Guild (34)* 28-30. Retrieved January 4, 2019, from https://issuu.com/petprofessionalguild/docs/bftg_january_2019_online_edition_op/28

Brambell, R. (1965). Report of the technical committee to enquire into the welfare of animals kept under intensive livestock husbandry systems. London: Her Majesty's Stationery Office

Brewer, P. (2019). Do let the dogs out: Huge fines for pet confinement part of ACT animal welfare overhaul. Retrieved May 22, 2019, from https://www.canberratimes.com.au/story/6124428/do-let-the-dogs-out-huge-fines-for-pet-confinement-part-of-act-animal-welfare-overhaul/

British Columbia Society for the Prevention of Cruelty to Animals. (2019). Position Statement on Animal Training. Available at: https://spca.bc.ca/programs-services/leaders-in-our-field/position-statements/position-statement-on-animal-training/

British Small Animal Veterinary Association. (2019). Position Statement on Aversive Training Methods. Retrieved February 12, 2019, from https://www.bsava.com/Resources/Veterinary-resources/Position-statements/Aversive-training-methods

British Veterinary Association. (2018). Aversive training devices for dogs. Retrieved February 12, 2019, from https://www.bva.co.uk/uploadedFiles/Content/News,_campaigns_and_policies/Policies/Ethics_and_welfare/BVA%20position%20on%20Aversive%20training%20devices%20for%20dogs_PS20JUL2016.pdf

Canadian Veterinary Medical Association. (2015). Humane Training Methods for Dogs – Position Statement. Retrieved May 25, 2019, from https://www.canadianveterinarians.net/documents/humane-training-methods-for-dogs

Casey, J. (2012, March). Can Shock Collars Burn? *BARKS from the Guild (1)* 21-22. Retrieved May 28, 2019, from issuu.com/petprofessionalguild/docs/bbtg-march2012-final/21

Chance, P. (2008). Learning and Behavior. Belmont, CA: Wadsworth Cengage Learning

Cooper, J.O., Heron, T.E., & Heward, W.L. (1987). Applied Behavior Analysis. Upper Saddle River, NJ: Merrill

Deldalle, S., & Gaunet, F. (2014). Effects of 2 training methods on stress-related behaviors of the dog (Canis familiaris) and on the dog-owner relationship. *Journal of Veterinary Behavior (9)* 58-65. Retrieved January 4, 2019, from https://www.journalvetbehavior.com/article/S1558-7878(14)00007-0/abstract

Department for Environment, Food and Rural Affairs. (2017). Code of practice for the welfare of dogs. Retrieved May 25, 2019, from https://assets.publishing.service.gov.uk/government/uploads/system/uploads/attachment_data/file/697953/pb13333-cop-dogs-091204.pdf

Dodds, W.J. (2013). Q&A with Dr. Dodds: Can Collars Really Damage the Thyroid? Retrieved May 28, 2019, from https://www.hemopet.org/dog-collars-thyroid/

Donaldson, J. (2017, January 5). Talk Softly and Carry a Carrot, Not a Stick. Retrieved January 2, 2019, from https://academyfordogtrainers.com/blog/talk-softly-and-carry-a-carrot-not-a-stick

Elliott, P. (2017). How Choke Collars Can Cause Real Damage to Your Dog. Retrieved May 28, 2019, from https://www.petful.com/pet-health/cautionary-tale-choke-collars/

European Society of Veterinary Clinical Ethology. (2017). ESVCE Position Statement: Electronic Training Devices. Retrieved May 28, from http://www.esvce.org/wp-content/uploads/2017/11/ESVCE-Position-Statement-e-collar.pdf

Foubert, E. (2016). Occupational Licensure for pet Dog Trainers: Dogs are not the only ones who should be licensed. Chicago, IL: The John Marshall Law School

Friedman, S. (2004, November). Straight Talk about Parrot Behavior. StopPDD Conference. Retrieved January 4, 2019, from http://behaviorworks.org/files/articles/Straight%20Talk%20About%20Behavior.pdf

Friedman, S. (2005). He Said, She Said, Science Says. *Journal of Applied Companion Animal Behavior (5)* 1 25-31. Retrieved January 4, 2019, from http://www.associationofanimalbehaviorprofessionals.com/vo5no1friedmana.pdf

Garrod, D. (2015, January). The Argument against Prong Collars. *BARKS from the Guild (10)* 26-29. Retrieved May 28, 2019, from https://issuu.com/petprofessionalguild/docs/bftg_jan_2015flattened_opt_opt/26

Gershoff, E.T., & Font, S.A. (2016). Corporal Punishment in U.S. Public Schools: Prevalence, Disparities in Use, and Status in State and Federal Policy. Social Policy Report 30:1. Retrieved February 12, 2019, from https://www.ncbi.nlm.nih.gov/pmc/articles/PMC5766273/

Global Initiative to End All Corporal Punishment of Children. (2018). Global progress towards prohibiting all corporal punishment. Retrieved February 12, 2019, from http://endcorporalpunishment.org/wp-content/uploads/legality-tables/Global-progress-table-commitment.pdf

Ha, J.C., & Campion, T.L. (2019). Dog Behavior: Modern Science and Our Canine Companions. London, UK: Elsevier

Herron, M.E., Shofer, F.S., & Reisner, I.R. (2009). Survey of the use and outcome of confrontational and non-confrontational training methods in client-owned dogs showing undesired behaviors. *Applied Animal Behavior Science (117)* 47-54. Retrieved January 4, 2019, from https://vet.osu.edu/assets/pdf/hospital/behavior/trainingArticle.pdf

Lang, P.J., Bradley, M.M., & Cuthbert, B.N. (1990, July). Emotion, attention, and the startle reflex. *Psychological Review 97* (3) 377-395. Retrieved January 4, 2019, from http://dx.doi.org/10.1037/0033-295X.97.3.377

Low, P. (2012, July 7). The Cambridge Declaration on Consciousness. Retrieved January 4, 2019, from http://fcmconference.org/img/CambridgeDeclarationOnConsciousness.pdf

Masson, S., La Vega, S., Gazzano, A., Mariti, C., Da Graça Pereira, G., Halsberghe, C.,…Schoening, B. (2018). Electronic training devices: Discussion on the pros and cons of their use in dogs as a basis for the position statement of the European Society of Veterinary Clinical Ethology. *Journal of Veterinary Behavior 25* 71-75. Retrieved May 28, from https://www.sciencedirect.com/science/article/pii/S1558787818300108?fbclid=IwAR0rsVM-689ZbE2CFDUuMAmatkmEKiIk9id15xbJrTiLac9Nj5UGtPZW9ho

McKeon, S. (2017, March). Great Expectations. *BARKS from the Guild (23)* 33-35. Retrieved January 4, 2019, from https://issuu.com/petprofessionalguild/docs/bftg_mar_2017_online_opt/33

Mech, L.D. (1999). Alpha status, dominance, and division of labor in wolf packs. Retrieved January 4, 2019, from http://67.222.97.186/267alphastatus_english.pdf

New Zealand Veterinary Association. (2018). Use of behaviour modifying collars on dogs. Retrieved February 12, 2019, from https://www.nzva.org.nz/page/policybehavcollar

O'Heare, J. (2005). Canine Neuropsychology. Ottawa, ON: DogPsych Publishing

O'Heare, J. (2011). Empowerment Training. Ottawa, ON: BehaveTech Publishing

Overall, K. L. (2013). Manual of Clinical Behavioral Medicine for Dogs and Cats. St. Louis, MO: Mosby Inc.

Overall, K.L. (2016, November). Current Trends: Beyond Dominance and Discipline. Pet Professional Guild Summit Keynote Presentation, Tampa, FL. In S. Nilson. (2017, January). #PPGSummit 2016: Beyond Dominance. *BARKS from the Guild (22)* 10-11. Retrieved January 4, 2019, from https://issuu.com/petprofessionalguild/docs/bftg_jan_2017_online_edition_lores/10

Overall, K.L. (2017, November). Why Balanced Training Can Unbalance Dogs. Pet Professional Guild Summit Keynote Presentation, Orlando, FL. In S. Nilson. (2018, January). A Time to Revitalize, Re-energize and Rejuvenate. *BARKS from the Guild (28)* 10-11. Retrieved January 4, 2019, from https://issuu.com/petprofessionalguild/docs/bftg_january_2018_online_edition_op/10

Panksepp, J. (2012). [Discover Interview with Pamela Weintraub] Jaak Panksepp Pinned Down Humanity's 7 Primal Emotions. Retrieved January 4, 2019, from http://discovermagazine.com/2012/may/11-jaak-panksepp-rat-tickler-found-humans-7-primal-emotions

Patel, C. (2016, November). Behavior Science beyond the Quadrant. Pet Professional Guild Summit Presentation, Tampa, FL. In S. Nilson. (2017, January). New Look for 2016: Guest Speaker and

General Presenters - What They Said. *BARKS from the Guild (22)* 10. Retrieved May 14, 2019, from https://issuu.com/petprofessionalguild/docs/bftg_jan_2017_online_edition_lores/10

Patel, C. (2018, April). Rethinking Dog Training. Pet Professional Guild Training and Behavior Workshop Presentation, Kanab, UT. In S. Nilson. (2018, July). Lecture Notes: What They Said. *BARKS from the Guild (31)* 12-13. Retrieved May 14, 2019, from https://issuu.com/petprofessionalguild/docs/bftg_july_2018_online_edition_opt_1/12

Pet Professional Guild. (2018). Dominance Theory in Animal Training. Retrieved May 14, 2019, from https://petprofessionalguild.com/DominanceTheoryPositionStatement

Pet Professional Guild. (2018). The Use of Pet Correction Devices. Retrieved May 14, 2019, https://petprofessionalguild.com/Equipment-Used-for-the-Management-Training-and-Care-of-Pets

Polsky, R.H. (1994). Electronic shock collars: Are they worth the risks? *Journal of the American Animal Hospital Association 30* (5) 463-468

Ramirez, K. (2016, November). Evolving Challenges for the Positive Reinforcement Trainer in the Modern World. Pet Professional Guild Summit Presentation, Tampa, FL. In S. Nilson. (2017, January). New Look for 2016: Guest Speaker and General Presenters - What They Said. *BARKS from the Guild (22)* 10. Retrieved May 14, 2019, from https://issuu.com/petprofessionalguild/docs/bftg_jan_2017_online_edition_lores/10

Ramirez-Moreno, D.F., & Sejnowski, T.J. (2012, March). A computational model for the modulation of the prepulse inhibition of the acoustic startle reflex. *Biological Cybernetics 106* (3) 169-176. Retrieved January 4, 2019, from http://link.springer.com/article/10.1007/s00422-012-0485-7

Rooney, N.J., & Cowan, S. (2011). Training methods and owner-dog interactions: links with dog behaviour and learning ability. *Applied Animal Behavior Science 132* 169-177. Retrieved January 4, 2019, from https://www.appliedanimalbehaviour.com/article/S0168-1591(11)00087-6/abstract

Sege, R.D., & Siegel, B.S. (Council on Child Abuse and Neglect, Committee on Psychosocial Aspects of Child and Family Health). (2018) Effective Discipline to Raise Healthy Children. *Pediatrics*. Retrieved January 4, 2019, from http://pediatrics.aappublications.org/content/early/2018/11/01/peds.2018-3112

Shock-Free Coalition. (2018). It's Time to Say NO to the Use of Shock Devices! Retrieved January 4, 2019, from https://www.shockfree.org

Shock-Free Coalition. (2018). What Is Shock Training? Retrieved May 28, 2019, from https://www.shockfree.org

Steimer, T. (2002). The biology of fear- and anxiety-related behaviors. Dialogues in *Clinical Neuroscience 4* (3) 231-49. https://www.ncbi.nlm.nih.gov/pmc/articles/PMC3181681/

The Kennel Club. (2018). The Kennel Club and Scottish Kennel Club Welcomes the Scottish Government's Effective Ban on Shock Training Devices. Retrieved January 4, 2019, from https://www.thekennelclub.org.uk/press-releases/2018/october/the-kennel-club-and-scottish-kennel-club-welcomes-the-scottish-government-s-effective-ban-on-shock-training-devices/

Tudge, N.J. (2008). What is the difference between escape and avoidance behavior? The DogSmith. Retrieved January 4, 2019, from https://www.dogsmith.com/what-is-the-difference-between-escape-and-avoidance-behavior

Tudge, N.J. (2009). An outline of the four quadrants of operant conditioning. The DogSmith. Retrieved January 4, 2019, from https://www.dogsmith.com/an-outline-the-four-quadrants-of-operant-conditioning/

Tudge, N.J. (2010). Professional Ethics in Dog Training - A Few Thoughts to Ponder! Retrieved November 20, 2018, from https://www.dognosticscareercenter.com/Blogs/6915713

Tudge, N.J. (2017). Training Big for Small Business. (n.p.) Ingram Spark Self-Publishing

Tudge, N.J, & Nilson, S.J. (2016). The Use of Shock in Animal Training. Retrieved February 12, 2019, from https://petprofessionalguild.com/shockcollars

United Nations Committee on the Rights of the Child. (2006). General Comment No. 8: The right of the child to protection from corporal punishment and other cruel or degrading forms of punishment (arts. 19; 28, para. 2; and 37, inter alia). Retrieved February 12, 2019, from https://www.refworld.org/docid/460bc7772.html

Wächter, T., Lungu, O.V., Liu, T., Willingham, D.T., & Ashe, J. (2009). Differential Effect of Reward and Punishment on Procedural Learning. *Journal of Neuroscience 14* 29 (2) 436-443. Retrieved May 23, 2019, from http://www.jneurosci.org/content/29/2/436

Vet West Animal Hospitals. (2019). Skin - The Difference Between Canine and Human Skin. Retrieved May 28, From https://www.vetwest.com.au/pet-library/skin-the-difference-between-canine-and-human-skin

Wood, A. (2016). How Fear Becomes Aggression in Dogs and Humans. Retrieved January 4, 2019, from http://adriennerixwood.com/psychologists-best-friend/2016/7/18/how-fear-becomes-aggression-in-dogs-and-humans#citation1

Yin, S. (2012). How Technology from 30 Years Ago is Helping Military Dogs Perform Better Now. Retrieved May 28, 2019, from https://drsophiayin.com/blog/entry/how-technology-from-30-years-ago-is-helping-military-dogs-perform-better-no/

Ziv, G. (2017). The Effects of Using Aversive Training Methods in Dogs – A Review. *Journal of Veterinary Behavior: Clinical Applications and Research (19)* 50-60. Retrieved January 4, 2019, from http://www.journalvetbehavior.com/article/S1558-7878(17)30035-7/fulltext

Chapter Five: A Call for an Industry Wide, Professionally Acknowledged Best Practice

In addition to the moral and ethical concerns about mental and physical damage to animals subjected to methods using force, fear and/or pain (see *Chapter Four: How Pets Learn and the Consequences of Methodology, Equipment and Philosophical Choice*), the growing body of scientific data we now have available to us has encouraged a number of representing organizations worldwide to advocate for the adoption of approaches humane and ethical practices and to avoid, or eliminate altogether, forceful and painful methods and/or equipment, including the Pet Professional Guild (PPG) in the United States, United Kingdom and Australia, the Institute of Modern Dog Trainers (IMDT) and the Association of Pet Dog Trainers (APDT) in the United Kingdom, and the Association of Pet Dog Trainers (APDT) in Australia. (See *Chapter Four: How Pets Learn and the Consequences of Methodology, Equipment and Philosophical Choice / Where It Begins* for more on credible studies and methods.)

According to Millikan (2012), the definition of best practice "varies across differing sources" and, for some, is "purely result driven." Millikan summarizes the following definitions:

> The question of how a best practice is defined in the currently unregulated pet industry is historically troubling and has continually been one of the key sticking points between and across key industry associations and credentialing bodies.

- "Methods and techniques that have consistently shown results superior to those achieved with other means and which are used as benchmarks to strive for." (Business Dictionary, 2011).
- "A process, method, technique or activity that conventional wisdom considers to be '...more effective at delivering a particular outcome than any other technique, method, process etc. when applied to a particular condition or circumstance. The idea is that with proper processes, checks, and testing, a desired outcome can be delivered with fewer problems and unforeseen complications...A given best practice is only applicable to particular condition or circumstance and may have to be modified or adapted for similar circumstances. In addition, a 'best' practice can evolve to become better as improvements are discovered.'" (Wikipedia, 2011).

- "Without such a standard, we are likely to intervene on the basis of effectiveness alone, without due consideration of humaneness. To be maximally humane, our interventions should be as unintrusive for the learner as possible and still be effective." (Friedman, 2010).

The question of how a best practice is defined in the currently unregulated pet industry is historically troubling and has continually been one of the key sticking points between and across key industry associations and credentialing bodies. Because these entities play a critical role in establishing and recommending best practices, codes of practice, education, leadership and technical standards that interface directly with the general public, it is a responsibility that should be taken very seriously.

In an Open Letter Regarding the Use of Shock in Animal Training, the Pet Professional Guild (PPG) (2017) states that the organization "has an obligation to provide transparent and consistent positions on important and urgent issues, such as training practices and equipment use." PPG's Guiding Principles (2012) clearly state that methods using shock, pain, choke, fear, physical force, or compulsion should never be employed to train or care for a pet. They are specific, measurable and forward thinking and provide a clear way ahead for the industry while supporting professional autonomy and without sacrificing unambiguous ethical guidelines. In a business environment where certifications are rife and new associations emerge annually, it is critical that professional organizations representing professionals do so to the benefit of the professional, the client, and the industry as a whole, not just in the interests of the singular organization. (Tudge & Nilson, 2019).

> *Progressing up the hierarchy to more invasive and aversive protocols is merely a matter of time for individuals who are not proficient in their trade, or do not have the requisite scientific knowledge or education to understand why this strategy is so problematic in the first place.*

The Humane Hierarchy

A common trend across some of the more forward acting professional animal training and behavior associations is the promotion and application of a so-called humane hierarchy, and various versions of this hierarchy have been published from a variety of sources. Some of the models are accompanied by pages of explanation, detail and academic citations, while others are wonderfully graphic and explain each level of the hierarchy, which generally begins with positive reinforcement (i.e. rewarding a desirable behavior to increase the likelihood of that behavior being repeated), and gradually goes through a number of steps before landing at positive punishment to stop an undesirable behavior via the use of force or pain or any other aversive (to the animal) means. In many cases, members of any given professional body are encouraged to work within the guidelines of these hierarchies, which are promoted as a tool to utilize when initiating training and behavior change programs (Tudge & Nilson, 2019).

Some industry associations, such as the International Association of Canine Professionals (IACP) (2018), have taken positions where members "may not seek to deprive any canine professional of his or her ability to conduct his or her business by seeking to restrict or ban accepted and established tools of the trade, or by seeking to restrict or ban accepted and established techniques and practices within the industry through calls for boycotts, restrictions, bans, or other actions designed to interfere with free marketplace participation of a canine professional in his or her business. Accepted and established tools of the trade include, but are not limited to, leashes, harnesses, training collars, slip collars, prong collars, head halters, remote electronic collars, and electronic pet containment systems."

> *What is of most concern regarding the various humane hierarchies which have been adopted and promoted by industry organizations is that said organizations are not shown themselves to be either willing or prepared – even in the face of the increasing academic body of knowledge regarding punishment – to remove specific tools, such as electric shock, from being a publicly endorsed and acceptable option for professionals and pet owners.*

Pet professionals who are affiliated with or represented by an organization that promotes the use of a humane hierarchy are generally urged to begin training and behavior change programs with the least invasive and aversive protocols available and work up to the more aversive levels – as deemed necessary by the individual trainer involved. These ratcheting up strategies can serve to justify, in the individual's mind, the use of more aversive and invasive protocols. However, if these types of hierarchies work in isolation of any non-negotiable best practices, then they fail the pet, the pet owner, the professional, and the entire industry. Progressing up the hierarchy to more invasive and aversive protocols is merely a matter of time for individuals who are not proficient in their trade, or do not have the requisite scientific knowledge or education to understand why this strategy is so problematic in the first place. Indeed, it could be argued that the humane hierarchy model simply provides an expressway – with nominal warning signs – to highly aversive practices. Going a step further, one could also argue that the representation of any level of invasive and/or aversive practices on a humane hierarchy surely legitimizes such practices and sets forth that their eventual use is an acceptable standard operating procedure – albeit under certain conditions.

What is of most concern regarding the various humane hierarchies which have been adopted and promoted by industry organizations is that said organizations are not showing themselves to be either willing or prepared – even in the face of the increasing academic body of knowledge regarding punishment – to remove specific tools, such as electric shock, from being a publicly endorsed and acceptable option for professionals and pet owners.

In addition, not only are there no ramifications for members who misrepresent their services through the omission of information about their chosen training methods in a membership directory or through their individual professional websites, organizations themselves are abstaining from taking a stand on any piece of equipment or training technique that any individual professional decides to use. This begs the question as to how consumers are protected in the absence of compulsory transparency across, or within membership organizations, given that a variety of methods and equipment, ranging from positive to negative, humane to aversive, may be used by a professional without gaining informed consent. As it stands, pet owners who are steered toward a professional organization through its own marketing efforts search, at their own peril, through an assortment of trainers operating at opposite ends of the ethical and moral spectrum.

> *As it stands, pet owners who are steered toward a professional organization through its own marketing efforts search, at their own peril, through an assortment of trainers operating at opposite ends of the ethical and moral spectrum.*

LIEBI and LIMA

Significantly, there is no consensus across the pet industry with regards to the suitability and appropriateness of the differing best practice models. In 2012, PPG worked in conjunction with Dr. James O'Heare, president of the Companion Animal Sciences Institute (CASI) and director of the Association of Animal Behavior Professionals (AABP), to deliver to its members a guided delivery system for best practice within the parameters of its Guiding Principles.

> *According to Donaldson (2017), dog training is a divided profession: "We are not like plumbers, orthodontists or termite exterminators who, if you put six in a room, will pretty much agree on how to do their jobs*

This best practice works through an algorithm and levels of intrusiveness model known as Least Intrusive Effective Behavior Intervention, or LIEBI. Meanwhile, in September 2018, the International Association of Animal Behavior Consultants (IAABC), the Certification Council for Professional Dog Trainers (CCPDT) and the Association of Pet Dog Trainers (APDT) in the United States made a joint announcement regarding their newly adopted best practice model. The organizations stated that they were "incredibly proud" to announce their agreement of a Standard of Practice: "Through our unified Code of Ethics and LIMA (Least Intrusive, Minimally Aversive) guidelines, we promote, as a norm and a fundamental tenet, positive reinforcement training, and giving a voice to our learners as well as our clients."

It becomes clear, then, that some of the key organizations representing pet professionals have taken somewhat differing approaches to how their members should approach the modification of behaviors and implementation of training programs. Some have provided parameters within which members should work whereas others have provided models that allow complete autonomy for their members regarding tools, equipment and philosophy.

Scientific Approach – Tactical Approach and Methodology

According to Donaldson (2017), dog training is a divided profession: "We are not like plumbers, orthodontists or termite exterminators who, if you put six in a room, will pretty much agree on how to do their jobs. Dog training camps are more like Republicans and Democrats, all agreeing that the job needs to be done but wildly differing on how to do it. The big watershed in dog training is whether or not to include pain and fear as means of motivation."

To compound the differences of opinion regarding the philosophical approach and structure toward pet training, there are also several factions within the professional population regarding the tactical approach to training pets and much conflict on the application of how the science is utilized. In *Chapter Four: How Pets Learn and the Consequences of Methodology, Equipment and Philosophical Choice*, the science is covered in its application to learning. Now, we will provide an overview of how to put the science into a context of working best practice.

Key Learning Theory

The key methods of learning that are applied and used for changing behavior are operant and respondent conditioning. In respondent (or classical) conditioning, the presence of one stimulus begins to reliably predict the presence of a second stimulus (Tudge, 2017). This is not a consciously learned process; it happens automatically and without thought, e.g. Pavlov's dogs started to salivate as they began to associate the sound of a bell with the delivery of food. In respondent conditioning, we are managing and changing emotions. In operant conditioning, meanwhile, we are managing and changing behaviors through the control and manipulation of consequences, the environment. Operant conditioning, defined as such because the behavior operates on the environment, takes place when a response in a given situation is reliably reinforced or punished, so there is a contingency between the response and the reinforcer/punisher.

There are four types of operant learning (known as the four quadrants): positive reinforcement, negative reinforcement, positive punishment, and negative punishment. In the descriptions detailed in *Fig. 4*, the terms positive and negative do not describe the consequence, rather, they indicate whether a stimulus has been added (positive) or subtracted (negative) to increase/strengthen or decrease/weaken the preceding behavior (Chance, 2008, p.126).

> *Operant conditioning, defined as such because the behavior operates on the environment, takes place when a response in a given situation is reliably reinforced or punished, so there is a contingency between the response and the reinforcer/punisher.*

Fig. 4: The Four Quadrants of Operant Conditioning

© Niki Tudge

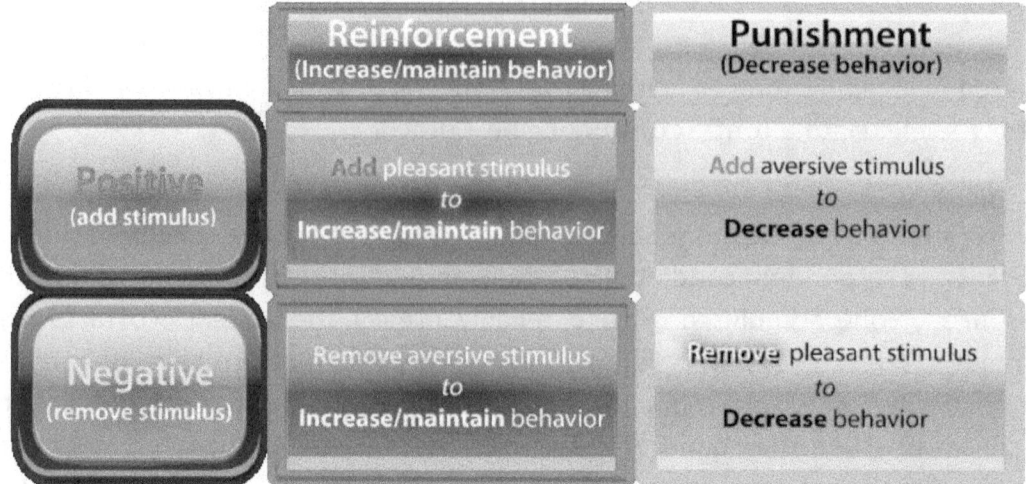

The quadrants that strengthen behaviors are referred to as reinforcements. Both positive and negative reinforcement increase the strength of a behavior due to the consequence. In positive reinforcement, a behavior is followed by the appearance of or an increase in the intensity of a stimulus. The stimulus is something a pet seeks out, i.e. something he finds attractive or desirable, and, therefore, it reinforces the behavior that precedes it. In negative reinforcement, a behavior is strengthened by a pet's ability to avoid or escape an aversive stimulus, i.e. something he finds unpleasant or frightening. It is thus sometimes referred to as escape/avoid learning (Chance, 2008, p.129). We discussed escape/avoid learning in greater detail in *Chapter Four: How Pets Learn and the Consequences of Methodology, Equipment and Philosophical Choice / Escape/Avoid Learning*.

The remaining two quadrants weaken behavior and are referred to as punishments. Both positive and negative punishment decrease the strength of a behavior due to the consequence. Punishers are aversive and something a pet works to avoid. When an aversive event is added to a situation, then positive punishment has taken place. Negative punishment subtracts something from a situation, such as privileges, and is sometimes called penalty training (Chance, 2008, p.208).

Pet Training and Behavior Consulting: A Model for Raising the Bar to Protect Professionals, Pets and Their People

> *In animal training, chasms can develop due to the fact that the application of each of the four quadrants is totally dependent on the individual trainer. Each professional has their own line in the sand in terms of how they will determine, apply and justify (or not) the use of aversives, i.e. stimuli that are scary or painful for the pet.*

In animal training, chasms can develop due to the fact that the application of each of the four quadrants is totally dependent on the individual trainer. Each professional has their own line in the sand in terms of how they will determine, apply and justify (or not) the use of aversives, i.e. stimuli that are scary or painful for the pet. While blanket statements such as, "We should never use positive punishment," may be made, aversive stimuli are ever present and even the "simple use of the word 'no' can function as positive punishment." (O'Heare, 2016, p.19). How fear-provoking the word "no" is will be based purely on an individual animal's conditioning history. If it has been paired with an electric shock, loud shout, or physical punishment, for example, then its future use will most likely elicit fear. And while a gentle use of the same word "no" prior to removing a shoe from a pet's mouth may also technically function as positive punishment, on a scale of pain or fear, this cannot be compared to the previous example. States O'Heare (2016, p.19): "It is important to avoid exaggeration or excessive simplicity in the analysis. Accepting extreme arguments such as all forms of aversive stimulation are always sure to cause irreparable harm or that aversive stimulation is necessary to succeed in training leads to dogmatic positions."

A critical point to understand here is that reinforcement and punishment are defined by the pet, not the trainer. For some dogs, being sprayed in the face with water may be applied as a punishment by a trainer but may be a reinforcing contingency to the dog (i.e. the dog enjoys it). In everyday life, we are all faced with aversive stimuli from the moment we wake till the moment we go to sleep. These come in various forms, such as the alarm clock, droning or beeping signals that remind us to fasten our seat belts, arguments with colleagues or spouses, and honking horns can all serve to frustrate or irritate us and have an impact on our behavior.

It should be noted that some stimuli (for both humans and pets) are socially mediated and cannot be foreseen and/or prevented. Other stimuli, meanwhile, are contingent on our own behavior and, it may be argued, serve some greater function, such as the unpleasant taste of a poisonous plant that may prove useful as part of our survival strategy. While everyday unpleasantness cannot be avoided, the application of aversive stimuli in a strategic and purposeful training, management or care plan most certainly can be. There are perfectly humane and positive alternatives that are not packaged with problematic emotional consequences such as fear, anxiety and pain.

We must also recognize that some aversive stimuli are merely irritating, whereas others may generate a strong emotional response and be completely unproductive. Again, dependent on a pet's conditioning history, what is merely an irritant for one can be devastating for another. This argues for why, as an industry and as training and behavior professionals, we need to avoid making dogmatic statements and generalizations about the behavioral sciences with no regard for the individual pet in our care. Instead, we must avoid risking negligence by focusing purely on the animal in front of us as well as his immediate welfare needs at the hands of our training and care procedures. This means that, rather than just speaking to the four quadrants, we must determine the impact of our intervention choices by studying the immediate emotional and behavioral welfare of each pet.

> *While everyday unpleasantness cannot be avoided, the application of aversive stimuli in a strategic and purposeful training, management or care plan most certainly can be. There are perfectly humane and positive alternatives that are not packaged with problematic emotional consequences such as fear, anxiety and pain.*

When structuring hypothetical arguments on a wholesale front about training approaches, it is also important to be careful not to apply generalizations on paper that do not play out in a training scenario. Professionals can achieve this by possessing a comprehensive knowledge and thorough understanding of canine social behavior and communication. We will talk more about this in *Chapter Six: Canine Communication and Social Behavior*.

As already outlined in *Chapter Four: How Pets Learn and the Consequences of Methodology, Equipment and Philosophical Choice / A Review of the Science*, **Ziv** (2017) reviewed data from a number of studies and surveys on the relationship between the use of a variety of tools and methods in dog training. The results show that using aversive training methods (e.g., positive punishment and negative reinforcement) can jeopardize both the physical and mental health of dogs (Tudge & Nilson, 2017). In addition, although positive punishment is known to be effective, there is no real evidence that it is more effective than positive reinforcement-based training. Nevertheless, despite the decades of studies we now have access to, there are still organizations, associations and councils responsible for the representation, guidance and certification of pet industry professionals that adhere to the belief that using scary and painful aversives is an acceptable – and even necessary – way to train, care for, and manage pets (*see Chapter Three: Professionals Should Exemplify and Promote Anti-Cruelty Statutes / Abusive Training Practices*.) (*Note: A list of some of the key studies can be found in Chapter Eight: Ethics in Pet Training and Behavior Consulting / Ethics and the Detrimental Effect of Aversives*.)

> *As an industry and as training and behavior professionals, we need to avoid making dogmatic statements and generalizations about the behavioral sciences with no regard for the individual pet in our care.*

These same associations play a critical role in establishing and recommending best practices, education, leadership and technical standards in their respective arenas and with this role comes the obligation to take a transparent and consistent position on important and urgent issues, including training practices and equipment use. This does not mean said organizations need to remove or even inhibit professional autonomy. However, a line based on research, science, and ethics should be drawn as to what are, and are not, acceptable business practices in terms of applied animal behavior (ABA) (*see Chapter Four: How Pets Learn and the Consequences of Methodology, Equipment and Philosophical Choice / Applied Behavior Analysis*), core principles, and informed consent. And, wherever possible "practitioners should base their choices of training methods on scientific data." (Ziv, 2017).

Among professionals, it should not even need to be debated that, in the process of training, one must not physically or emotionally harm an animal. This should not even be an issue. As such, it is our view that local authorities, animal welfare organizations, municipal animal control facilities and professional pet industry associations can no longer remain as passive observers here, but, rather, must actively shape the change in the industry by stepping forth and making the difficult and necessary decisions regarding tools, equipment and training approaches. (See *Chapter Four: How Pets Learn and the Consequences of Methodology, Equipment and Philosophical Choice / Summary* for further discussion on choice of training method and equipment.)

> *Across these differing approaches to dog training and behavior modification, professionals may commonly be insistent on using the tools they deem to be best or most appropriate with little concern to the emotional state expressed by the pet in front of them. All too often there is a myopia to what the pet is actually communicating, feeling, or even how he is reacting or responding. As such, subtle signs of stress, anxiety or fear may be missed due to the insistence that the chosen approach is acceptable.*

Summary

While pet professional membership bodies, industry associations and credentialing bodies should be taking full responsibility for the fact that pet owners are encouraged to purchase services from their members purely by association, and through their efforts to market said members to the general pet owning public, what this does not take into consideration, unfortunately, are the vast differences in methodology and philosophy that may exist across the membership. In other words, there is no stated transparency in terms of the risks and benefits associated with the services provided, nor any differentiation between those members who practice a positive training philosophy and those who still risk physical and/or psychological harm to pets through their approach, philosophy and/or choice of tools.

Across these differing approaches to dog training and behavior modification, professionals may commonly be insistent on using the tools they deem to be best or most appropriate with little concern to the emotional state expressed by the pet in front of them. All too often there is a myopia to what the pet is actually communicating, feeling, or even how he is reacting or responding. As such, subtle signs of stress, anxiety or fear may be missed due to the insistence that the chosen approach is acceptable. For example, feeding a dog treats while undergoing a training session in a stressful environment, or with a rough hand, is not going to constitute a positive approach to the training task. Indeed, we often see in such scenarios that the pet is too emotionally aroused to even take interest in a treat, much less actually consume one. We will talk more about behavior myopia in *Chapter Six: Canine Communication and Social Behavior / Dog-Human Interaction*.

A possible resolution to common situations such as these may be found in the adoption of a Best Practice Model that covers the need for efficacy and efficiency in pet training while avoiding industry dogma and taking into consideration the welfare of our family pets. With this at its foundation, we set forth our proposed Best Practice Model in *Appendix A: The Recommended Best Practice Model for Pet Training and Behavior Consulting*. (**See also** *Chapter Ten: Pet Industry Oversight Recommended Implementation Model*.)

Bibliography

Best Practice [Def]. (2010). In Business Dictionary. Retrieved May 14, 2019, http://www.businessdictionary.com/definition/best-practice.html

Best Practice [Def]. (2010). Wikipedia. Retrieved May 14, 2019, from https://en.wikipedia.org/wiki/Best_practice

Chance, P. (2008). Learning and Behavior. Belmont, CA: Wadsworth Cengage Learning

Donaldson, J. (2017, January 5). Talk Softly and Carry a Carrot, Not a Stick. Retrieved January 2, 2019, from https://academyfordogtrainers.com/blog/talk-softly-and-carry-a-carrot-not-a-stick

Friedman, S. (2010). What's wrong with this picture? Effectiveness is not enough. *APDT Journal*. Retrieved January 2, 2019, from http://behaviorworks.org/files/articles/APDT%20What%27s%20Wrong%20with%20this%20Picture%20-%20Dogs.pdf

International Association of Animal Behavior Consultants. (2018). Announcing a new Joint Standards of Practice for professional animal behavior consultants and trainers. Retrieved November 28, 2018, from https://m.iaabc.org/joint-standards-of-practice

International Association of Canine Professionals. (2018). IACP Code of Conduct. Retrieved November 28, 2018 from https://www.canineprofessionals.com/code-of-conduct

Millikan, D.A. (2012). Defining, Determining and Maintaining Best Practices within Our Force-Free Organization. Retrieved January 2, 2019, from https://petprofessionalguild.com/PPG-Best-Practice

O'Heare, J. (2014). The least intrusive effective behavior intervention (LIEBI) algorithm and levels of intrusiveness table: a proposed best practices model. Version 6.0. Retrieved January 2, 2019, from https://pdfs.semanticscholar.org/88a4/1389d24c4a2802faeae02fce472d1b017f91.pdf

O'Heare, J. (2016). Minimally Aversive Contingency Management. *Journal of Animal Behavior Technology (6)* 1 19-35. Retrieved January 2, 2019, from http://www.associationofanimalbehaviorprofessionals.com/jabtvol6no1.pdf

Pet Professional Guild. (2012). Guiding Principles. Retrieved January 2, 2019, from https://petprofessionalguild.com/PPGs-Guiding-Principles

Pet Professional Guild. (2017). Open Letter Regarding the Use of Shock in Animal Training. Retrieved January 2, 2019, from https://petprofessionalguild.com/Open-Letter-to-Pet-Industry-Representatives-Regarding-the-Use-of-Shock-in-Animal-Training

Tudge, N.J. (2017). Training Big for Small Business. (n.p.) Ingram Spark Self-Publishing

Tudge, N.J., & Nilson, S.J. (2017). Open Letter Regarding the Use of Shock in Animal Training. Pet Professional Guild. Retrieved January 2, 2019, from https://petprofessionalguild.com/Open-Letter-to-Pet-Industry-Representatives-Regarding-the-Use-of-Shock-in-Animal-Training

Tudge, N.J., & Nilson, S.J. (2019). The Case for Scientifically-Informed, Kind Practices. *BARKS from the Guild (34)* 18-26. Retrieved January 2, 2019, from https://issuu.com/petprofessionalguild/docs/bftg_january_2019_online_edition_op/18

Ziv, G. (2017). The Effects of Using Aversive Training Methods in Dogs – A Review. *Journal of Veterinary Behavior: Clinical Applications and Research (19)* 50-60. Retrieved January 2, 2019, from https://www.sciencedirect.com/science/article/pii/S1558787817300357

Chapter Six: Canine Communication and Social Behavior

Dogs are master communicators and exhibit a wide range of both overt and covert signals via their body language and facial expression. It is essential that dog training and behavior professionals are fluent in reading canine communications so they can understand a dog's emotional state at any given moment in any given context, as well as be able to educate owners when a dog is experiencing a negative emotional state, such as fear, stress, or anxiety. This ability is essential both for safety reasons (i.e. to avoid a potential escalation of emotions to a point where a dog feels he has no other choice but to snap or bite) and to enhance the dog-human bond via helping dogs and their families achieve mutual understanding to live happily and harmoniously together in the home.

Communication involves "a wide range of behaviors that animals emit in their daily lives and can take place between different species," as in the case of domestic dogs and humans (Elgier, Jakovcevic, Barrera, Mustaca & Bentosela, 2009). Canine communication systems have evolved specifically to avoid or cut off conflict and are greatly ritualized. Historically, this has ensured the pack's smooth functioning and successful hunting and made dogs, as a species, very successful in terms of their numbers, variety, and adaptability.

Some of the methods dogs use to communicate include:

- Scent: Includes scent markers such as pheromones, urine, feces and anal gland secretions, and undoubtedly others we are unaware of.
- Vocalizations: Include barking, whining, yelping, howling, growling, grumbling and general muttering.
- Visual Signals: Include body postures, appearance of facial features such as eyes, ears, and mouth, and appearance of other body features such as tail and hair. Each of these visual signals is an indication as to how a dog is feeling.
- Body Movements: Can be fast or slow, face-to-face or indirect, closeness of physical contact, and use of the mouth for licking, snapping, or biting.

Sadly, human understanding of canine communication signals often remains limited either because people do not see them or, when they do see them, do not comprehend them or are unaware of what they mean. Indeed, it can be hard for owners to know what another dog is saying to their dog or what their dog is saying to them because much of canine communication happens so quickly or is simply unseen or indecipherable to the untrained eye.

States Rugaas (2013): "[Dogs] easily perceive tiny details - a quick signal, a slight change in another's behavior, the expression in our eyes. Pack animals are so perceptive to signals that a horse can be trained to follow the contraction in our pupils and a dog can be trained to answer your whispering voice. There's no need to shout commands, to make the tone of our voice deep and angry - what Karen Pryor refers to as swatting flies with a shovel."

Interspecific miscommunications and misunderstandings can lead to situations where owners have no idea why their dog responds to a stimulus in a certain way and may as a consequence label his behavior "unpredictable." Things can go awry very quickly when humans ignore or misread the signals dogs send them, leaving their pets struggling to effectively communicate their current emotional state.

Dogs exhibit behaviors designed either to access pleasurable situations and desirable objects, or, conversely, to avoid and escape unpleasant situations and undesirable objects. This is based on what any individual dog considers to be pleasant/desirable or unpleasant/undesirable, and it is important to note that canine opinion may differ from human opinion on this.

> *Interspecific miscommunications and misunderstandings can lead to situations where owners have no idea why their dog responds to a stimulus in a certain way and may as a consequence label his behavior "unpredictable."*

The types of social behaviors dogs demonstrate can be broadly grouped into the following two possibilities:

Distance Decreasing

Dogs use distance decreasing behaviors to promote approach, play and continued interaction. A lumbering soft gait, relaxed body and a relaxed face where the muscles are loose indicate the dog is encouraging interaction, as does a dog who is moving toward or leaning into a person. A dog may also offer a paw or rub against a person, soliciting attention. In a consent test, this would be interpreted as a dog saying "yes." Consent testing is an "informal experiment which allows a dog to offer consent regarding a specific situation. Via his/her body language the dog communicates a yes or no response...If consistently applied, consent testing creates a partnership with the dog, which is critically important, especially for dogs with behavior issues." (Steinker, 2016).

Another commonly seen canine communication signal is the "play bow," a posture where the dog literally bows the front of his body so the front legs are parallel to the ground while the hindquarters remain in the standing position. Dogs who want to engage in play will demonstrate the play bow to other dogs as a so-called meta signal, indicating that any ensuing actions are meant in play, and not intended to be intimidating, threatening, or aggressive.

Some dogs may use the play bow when encouraging their owner or other humans to engage in play with them, but training history may also affect the way a dog plays with his owner. Rooney and Cowan (2011) observe "a significant difference in play behaviour between owner-dog partnerships which reported using physical punishment and those which did not," in that play was "less interactive in partnerships which use some physical punishment." This may suggest that training using punishment is "associated with a reduced quality of dog–human relationship." (Rooney & Cowan, 2011).

> Dogs use appeasement behaviors to make friendly encounters more predictable and to help them diffuse what they anticipate might be a hostile encounter if escape is impossible. These behaviors are a nonaggressive way to "cut off" conflict.

Distance Increasing

Canine distance increasing signals vary and can be easily misread. In a consent test, distance increasing signals "are interpreted as a dog saying 'no.' Conflicted behaviors are also a 'no.'" (Steinker, 2016). Signals such as a dog standing tall, making each part of his body appear as large as possible with the weight on the front legs, displaying an upright tail and ears, stiffened musculature, and piloerection (i.e. the hair along the spine stands up, a.k.a. raised hackles), are rather obvious distance increasing signals even to the untrained eye. The dog may also vocalize (e.g. bark or growl). Humans often instinctively react to signals such as these and take them as the warnings they are intended to be.

There are, however, a number of distance increasing signals humans commonly seem to misinterpret. These include the more appeasing behaviors dogs demonstrate. Dogs use appeasement behaviors to make friendly encounters more predictable and to help them diffuse what they anticipate might be a hostile encounter if escape is impossible. These behaviors are a nonaggressive way to "cut off" conflict. When dogs display appeasement behaviors, it is their way of showing they are unsure and a little scared, and it is up to humans to acknowledge this and react accordingly and appropriately. Significantly, according to Rooney and Cowan (2011), "the type of training methods employed may affect the way in which a dog behaves in numerous situations. For example, punishment-based training methods may lead to general anxiety (Blackwell et al., 2008), which may affect a dog's social behaviour towards both its owner and towards other people, or its response to denial of contact or attention from its owner."

Appeasement Signals

Appeasement signals are manifested in two ways:

Passive Appeasement

Passive appeasement behaviors are commonly misunderstood and may be labeled by owners as "submissive." Dogs displaying passive appeasement may present themselves in a hunched or recumbent position exposing the underside of their body. The ears are typically back and down against the head and the tail is often tucked between the upper legs. Sometimes, the dog will expel a small amount of urine while he waits for the attention or situation he perceives to be hostile to cease.

Active Appeasement

Dogs displaying active appeasement gestures are often incorrectly labeled in anthropomorphic terms, such as "excited," "overly friendly," or even "pushy." They will often approach with their whole rear-end wagging in a "U" shape allowing both their face and genital area to be inspected. They may be desperate to jump up and get "in your face."

For humans, then, it is important when meeting and greeting dogs to be able to recognize if a dog is genuinely friendly and wanting to greet them, or if he is experiencing stress, anxiety or fear. The latter are all signs that a dog is saying "no," and should be respected as such.

Specific Signs of Stress or Anxiety

Dogs often feel stressed or anxious in certain situations and will give signs to indicate their discomfort. In such cases, there is a need for awareness and, if appropriate, intervention to prevent pushing a dog to the point where he feels compelled to bite to make the discomfort stop or go away. The goal in such situations is for the dog to attain a positive emotional state (i.e. happy) and not a negative emotional state (i.e. stressed or anxious).

> *States Miller (2005): "Most dogs don't want to bite or fight. The behaviors that signal pending aggression are intended first and foremost to warn away a threat. The dog who doesn't want to bite or fight tries his hardest to make you go away."*

Here are just two examples of the more subtle or commonly misinterpreted signs a dog may give when feeling stressed or anxious:

- One Paw Raised: This may look "cute," but the dog who raises his paw is not happy and does not want to be petted or bothered. A raised paw is a sign that the dog is worried.
- Half-Moon Eye: Also known as whale eye, this is when the whites of the dog's eyes are visible. This is a common expression in dogs that are being hugged, when children are playing too roughly with him, or are too noisy or close to him. If the half-moon eye is seen when approaching or interacting with a dog, it is time back off as he wants to be left alone.

A dog may also vocalize stress, fear or anxiety in the form of a whine, growl or bark, a tongue flick, looking away, yawning, or by licking his lips. It is imperative that a dog is not punished for showing he wants to be left alone, by growling, leaving the area, or demonstrating any of the more subtle signs highlighted above in order to avoid the risk of suppressing his warning system. It is always a good thing that a dog shows when he is anxious or uncomfortable and gives a person the chance to change the situation, rather than put him in a position where he feels there is no other option but to bite to put an end to the uncomfortable situation once and for all. States Miller (2005): "Most dogs don't want to bite or fight. The behaviors that signal pending aggression are intended first and foremost to warn away a threat. The dog who doesn't want to bite or fight tries his hardest to make you go away."

Other signs of anxiety, stress and/or fear include:

- Tail between the legs.
- Tail low and only the end is wagging.
- Tail between the legs and wagging.
- Tail down or straight for curly-tailed dogs (husky, malamute, pug, chow, spits-type dogs etc.)
- Ears sideways for an erect-eared dog.
- Ears back and very rapid panting.
- The dog goes into another room away from the person.
- The dog goes into another room away from the person and urinates or defecates.
- Freezing.

Masson et al. (2018) note that a number of behaviors such as these, "associated with a negative emotional state," have been reported as an effect of e-collar use, including "lowered body postures (Beerda et al., 1998; Schilder and van der Borg, 2007; Salgirli et al., 2012) as well as avoidance, paw lifting, tongue flicking, yawning, panting, behavioral inhibition, or reduced exploration (DEFRA AW1402, 2013)." Masson et al. (2018) state that these behaviors "can be seen in dogs trained with e-collars even under the most benign and controlled training conditions (Cooper et al., 2014)."

Displacement Behaviors

Displacement behaviors are behaviors that a dog would normally do in another context. As such, it is important to look at the whole situation to determine whether the dog is feeling anxious. For example:

- If the dog gets up, stretches, yawns and goes to his bed to rest or sleep, then that yawn was not a displacement behavior.
- If children are hugging the dog or lying on him and he yawns or starts licking at them over and over, then these are displacement behaviors. The dog wants to get up and leave, or perhaps even to bite to put an end to the unpleasant situation, but instead displaces that urge with yawning or licking either the children or himself. In this context, the licking or yawning behavior tells us that the dog is uncomfortable, and it is time to intervene. (*Note: Children should never lie on, sit on, or stand on any dog.*)

As well as being typical behaviors that are displayed out of context, displacement behaviors also indicate conflict and anxiety, i.e. the dog wants to do something, but is suppressing the urge to do it. He may, then, displace the suppressed behavior with something else such as a lick or a yawn. For example, an owner is getting ready to leave the house and the dog either wants to go too, does not want to be left alone, or does not want the person to leave. He is not sure what will happen next and may want to jump on the owner or run out the door, but instead he yawns. The uncertainty of the situation causes conflict for the dog, and the displacement behaviors are a manifestation of that conflict.

Some examples of displacement behaviors include:

- Yawning when not tired.
- Licking chops without the presence of food.
- Sudden scratching when not itchy.
- Sudden biting at paws or other body part.
- Sudden sniffing the ground or other object.
- All over body shake when not wet or dirty.

Avoidance Behaviors

Sometimes dogs are more overt when they feel anxious and want to remove themselves from a situation. Examples include:

- Getting up and leaving an uncomfortable situation.
- Turning the head away.
- Hiding behind a person or object.
- Barking and retreating.
- Rolling over on the back in a submissive way.

Dogs should not be forced to stay in any situation where they feel anxious. All dogs should have a safe place, such as a crate or mat, or even a separate room, where they can go when they want to be left alone. All family members and guests should be taught not to bother the dog when he is in his safe place.

Calming Signals

Rugaas (2013) talks of approximately 30 canine calming signals used by dogs to reduce stress. These include many of the behaviors outlined above and below. Rugaas (2013) explains thus: "For species who live in packs it's important to be able to communicate with its own kind. Both in order to cooperate when they hunt, to bring up their offspring, and perhaps most importantly: to live in peace with each other. Conflicts are dangerous - they cause physical injuries and a weakened pack, which is something that no pack can afford - it will cause them to [become] extinct."

> When looking at the topography of a dog's body and his communication signals, one must look at the entire package, i.e. all of the body parts. A wagging tail does not always mean that a dog wants to be friends and is safe to approach.

Cutoff Behaviors

Cutoff behaviors are designed to end social contact. If, when greeting a dog, a person does not recognize that he is scared or stressed, or they choose to ignore his signals and push forward with their approach, they are unfairly pushing him into a situation where he may feel he is only left with one option – to bite. Thus, the onus is on owners and professionals to understand and respond to a dog's communication signals so he does not reach that point.

Tail Carriage

One of the biggest misconceptions about canine body language is that a dog wagging his tail is a happy dog. A dog's tail can indeed indicate that he feels happy and relaxed. When looked at in isolation, however, the tail is one of least reliable indicators of how a dog is feeling. When looking at the topography of a dog's body and his communication signals, one must look at the entire package, i.e. all of the body parts. A wagging tail does not always mean that a dog wants to be friends and is safe to approach.

General Meeting and Greeting

When meeting and greeting a dog, it is important to have a relaxed posture. The person should allow the dog to approach them (only if/when the dog wants to) and turn slightly to the side, as this is less threatening than standing in a full-frontal position, leaning over the dog and/or staring directly at him. The person can then talk gently to the dog without making eye contact, which the dog may perceive to be threatening.

Dogs should not be approached head on or in a straight line as this may be viewed as hostile or threatening. In general, when they have the option, dogs will approach each other indirectly, meandering, or walking "in curves" (Rugaas, 2013).

When meeting a new dog who is happy to proceed, it helps to crouch down and keep one's hands by one's side without making any sudden movements. When it is determined the dog is not showing any signs of stress or fear and his body language is relaxed and happy, then the person can allow the dog to sniff their hand. If he does so and continues to encourage the contact, they can then slowly move their hand to the side of his body, just below the neck, and stroke him gently across his chest and side. If at any time the dog shows passive appeasement signals (i.e. signs of unease or fear) such as those described above, the person should slowly stop and/or retreat, give the dog space and allow him to approach them on his terms and at his preferred timing. If he chooses not to, then the person must respect that, accept that he is not ready to interact at that moment and is saying "no."

> *People may think that a bite happened "out of nowhere," but this is rarely the case. It is more likely to be the case that the dog showed initial signs of distress that were either unseen, unacknowledged, or ignored*

Conflicted Dogs

A dog in conflict will want to approach but at the same time may be too scared or unsure of the outcome. His body language will vacillate between displays of distance decreasing behaviors and distance increasing behaviors. "Some dogs feel two things at the same time. It is not uncommon, especially for herding breeds, to exhibit both distance-increasing and distance-decreasing behaviors at the same time. These dogs will approach, lick and then retreat. Conflicted body language must be interpreted as a 'no.'" (Steinker, 2015).

Interacting with a dog that is conflicted can be risky. If one makes a wrong move and the dog cannot avoid the approach, then he may become aggressive. This can happen very quickly and is often the case with a "fear biter." People may think that a bite happened "out of nowhere," but this is rarely the case. It is more likely to be the case that the dog showed initial signs of distress that were either unseen, unacknowledged, or ignored: "As a consequence, a so-called 'unpredictable' aggressive response, without any obvious preamble, may occur in any context which predicts inescapable threat to the dog, when in reality it was entirely predictable." Shepherd (2009, p.13-16).

Cullinan, Blackwell and Casey (2004) report that the highest instances of aggressive behavior were found in "dogs whose owners used a combination of positive reinforcement and positive punishment." According to Ha and Campion (2019), using both positive reinforcement and positive punishment is "one of the worst things you can do to your dog…Some of the most confused dogs, showing the strangest behaviors or responses to their environment, have turned out to be those that were facing significant levels of training: punishment or aversive based training as well as positive reinforcement training." Cullinan, Blackwell and Casey (2004) hypothesize that "aggressive responses in dogs can develop as a result of 'conflict,' or anxiety about an uncertain response to their behaviors from inconsistent owners." Ha and Campion (2019) speak of "conflicting [neural] pathways for the learning involved with each method" (*see Chapter Four: How Pets Learn and the Consequences of Methodology, Equipment and Philosophical Choice / Summary*) and also reference the risk of using both methods in tandem as simply teaching the dog that their owner (or, indeed, trainer) is "inconsistent" and "unpredictable."

> *It is essential that anyone working with dogs in any capacity is schooled in canine communication, body language, and facial expression, and is able to understand the signals given by the dogs in their care at any time so they can manage the environment accordingly.*

In her Canine Ladder of Aggression, Shepherd (2004) details how a dog reacts to stress or threats and how his emotional state can escalate if early warnings (ranked here from mild to severe) are not heeded:

- Yawning, blinking, nose licking.
- Turning head away.
- Turning body away, sitting, pawing.
- Walking away.
- Creeping, ears back.
- Standing crouched, tail tucked under.
- Lying down, leg up.
- Stiffening up, stare.
- Growling.
- Snapping.
- Biting.

A dog may not display every signal, and signals displayed by an individual dog at different times and in different contexts may vary. Depending on the situation, dogs may progress up the ladder within mere seconds, which does not necessarily give enough time for the untrained eye to acknowledge them or react appropriately, if, indeed, the signals are observed and understood in the first place. "It is most important to realize that these gestures are simply a context and response-dependent sequence which will culminate in threatened or overt aggression, only if all else fails." (Shepherd, 2009, p.13-16).

It is essential that anyone working with dogs in any capacity is schooled in canine communication, body language, and facial expression, and is able to understand the signals given by the dogs in their care at any time so they can manage the environment accordingly (a.k.a. antecedent control) to ensure a dog never feels the need to escalate up the ladder to the more severe warning signals. This knowledge must also be passed on to their dog owner clients, both adults and children.

> *According to current scientific literature, "canine aggression and other behavior problems are not a result of dominant behavior or lack of the owner's 'alpha' status but rather a result of fear (self-defense) or underlying anxiety problems." - Herron, Shofer & Reisner, (2009)*

Many dogs who bite, bite out of fear. Movement toward them, or even the mere presence of a person may be scary to them, and they bite as a last resort to encourage the person to leave because they feel that, in that moment, they have no other option. A dog in this state is highly emotionally aroused and virtually incapable of rational thought. As already detailed in *Chapter Four: How Pets Learn and the Consequences of Methodology, Equipment and Philosophical Choice / Where It Begins*, in cases of extreme emotional arousal where the emotional brain inhibits the rational brain, an animal will go into fight or flight mode, meaning it is difficult, if not impossible, for them to select an appropriate behavior or to learn productively. Because they know this, "positive trainers focus on building relationships with pets by using positive reinforcement to train new skills, and to build new behaviors as replacements for problematic ones." (Tudge & Nilson, 2019).

When a dog is experiencing fear, it is advisable to avoid sudden movements, and to allow him an escape route. It is essential that owners and professionals – and, indeed, anyone wishing to interact with a dog – do not force a meet and greet by moving toward the dog, have the dog's handler manipulate the dog into moving toward them, or try to touch the dog in any way.

According to current scientific literature, "canine aggression and other behavior problems are not a result of dominant behavior or lack of the owner's 'alpha' status [(see Chapter Four: How Pets Learn and the Consequences of Methodology, Equipment and Philosophical Choice / Outdated Approach)], but rather a result of fear (self-defense) or underlying anxiety problems." (Herron, Shofer & Reisner, 2009). It is imperative that dog training and behavior professionals understand this so they can work with the owners to change a dog's current emotional state and overall mood state, as well as elevate confidence levels, so he no longer feels motivated to react aggressively in specific contexts to specific stimuli "because many behavior problems are associated with increased anxiety levels." (Blackwell, Bolster, Richards, Loftus & Casey, 2012). Punitive and outdated "training" techniques "such as forcing a dog down by the collar or by pushing on its neck and back—as, for example, in the 'dominance down'—are associated with increased physiological stress (Beerda et al., 1998). Frightened animals are often self-defensively aggressive; it would not be unexpected, then, that dogs respond aggressively to such provocative handling." (Herron, Shofer & Reisner, 2009).

> *It is also important to note that using aversive stimuli to reduce distance increasing behaviors "may suppress signals that warn of a more serious, and potentially imminent behavior, such as biting. Without ritualized aggression behaviors, people and other pets will receive no warning before the pet subjected to punishment feels forced to resort to biting." (Tudge & Nilson, 2017).*

Canine Warnings

As we have explained, dogs will typically give plenty of warning if they are uncomfortable with something another dog or a person is doing, or with a certain situation. Warning signs may include a direct stare, a rigid face or body, a growl, a curled lip (this can be minimal and hard to spot), or "whale eye" (i.e. flashing the whites of the eyes, also known as half-moon eye). The dog's ears may be flat against his head and he may have a closed, tense mouth. When any of these signals are seen, the person should stop what they are doing immediately, back away and/or allow the dog to slowly back away. Dogs can make signals extremely quickly, within nanoseconds, and because of this it is not always easy to spot them.

States Shepherd (2009, p.13-16): "In all dogs, inappropriate social responses to appeasement behaviour will result in its devaluing and the necessity, from a dog's perspective, to move up the ladder [of aggression]. Aggression is therefore created in any situation where appeasement behavior is chronically misunderstood and not effective in obtaining the socially expected outcome. Dogs may progress to overt aggression within seconds during a single episode if the perceived threat occurs quickly and at close quarters or learn to dispense with lower rungs on the ladder over time, if repeated efforts to appease are misunderstood and responded to inappropriately."

> *It is also important to note that using aversive stimuli to reduce distance increasing behaviors "may suppress signals that warn of a more serious, and potentially imminent behavior, such as biting*

It is also important to note that using aversive stimuli to reduce distance increasing behaviors "may suppress signals that warn of a more serious, and potentially imminent behavior, such as biting. Without ritualized aggression behaviors, people and other pets will receive no warning before the pet subjected to punishment feels forced to resort to biting." (Tudge & Nilson, 2017).

Dog-Human Interaction

Ha and Campion (2019, p.48) propose the ethogram as "one of the most reliable and effective ways to get a glimpse into another species' possible emotional states, thoughts, perspective and actions." The ethogram "catalogues an animal's behavior, comprising the placement, configuration, and movements of body parts and behavioral contexts, including locomotion and travel. The behaviors included in an ethogram are typically defined as objective and mutually exclusive, thus making them individually recognizable to any observer."

It is likely that dogs were the "first animals to be domesticated and as such have shared a common environment with humans for over ten thousand years." (Udell & Wynne, 2008). They are social animals whose personalities range from being social butterflies to shy wallflowers. They are very clear with their intentions and emotions and respond accordingly to those of humans. Indeed, human body language and approach speak much louder than words and dogs are expert readers of human body language and nonverbal communication.

Domestic dogs kept as pets today remain "dependent on humans for primary reinforcers, such as food, water, access to mates, and even touch, throughout their lifetimes. Consequently, their access to reinforcers is contingent upon appropriate behavioral responses within the human social environment dependence and sensitivity to human contingencies are shaped quickly in domestic dogs in human households." (Udell & Wynne, 2008).

Udell and Wynne (2008) propose that "[o]ne of the most interesting behavioral characteristics of the modern domestic dog is its predisposition to attend and respond to human social gestures and cues." They cite examples of common human gestures, such as a signal to stop, pointing, nodding, reaching toward something, or glancing between an object and another individual. "The degree to which individual dogs attend to human social cues and their tendency to rapidly integrate new behaviors into their repertoire based on the consequences that follow from them, says something about both their development and their environment. For dogs to provide adaptive responses to human gestures requires not only attentiveness and close proximity to human action, indicative of some sort of social attachment to humans, but also sensitivity to context within a human environment." (Udell & Wynne, 2008).

Dogs can thus display social behaviors "adjusted to the living constraints of the human environment. For example, research has shown that dogs can learn to communicate with humans, whether incidentally or explicitly." (Deldalle & Gaunet, 2014). Reid (2009), giving the example of locating hidden food, points out that dogs are "more skillful than a host of other species at tasks which require they respond to human communicative gestures." Further, dogs "produce apparent referential and attention-getting signals to let humans know which object or action they desire from their owner (Gaunet, 2010; Gaunet & Deputte, 2011)." (Deldalle & Gaunet, 2014). Dogs have also "shown to be successful at following human cues to solve the object choice task" (Elgier et al., 2009), and "tend to look at the human face in situations of conflict and uncertainty." (Barrera, Mustaca & Bentosela, 2011). Data collected in a study by Siniscalchi, d'Ingeo and Quaranta (2018) found that "dogs displayed a higher behavioral and cardiac activity in response to human face pictures expressing clear arousal emotional states," leading the authors to suggest that dogs are "sensitive to emotional cues conveyed by human face."

Pet Training and Behavior Consulting: A Model for Raising the Bar to Protect Professionals, Pets and Their People

Summary

According to Steinker and Anderson (2014), the fundamental goal of any behavior change program should be to "improve the dog's and owner's emotional states, both during and after the process." They highlight the importance of professionals being able to read dogs' communication signals, noting that it can be "particularly catastrophic when covert or subtle behaviors are ignored as, arguably, they are the most important information a behavior consultant has. But we are all prone to focusing on what is most obvious. For example, if a dog is engaging in overt behaviors such as barking and lunging, it can overshadow nuance and make us miss the more subtle behaviors. When this occurs however, we overlook our obligation to improve the animal's quality of life – even though we might be presenting a potentially effective behavior modification program." (Steinker & Anderson, 2014).

Steinker and Anderson (2014) refer to this as "behavior myopia" of which the "most damaging aspect...is the complete disregard for [the dog's] emotional state." They cite disregard or ignorance of canine body language as a key cause of behavior myopia: "In order to interpret subtle behaviors, dog trainers need to understand canine body language. Some dogs are just hard to read, no matter how experienced the trainer. Certain breeds are stoic and simply 'quiet' in their nonverbal communication. Sometimes a dog's behavior can be globally suppressed from the use of punishment and/or negative reinforcement. Such dogs can be particularly dangerous and difficult to work with." (Steinker & Anderson, 2014).

Another cause of behavior myopia cited by Steinker and Anderson (2014) is a lack of consideration of a dog's emotions and their subtle indicators: "If a dog is barking and lunging at a stimulus then he is usually fearful or angry. If the behavior modification protocol does not address the dog's emotional state then it is flawed…Often, trainers are only aware of obvious, reactive behaviors and unaware of the small changes that occur as a stimulus becomes gradually more aversive to the animal." They state that dog trainers have an "ethical obligation" to do everything they can to improve the quality of life for both the dog and owner, and that having completed a behavior modification program, "dogs should feel safer and happier. Similarly, the process should create dogs who are more resilient because of the improved baseline regarding joy and happiness – which also leads to a more desirable result for the owner. (Steinker & Anderson, 2014).

Rugaas (2013) highlights the fact that dogs live in a "world of sensory input: visual, olfactory [and] auditory perceptions," leading Ha and Campion (2019) to conclude that the "key to a successful relationship with our dogs is fluency in both canine communication signs and in their unique sensory perspectives." Dogs use their communication systems towards humans, "simply because it's the language they know and think everyone understands." (Rugaas, 2013). It is when humans fail to see the signals, to understand or acknowledge them, or worse still, punish the dog, that problems can start to occur.

Bibliography

Barrera, G., Mustaca, A., & Bentosela, M. (2011). Communication between domestic dogs and humans: effects of shelter housing upon the gaze to the human. *Animal Cognition 14* 5 727–734. Retrieved May 20, 2019, from https://link.springer.com/article/10.1007%2Fs10071-011-0407-4

Blackwell, E.J., Bolster, C., Richards, G., Loftus, B.A., & Casey, R.A. (2012). The use of electronic collars for training domestic dogs: estimated prevalence, reasons and risk factors for use, and owner perceived success as compared to other training methods. *BMC Veterinary Research (8)* 93. Retrieved January 6, 2019, from https://bmcvetres.biomedcentral.com/articles/10.1186/1746-6148-8-93

Cullinan, P., Blackwell, E. J., & Casey, R. A. (2004, October 22). The relationships between owner consistency and 'problem' behaviors in dogs: a preliminary study. Cremona, Italy: Proceedings of 1st meeting of the European College of Veterinary Behavioral Medicine – Companion Animals

Deldalle, S., & Gaunet, F. (2014). Effects of 2 training methods on stress-related behaviors of the dog (Canis familiaris) and on the dog-owner relationship. *Journal of Veterinary Behavior (9)* 58-65. Retrieved January 6, 2019, from https://www.journalvetbehavior.com/article/S1558-7878(14)00007-0/abstract

Elgier, A.M., Jakovcevic, A. Barrera, G., Mustaca, A.E., & Bentosela, M. (2009). Communication between domestic dogs (Canis familiaris) and humans: Dogs are good learners. *Behavioural Processes (81)* 3 402-408. Retrieved January 6, 2019, from https://www.sciencedirect.com/science/article/abs/pii/S0376635709000965

Ha, J.C., & Campion, T.L. (2019). Dog Behavior: Modern Science and Our Canine Companions. London, UK: Elsevier

Herron, M.E., Shofer, F.S., & Reisner, I.R. (2009). Survey of the use and outcome of confrontational and non-confrontational training methods in client-owned dogs showing undesired behaviors. *Applied Animal Behavior Science (117)* 47-54. Retrieved January 6, 2019, from https://www.sciencedirect.com/science/article/abs/pii/S0168159108003717

Masson, S., La Vega, S., Gazzano, A., Mariti, C., Da Graça Pereira, G., Halsberghe, C.,...Schoening, B. (2018). Electronic training devices: Discussion on the pros and cons of their use in dogs as a basis for the position statement of the European Society of Veterinary Clinical Ethology. *Journal of Veterinary Behavior 25* 71-75. Retrieved May 28, from https://www.sciencedirect.com/science/article/pii/S1558787818300108?fbclid=IwAR0rsVM-689ZbE2CFDUuMAmatkmEKiIk9id15xbJrTiLac9Nj5UGtPZW9ho

Miller, P. (2005). Understand Why Your Dog Growls. *Whole Dog Journal*. Retrieved May 20, from https://www.whole-dog-journal.com/behavior/understand-why-your-dog-growls/

Reid, P.J. (2009). Adapting to the human world: Dogs' responsiveness to our social cues. *Behavioural Processes (80)* 3 325-333. Retrieved January 6, 2019, from https://www.sciencedirect.com/science/article/abs/pii/S0376635708002623

Rooney, N.J., & Cowan, S. (2011). Training methods and owner-dog interactions: links with dog behaviour and learning ability. *Applied Animal Behavior Science 132* 169-177. Retrieved January 6, 2019, from https://www.appliedanimalbehaviour.com/article/S0168-1591(11)00087-6/

Rugaas, T. (2013). Calming Signals - The Art of Survival. Retrieved May 20, 2019, from http://en.turid-rugaas.no/calming-signals---the-art-of-survival.html

Shepherd, K. (2004). The Canine Ladder of Aggression. Retrieved January 5, 2019, from https://www.kendalshepherd.com/app/download/5741399162/Ladder+of+Aggression+and+text.pdf?t=1363339642

Shepherd, K. (2009). Behavioural medicine as an integral part of veterinary practice. BSAVA Manual of Canine and Feline Behaviour (2nd edn.). (Eds: Debra F. Horwitz and Daniel S. Mills). Quedgeley, UK: British Small Animal Veterinary Association

Siniscalchi, M., d'Ingeo, S., & Quaranta, A. (2018). Orienting asymmetries and physiological reactivity in dogs' response to human emotional faces. *Learning & Behavior 46* 4 574–585. Retrieved May 20, 2019, from https://link.springer.com/article/10.3758%2Fs13420-018-0325-2

Steinker, A. (2015, July). The Art and Science of Consent Testing. *BARKS from the Guild (13)* 52-53. Retrieved January 5, 2019, from https://issuu.com/petprofessionalguild/docs/bftg_july_2015_online_version_opt_1/52

Steinker, A. (2016, January). The Value of Non-Verbal Communication. *BARKS from the Guild (16)* 26-31. Retrieved January 5, 2019, from https://issuu.com/petprofessionalguild/docs/barks_from_the_guild_january_2016/26

Steinker, A., & Anderson, E. (2014, October). Avoiding Behavior Myopia: Recognizing the Subtle Signs. *BARKS from the Guild (9)* 14-19. Retrieved January 6, 2019, from https://issuu.com/petprofessionalguild/docs/barks_october_2014_pet_professional/14

Tudge, N.J., & Nilson, S.J. (2017). Open Letter Regarding the Use of Shock in Animal Training. Retrieved January 5, 2019, from https://petprofessionalguild.com/Open-Letter-to-Pet-Industry-Representatives-Regarding-the-Use-of-Shock-in-Animal-Training

Tudge, N.J., & Nilson, S.J. (2019). The Case for Scientifically-Informed, Kind Practices. *BARKS from the Guild (34)* 18-26. Retrieved January 5, 2019, from https://issuu.com/petprofessionalguild/docs/bftg_january_2019_online_edition_op/18

Udell, M., & Wynne, C. (2008). A Review of Domestic Dogs' (Canis Familiaris) Human-Like Behaviors: Or Why Behavior Analysts Should Stop Worrying and Love Their Dogs. *Journal of the Experimental Analysis of Behavior 89* (2) 247–261. Retrieved January 6, 2019, from https://www.ncbi.nlm.nih.gov/pmc/articles/PMC2251326

Chapter Seven: Competency Is Mission Critical

In 1953, American psychologist, academic and scientist David McClelland referenced, for the first time, "a human trait that he called 'competence.'" (Chouhan & Srivastava, 2014, p.14). As such, the development of competence as a concept originated in the United States and was then followed by developments in the United Kingdom.

Pet Industry Competence Is Paramount to Industry Professionalism

The terms competence and competency have a tendency to be used interchangeably and this, not surprisingly, can be a source of confusion. According to Le Deist and Winterton (2005, p.29), there is "such confusion and debate concerning the concept of 'competence' that it is impossible to identify or impute a coherent theory or to arrive at a definition capable of accommodating and reconciling all the different ways that the term is used." Armstrong (2003, p.147), meanwhile, discusses how the concept of competence is essentially about performance, quoting Mansfield (1999) who defines competence as "an underlying characteristic of a person that results in effective or superior performance."

> In the pet industry, it is highly unlikely that any one training or behavior professional will be competent across all the entire range of pet industry services as there are so many specialties, ranging from dog sports, canine fitness, hobby activities, training disciplines and various areas of expertise regarding behavior change protocols.

Delamare and Winterton (2005) note that "'competence' generally refers to functional areas and 'competency' to behavioral areas but usage is inconsistent." Eraut (1994, p.179) makes a distinction between "competence," which has a generic or holistic meaning and refers to a person's overall capacity, and "competency," which refers to specific capabilities. Gonzi, Hager and Athanason (1993, p.5) take a slightly different view, stating that "performance is what is directly observable, whereas competency is not directly observable, rather is inferred from performance."

Rankin (2002) describes competencies as definitions of skills and behaviors: "Competencies represent the language of performance. They can articulate both the expected outcomes from an individual's efforts and the manner in which these activities are carried out." Boyatzis (1982) states that there is no single factor, but a range of factors that differentiate success from failure, defining competency as "a capacity that exists in a person that leads to behavior that meets the job demands and parameters of the organizational environment and that, in turn brings about the desired results." Finally, according to Armstrong (2003), competency is a person-based concept which refers to the dimensions of behavior lying behind competent performance; competencies are behavior characteristics, sometimes referred to as 'soft skills.'

What is Professional Competence?

How, then, does the concept of competence impact the work of professional dog trainers and pet care providers? Professional competence is the "broad professional knowledge, attitude, and skills required in order to work in a specialized area or profession. Disciplinary knowledge and the application of concepts, processes and skills are required in a test of professional competence in any particular field." (Reference, 2019). When speaking to the practice of counseling, Welfel (2009, p.81) points out that "professional competence is the most ethical obligation a professional has in their field of expertise."

> The pet is the vulnerable party in the consultation process as he cannot offer informed consent, and, therefore, the priority must always be to maintain an empathetic approach while practicing humane, effective, efficient and successful interventions. Not only should professionals ethically be competent, "competence is the most ethical obligation a professional trainer has in their field of expertise." (Welfel, 2009).

To be competent means a professional is knowledgeable, schooled in the theory and research of their industry, and has the necessary skills to apply that field of knowledge to a working situation with their clients (Tudge, 2010). Within the companion animal training and behavior field, "necessary skills" refers to the professional's interviewing skills, their ability to use applied behavior analysis to functionally analyze behavior via a professional functional assessment, and possess the technical skills and ability to support pet owners in their goals of improving and changing a pet's behavior (Tudge, 2010).

Furthermore, competence is "the measure of actual professional performance, not the level and amount of education the professional has achieved. The range of services offered by companion animal training and behavior professionals is referred to as 'scope of practice.' Competent professionals only work within the boundaries of their knowledge and skill body." (Tudge, 2010).

In the pet industry, it is highly unlikely that any one training or behavior professional will be competent across all the entire range of pet industry services as there are so many specialties, ranging from dog sports, canine fitness, hobby activities, training disciplines and various areas of expertise regarding behavior change protocols. The latter encompasses issues such as separation anxiety, aggression, reactivity, resource guarding, fearful behavior, and phobias, all of which attract and demand specialized knowledge to ensure competency of the service provider within their scope.

Client Attending Skills

There is also the issue of client attending skills, i.e. the ability of a professional to work with clients to impact positively the lives of their pets. The professional's role is to assess, implement and manage the training project and, in the process, educate clients in terms of the expectations and reasonableness of the agreed training or behavior change goal. This management process requires a set of individual skills such as communication, negotiation, time management, conflict resolution, listening, and basic project management. There is also the question of teaching skills versus training skills, i.e. the ability of the professional to competently teach the clients as well as support them training their pets. In actual fact, the animal training professional is a trainer of trainers.

> *In the pet industry, it is highly unlikely that any one training or behavior professional will be competent across all the entire range of pet industry services as there are so many specialties, ranging from dog sports, canine fitness, hobby activities, training disciplines and various areas of expertise regarding behavior change protocols.*

According to Welfel (2009, p.84), "professionals are diligent and focus their attention on the needs of the client." Tudge (2010) goes a step further, stating that, in companion animal training and behavior consulting, the term "client" must incorporate and include both the owner and the pet, and the needs and welfare of all parties must be met. When working in behavior counseling with pets and their owners, then, professionals must represent the needs of the pet and be his voice. The pet is the vulnerable party in the consultation process as he cannot offer informed consent, and, therefore, the priority must always be to maintain an empathetic approach while practicing humane, effective, efficient and successful interventions. Not only should professionals ethically be competent, "competence is the most ethical obligation a professional trainer has in their field of expertise." (Welfel, 2009).

> *The vision of the pet training body should ideally be one of an innovative leader that helps to shape the future of training regulations by protecting the public and promoting quality, ethical, scientifically proven training methods.*

Determining Competency

Determining what we mean by competence and competency in a fledgling industry is no small feat. Before we can begin to address various levels of competence, we must first speak to how competence is attained. The most diligent way of doing this is to review how other professional organizations determine their goals and standards. For example, medical boards and legal bar associations help protect human safety by ensuring the competence of their members.

In the United States, the Federal Bar Association Mission Statement (2018) declares that it exists to serve "…the interests and needs of the federal practitioner, both public and private, the federal judiciary and the public they serve." The Federation of State Medical Boards (FSMB) (2018), meanwhile, states that it supports its members "…as they fulfil their mandate of protecting the public's health, safety and welfare through the proper licensing, disciplining and regulation of physicians…" A stated goal of the FSMB is to "provide educational tools and resources that enhance the quality of medical regulation and raise public awareness of the vital role of the state medical boards."

The practice of veterinary medicine, the one consistently licensed job function in the pet industry, requires licenses in each state which are overseen by state boards. Each state (and Canadian province) has a regulatory board that is tasked with "regulating the practice of veterinary medicine. Regulators ensure that those entering the practice of veterinary medicine meet a minimum standard of practice by being properly educated, qualified, and are fit to be licensed." (American Association of Veterinary State Boards, 2018).

In Florida, for example, the Florida State Medical Board is overseen by the Department of Business and Professional Regulation. The Board of Veterinary Medicine works with the Department of Business and Professional Regulation to meet the mission to "license efficiently, regulate fairly" the 10,300 licensed professionals who engage in veterinary medicine in Florida (Florida Department of Business and Professional Regulation, 2016).

> *The vision of the pet training body should ideally be one of an innovative leader that helps to shape the future of training regulations by protecting the public and promoting quality, ethical, scientifically proven training methods.*

By reviewing these existing models as examples, we can draw similarities with the needs that must be met for attaining competence, maintaining competence, and governance of those in the pet training industry. If pet training is to professionalize and be a responsible part of the pet industry, visions and missions need to be similar. The vision of the pet training body should ideally be one of an innovative leader that helps to shape the future of training regulations by protecting the public and promoting quality, ethical, scientifically proven training methods. The mission of this body should be to support the industry by way of education, assessment, research, and advocacy while, at the same time, providing services and initiatives that promote animal welfare, safety, and quality of life, and industry best practice. (See *Chapter Eight: Ethics in Pet Training and Behavior Consulting / Ethics within the Framework of Competency* for further discussion of competency in the pet industry.)

We have already discussed the issue of occupational licensing and government oversight as well as the intended and unintended consequences thereof in *Chapter One: What Is Occupational Licensing?* Now, as we continue our discussion, we must consider salient points such as how to determine competency, how to measure it, and how it can and even must be demonstrated by those practicing as pet professionals.

Competency Models

A competency model is a collection of competencies that together define successful performance in a particular work setting. It is normal practice in business environments to use competency models not only to define and determine competencies across both hard and soft skills, but also to assess the performance of the competencies displayed by the professional. Competency models are a core function of human resource departments serving to support hiring and retention policies as well as talent and performance management activities.

Assessments of competency help form the basis for both formal and informal training programs and learning content and, ultimately, competency models have emerged as valuable tools to define skill and knowledge requirements for specific jobs and to then assess competencies and performances. This is the process of performance management (Armstrong, 2003). Career One Stop (2018) recommends that competency models are developed around a set of building blocks arranged in tiers, each representing a set of competencies. These tiers are stratified across a) foundational skills, b) industry related skills, and c) specific occupation skills (*see Fig. 5*).

Fig. 5: Competency Models

Foundational Competencies	Industry Related Competencies	Occupation Related Competencies
Tier 1: Personal Effectiveness Competencies	Tier 4: Industry-Wide Technical Competencies	Tier 6: Occupation-Specific Knowledge Competencies
Tier 2: Academic Competencies	Tier 5: Industry-Sector Technical Competencies	Tier 7: Occupation-Specific Technical Competencies
Tier 3: Workplace Competencies		Tier 8: Occupation-Specific Requirements
		Tier 9: Management Competencies

The Training Industry (2018) recommends that organizations seeking to build a competency model follow a five-step process:

1. Gather the background information. This includes cataloging existing resources, organizing resources, comparing contents to the building blocks framework, and determining commonalities for an industry model.
2. Develop a draft competency model framework. Identify themes and patterns in the information and relate the information to content areas.
3. Gather feedback from subject matter experts. If possible, select experts from across geographic and industry subsectors to gain the broadest perspective.
4. Refine the framework. Add or delete competencies as appropriate.
5. Validate the framework. This essential step ensures acceptance by the target community of users.

Assessment of Competencies

Once a competency model is in place, the question then posed, according to Miller (1990), concerns how competencies are assessed: When discussing competence and assessment, "…no single assessment method can provide all the data required for judgement of anything so complex as the delivery of professional services."

Miller (1990) also proposes a plan for the ethical assessment of competency and explains that, to fully assess a person's ability to perform the required tasks of their profession, a candidate should be assessed on:

- Knowledge.
- Competency.
- Performance.
- Action. (*See Fig. 6*)

Fig. 6: Framework for Assessment Adapted from Miller's (1990) Model

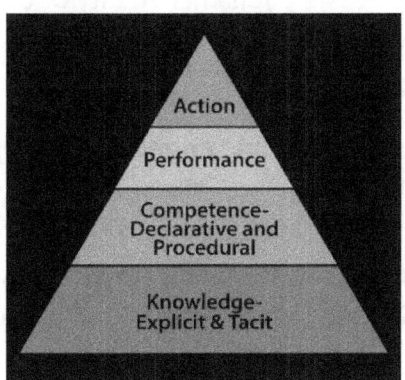

Knowledge

As can be seen in *Fig. 5*, the assessment of a candidate's knowledge forms the base of the assessment. The candidate must know the theory of their trade, yet most trades require a skill competency too. This can be the differentiating factor between academics and practitioners. Often, knowledge is the only method of assessment carried out and very frequently a written paper will suffice to prove competence. As Miller (1990) points out, however, "[t]ests of knowledge are surely important, but they are also incomplete tools in this appraisal if we really believe there is more to the practice of medicine than knowing." And the same must be said for the practice of animal training. Being well-informed and in the possession of explicit knowledge is not enough to be a competent animal trainer; knowledge must also be tacit. Both tacit knowledge based on common sense, and explicit knowledge based on academic accomplishment are critical (Smith, 2001).

Know-How (Competence)

> *Being well-informed and in the possession of explicit knowledge is not enough to be a competent animal trainer; knowledge must also be tacit. Both tacit knowledge based on common sense, and explicit knowledge based on academic accomplishment are critical (Smith, 2001).*

Competent animal trainers, like competent doctors, need to know how to apply their knowledge. Miller (1990) claims that "...graduates must know how to use the knowledge they have accumulated, for otherwise they may be little more than idiot savants." Miller (1990) goes on to say that, to be competent, candidates must develop the skill of acquiring information from a variety of sources, be able to interpret the data and then translate these findings into a rational management plan: "It is this quality of being functionally adequate, or of having sufficient knowledge, judgement, skill, or strength for a particular duty that Webster defines as *competence*."

In the field of animal training, candidates need to be skilled practitioners and thus need to be assessed on how they use their knowledge in practice. A Job Task Analysis (JTA) is used to identify what tasks within a job role are most important and are "often used to construct and validate certification programs, to ensure that the questions being asked are relevant to the job." (Question Mark, 2018). To be considered competent, a professional must be able to demonstrate the nominated skills determined critical by a Job Task Analysis.

Tudge (2017a) asserts that there is a difference between declarative and procedural knowledge. In other words, while a professional may understand some parts of learning theory, it does not mean they know when or how to apply that knowledge to an actual task. In other scenarios, an individual may have very competent mechanical skills but, if asked to explain what they are doing and why, will not be able to provide the reason or theory behind the skill. We may also notice differences in competence between, say, an academic who teaches theory versus a professional who works in the field practicing their skills with clients daily.

Show How (Performance)

To put acquired knowledge into practice requires an individual to visualize themselves performing the required skills for their level of competence. But what will they do when faced with a real client? They must demonstrate not only that they know, and know how, but that they can also "show how." (Miller 1990). Practical demonstrations in a real-life situation must thus be given and form an integral part of competency testing.

Does (Action)

What a candidate achieves in the artificial environs of an examination of practical skills is not necessarily predictive of they will do when functioning independently in practice. This can be one of the more difficult aspects of competence to assess, but ensuring the practical application takes place in a real-life setting that is not necessarily familiar to the candidate can help determine it. To support this area of candidate development prior to competency credentialing, there is a strong argument for supervised mentoring. (See *Appendix C: The Recommended Career Stage Mentoring Model*.)

Competency Standards

Understanding the areas of assessment is just the starting point for professional certification or accreditation. Competency is defined by a set of standards, which define the level of attainment at various levels (Trinder, 2008, p.165). The standards set can then test the effectiveness of training within many industries and are used by both professions and governments to define the qualifications required for individuals to practice in a particular discipline. The same standards work to define a range of levels of competency and the capabilities that are assumed to be achieved at these levels in order to provide the means to conduct Job Task Analysis and examination development, and to assess expert knowledge and competency standards for examination results. Altogether, these procedures ensure that measured competency equals the ability to apply knowledge and skills to produce a required outcome. In other words, it is the "ability to perform activities within an occupation, to function as expected for employment; and the ability to do a job under a variety of conditions, including the ability to cope with contingencies." (Trinder, 2008, p.165).

Increasingly, industries are demanding a proven level of competency for their employees while standards of competency are also used and maintained by professions and governments to "define the qualifications required for professionals to practice in a profession or discipline." (Trinder, 2008, p.165). As a result of this demand, the role of independent companies in guiding the development of competency assessments has grown to become critical to the ethics of accreditation and licensing and there are now specialist companies in place that provide these exact services.

> *No overriding and professional body determines a required level of competence within the pet industry and rarely are professional trainers held to account for any infractions or cruel practices. It is the unsuspecting, ill-informed, and – at times – misled, pet owners and their pets who suffer at the hands of so-called professionals due to this lack of credentialing and universal lack of educational standards.*

Currently, pet trainers and professional member associations are able to create their own framework for training approaches, methodology, standards, ethics, and equipment use, providing they do not encroach on any state or federal laws. No overriding and professional body determines a required level of competence within the pet industry and rarely are professional trainers held to account for any infractions or cruel practices. It is the unsuspecting, ill-informed, and – at times – misled, pet owners and their pets who suffer at the hands of so-called professionals due to this lack of credentialing and universal lack of educational standards. To address this, it must be determined what knowledge is needed, what skills are needed to be proven competent, what level of education is required, and what ongoing education the pet professional is undertaking to ensure correct and appropriate maintenance of appropriate knowledge, skills and ethical considerations.

There are a number of private certifying organizations and industry associations that provide education to the pet industry across many different disciplines and, on completion of programs or courses, offer certificates, diplomas, or attendance records to students. There are currently, however, only two nonprofit organizations that offer independent assessment and certifications for professional dog trainers and behavior consultants. (*Note: Certifications indicate that an individual has acquired the necessary knowledge, skills and sometimes personal attributes to perform a specific occupation or skill and are deemed competent and proficient across a collection of competencies.*) These are the Certification Council for Professional Dog Trainers (CCPDT), which follows the testing guidelines of the Institute of Credentialing Excellence and the Pet Professional Accreditation Board (PPAB), which assesses competencies through NOCTI Business Solutions. According to their website, NOCTI Business Solutions follow the best international industry practices and standards outlined in ISO 17024.

> Currently, and almost universally, unlike other counseling professions, pet training is not governed by "...state regulation or licensing, aside from the laws governing businesses in general." (Barry, 2008). Animal cruelty laws appear to be the only safety net for pets and, in all too many cases, these offer little protection.

Career One Stop (2018) states that competency models become the foundation for competency-based assessments, which inform the development of certification, licensure or assessments. The following steps outline how the process takes place:

1. Utilizing *Subject Matter Experts* to identify the basic literacy, numeracy, and academic competencies required for success in the industry and/or occupation.
2. Holding a *Job Task Analysis* to identify the specific foundational and workplace competencies expected in the job field.
3. Identifying the essential *Competency Components* to be included in professional certification and licensure requirements through a review of the scientific literature, industry standard operating procedures and required mechanical skills.

4. Coordinating and informing the development of achievement tests, *Competency Assessments* measure the desirable work-related knowledge and skills through a professional specialized and independent third party.

Given the vast monetary and employment gains of the pet industry over the last 20 years, it is essential that some level of oversight is introduced in the area of pet training. (*See the Executive Summary for industry statistics and growth projections.*) But what would this look like and how could it be applied? Currently, and almost universally, unlike other counseling professions, pet training is not governed by "...state regulation or licensing, aside from the laws governing businesses in general." (Barry, 2008). Animal cruelty laws appear to be the only safety net for pets and, in all too many cases, these offer little protection. Animal cruelty laws may be lacking in strength, are unique to individual states, and contain differing levels of fines and governmental oversight. In some states, animal cruelty laws have exceptions that apply to pet trainers, hunting dogs and/or other variables.

> *Most certainly some people enter the field of pet training out of a love for being around and working with animals in preference to being around or working with people. This can be an ill thought-out strategy, however, as pet training involves contact not only with the pet involved, but also their legal guardian, whether this be a rescue facility, a pet owner, or a referring professional. In other words, there is no avoiding people.*

The Role of Mentoring

Mentoring complements formal training and academia but does not replace the need for an apprentice to learn the required skills and knowledge required for their future role, as determined by a Job Task Analysis. There are several on-the-job training techniques that can help and support apprentices learn, grow and develop into competent professionals. These include:

- Demonstration: A technique whereby apprentices are told or shown how to do a job. It is very direct, and the apprentice is actively engaged in the task.
- Coaching: A person-to-person technique used to support and help an apprentice develop individual skills, knowledge and attitudes.
- Mentoring: A process whereby apprentices are partnered with individually selected and trained experts, so they can provide guidance and advice to help develop the individual careers (Armstrong, 2003). Mentoring may also

be described as a process whereby an experienced individual helps another person develop their goals and skills through a series of time-limited, confidential, one-on-one conversations and other learning activities (Murray, 2001).

Most certainly some people enter the field of pet training out of a love for being around and working with animals in preference to being around or working with people. This can be an ill thought-out strategy, however, as pet training involves contact not only with the pet involved, but also their legal guardian, whether this be a rescue facility, a pet owner, or a referring professional. In other words, there is no avoiding people. Tudge (2015, p.19) states that "our clients, the four-legged ones, live with the people who are our two-legged clients. They are supervised by people, cared for by people and trained by people. In fact, all these activities take place with and under the management of the human family and not the dog trainer."

> *In the roles of trainer and/or behavior consultant, the pet professional is both a teacher and a trainer. As such they have a unique role to play when clients seek help and expertise, and irrespective of how competent they are at their craft or how much knowledge they have, if they cannot adequately impart this onto their clients, then they are doing them a disservice (Tudge, 2017b).*

In the roles of trainer and/or behavior consultant, the pet professional is both a teacher and a trainer. As such they have a unique role to play when clients seek help and expertise, and irrespective of how competent they are at their craft or how much knowledge they have, if they cannot adequately impart this onto their clients, then they are doing them a disservice (Tudge, 2017b).

Working alongside the right professional mentor who has experience with both people and animals can be invaluable to an apprentice. In real life, pet trainers are often exposed to the inner workings of a family in their own home and, as a result, the challenges facing them can border on both professional and personal. This is a classic example where the personal influences the professional and the management of these situations requires an ability to operate effectively in times of stress and emotion. Real-life scenarios such as these are often not taught academically and require on-the-job mentoring to support the development of actual experience.

Mentoring Programs

A responsible mentoring program should meet the following criteria:

1. Is affiliated with and/or established under a reputable organization.
2. Has well-defined operating principles.
3. Has a program plan that encourages input from all stakeholders.
4. Includes documented eligibility criteria for program participation.
5. Has written administrative and program procedures.
6. Accounts for regular and consistent contact between mentor and mentee.
7. Employs/utilizes appropriately skilled personnel.
8. Has developed role statements for all staff and volunteer positions.
9. Fully adheres to local, state and federal laws.
10. Allows for program evaluations and continuous ongoing assessment.

To enable apprentices to fully transition into the pet industry as competent trainers and behavior consultants, a solid mentoring program is invaluable. Such a program will assist novice trainers in terms of how they acquire quality information as well as give them a means to seek guidance when they encounter any kind of problem. (See *Appendix C: The Recommended Career Stage Mentoring Model* for a more detailed breakdown.) In addition, when unsure of a training or behavior modification procedure, those new to the field will know there is someone knowledgeable they can turn to for help. Seeking different levels of peer guidance and support forms part of the Best Practice Model found in *Appendix A: The Recommended Best Practice Model for Pet Training and Behavior Consulting Professionals*. Gaining exposure and access to a professional industry mentor in the early stages of one's career is incredibly helpful and can bridge the networking void until such time as the professional's career allows for contact with other, more experienced professionals and supervisors.

Transitioning to workplace competency can be difficult. Dreyfus and Dreyfus (1986) advocate an outline that distinguishes an excellent performer from an average performer, and include these five stages:

(1) Novice.
(2) Advanced Beginner.
(3) Competence.
(4) Proficiency.
(5) Expertise.

To achieve competency and best practice in the pet industry, the authors propose three actual levels of transition. Each level provides for competency assessment across knowledge, skills and instruction with the higher levels providing for competency assessment across more competencies. The levels are set out below:

Level 1: Technician

A Technician is skilled in the manual application of science and artistic endeavor and delivers results through empathy and mutual respect for both client and pet. At this level, the Technician is capable of teaching pet manners classes with the knowledge of their own limitations in resolving behavior problems due to a lack of experience and/or further study. They have the ability to understand when a referral to a more qualified professional is necessary. This individual may operate a business specializing in group training services and/or work with, or for, a more qualified professional.

Level 2: Trainer

A Trainer is skilled in the application of science and artistic endeavor and delivers results through empathy and mutual respect for both client and pet, and also teaches obedience classes, pet manners classes, day training, private training sessions, and board and train programs that focuses primarily on pet dog skills and manners. This level of service to the community would offer similar abilities as the Technician, but with a deeper understanding of the scientific principles involved in training, as well as the ability to better understand and assist with minor behavioral problems and the knowledge of appropriate referral to an animal behavior consultant when necessary.

Level 3: Behavior Consultant

A Behavior Consultant is a professional who undertakes private consultations with pets and their owners and focuses primarily on modifying behavior problems that are elicited by the animal's emotional state in a given context (e.g. fear, anxiety). Behavior Consultants are often professional dog trainers who can competently teach pet manners classes, obedience classes, day training, private training sessions, and board and train programs that focus on pet dog skills and manners. For the purposes of this book, a Behavior Consultant is defined as a behavior and training professional skilled in the application of science and artistic endeavor who delivers results through empathy and mutual respect for both client and pet. The Behavior Consultant is aware of their limitations in terms of ability to prescribe psychotropic or any other kind of medication and diagnose illness, as well as their ethical responsibility in such cases, and can refer to a Veterinarian or Board Certified Veterinary Behaviorist with greater academic and expansive knowledge. It is considered unethical in pet counseling for a professional to engage in any discussion regarding the diagnosis or treatment of an illness, physical or mental. Only Veterinarians or Board Certified Veterinary Behaviorists are authorized to do this through the license and qualifications they hold.

> *Because of the importance of pets in people's lives, the body of scientific knowledge and research is ever growing on how best to ensure and maintain animal welfare. Keeping abreast of the science and industry techniques aids in delivering a professional service to both clients and the community.*

In brief:

- A Technician would refer to a Trainer or Behavior Consultant.
- A Trainer would refer to a Behavior Consultant, a Veterinarian, or Board Certified Veterinary Behaviorist.
- A Behavior Consultant would refer to a Veterinarian or Board Certified Veterinary Behaviorist.

Competency and Continuing Professional Development

As it stands, Continuing Professional Development (CPD) is often mandated by professional organizations or required by codes of ethics and/or conduct for various professions. However, at the core of CPD is a professional's personal responsibility to "...keep their knowledge and skills current so that they can deliver the high quality of service that safeguards the public and meets the expectations of customers and the requirements of their profession." (Kloosterman, 2014).

CPD activities should be designed to extend or update professionals' knowledge, skill and judgment in their area of practice. To take the example of Engineers Australia (2019), any well-designed CPD enables the professional to:

- Maintain technical competence.
- Retain and enhance effectiveness in the workplace.
- Be able to help, influence and lead by example.
- Successfully deal with changes in your career.

- Better serve the community.

CPD is an ongoing process and should continue throughout an individual's career. Correctly undertaken, valued and adhered to, it ensures continued competence in their chosen profession. "The ultimate outcome of well-planned continuing professional development is that it safeguards the public, the employer, the professional and the professional's career." (Kloosterman, 2014).

When relating CPD to pet trainers, it pays to consider the following:

- Without CPD, it is not possible to keep abreast of current professional standards. CPD enables a professional to maintain relevant and up-to-date knowledge and makes it easier to be aware of changing science and techniques within the profession.
    - Because of the importance of pets in people's lives, the body of scientific knowledge and research is ever growing on how best to ensure and maintain animal welfare. Keeping abreast of the science and industry techniques aids in delivering a professional service to both clients and the community.
- Experience is a great teacher but relying solely on experience can lead to repetition of the same service delivery. Well-planned and well-delivered CPD "opens you up to new possibilities, new knowledge and new skill areas." (Kloosterman, 2014).
    - Outdated skills do not lead to best practice delivery of a service.
    - A pet training professional needs to have many tools in their toolkit. One who relies only on experience does not have the advantage of multiple ways to overcome training problem situations when they occur.
- CPD can deliver "a deeper understanding of what it means to be a professional, along with a greater appreciation of the implications and impacts of your work." (Kloosterman, 2014).
- Kloosterman (2014) states that, in some high risk or specialized professions (and animal training can certainly be placed in these categories), "CPD contributes to improved protection and quality of life…" When you consider the safety and improvement of life quality for both pets and their owners when a perceived problem is resolved by a training professional, then this statement is decidedly relevant.

States Kloosterman (2014): "The importance of continuing professional development should not be underestimated – it is a career-long obligation for practicing professionals." CPD, then, should be the foundation of professional practice. It enables the professional to maintain and develop skills and ensures that their knowledge remains relevant and up to date. It also provides a form of quality assurance for members of the public seeking qualified trainers. It should thus be incumbent upon any animal training governing body to have CPD as an integral part of their professional conditions. Further, application of conditions or a refusal to renew registration for those who do not maintain their CPD should be applied, as is, indeed, already the case with a number of professional bodies.

Determining Continuing Professional Development through Continuing Education Units

There are many professions and professional organizations that require their members to earn a specific number of Continuing Education Units (CEU) each year in order to maintain registration. The exact number of required CEUs may vary between industries and states. CEUs help to ensure that members are up-to-date with current practices in their field and proof of CPD through CEUs most often comes by way certificates administered by an educating body. Submission of receipts for payment is not considered to be adequate proof. Copies, and in some cases certified copies, of attendance certificates are required.

Educating bodies or member-centric bodies who provide education to their members must often apply for CEUs from other organizations in their field. For example, a pet dog trainer may be a member of the Association of Pet Dog Trainers (APDT) and the Pet Professional Guild (PPG) and each of these organizations may weigh the same educational event differently, resulting in a different number of credits they each offer. Some educating facilities have an ongoing agreement with other bodies, meaning there is a predetermined number of CEUs assigned for any event held by that educating body. This may be something as simple as 1 hour = 1 CEU.

CEUs can be gained by attending seminars, workshops and conferences. In addition, some governing bodies accept the following for CEUs:

- Contributions to peer reviewed journals.
- Book or DVD reviews (usually with a predetermined word limit).

- Published letters to editors.
- Running workshops.
- Presenting at seminars or conferences.
- A quiz on relevant journal articles.
- Ongoing education by way of formal study.
- Client or peer review of the applicant's work.

Summary

In its Code of Ethics and Conduct, the European Society of Veterinary Clinical Ethology (ESVCE) (2017) states that its members shall "refrain from laying claim, directly or indirectly, to qualifications, competencies or affiliations they do not possess [and] recognize the boundaries of their own competence and do not execute activities they have no education or specialization for. Rather in such cases they will obtain services from others who are appropriately qualified to provide them."

As detailed in *Appendix A: The Recommended Best Practice Model for Pet Training and Behavior Consulting Professionals*, professionals committed to best practice will always take into consideration the following:

- Whether they have the required level of competency to be working with any individual training or behavior case.
- Whether they should only work on the case with support from a peer, or a peer with case-specific knowledge and/or experience.
- Whether they should work on the case under the supervision of a more experienced behavior consultant.
- Whether they should refer the case to a veterinary behaviorist.

While being aware of their current levels of competency, skills and knowledge, committed professionals will also be eager to keep learning and remain up-to-date, and thus will usually have no trouble reaching their required number of CEUs to maintain registration in a membership or educational body. As such, failure to maintain the predetermined number of CEUs should not go without penalty and some organizations refuse re-registration, while others inflict a consequence such as removing the individual from their public referral list.

CEUs may not be the perfect way to ensure updated knowledge, but their international use by many and varied organizations and professions would appear to be the most appropriate way at the current time. (*See Appendix B: The Recommended Model for the Assessment of a Professional's Knowledge and Skill* and *Appendix G: The Recommended Policy for Registration Renewal via Continuing Education* for more on the practical application of CEUs.)

Bibliography

Armstrong, M.A. (2003). A Handbook of Human Resource Management Practice (9th edn.). London, UK: Kogan Page

American Association of Veterinary State Boards. (2018). Look Up a License. Retrieved November 29, 2018, from https://www.aavsb.org/public-resources/look-up-a-license/

Barry, J. (2008). The Ethical Dog Trainer. Wenatchee, WA: DogWise Publishing

Boyatzis, R.E. (1982). The competent manager: a model for effective performance. London, UK: Wiley

Career One Stop. (2018). Competency Model Clearing House. Retrieved January 22, 2019, from https://www.careeronestop.org/CompetencyModel

Chouhan, V.S., & Srivastava, S. (2014). Understanding Competencies and Competency Modeling — A Literature Survey. *IOSR Journal of Business and Management (16)* 1 Version I 14-22. Retrieved January 22, 2019, from http://iosrjournals.org/iosr-jbm/papers/Vol16-issue1/Version-1/C016111422.pdf

Delamare, F., & Winterton, J. (2005) What is Competence? Retrieved December 30, 2018, from https://www.tandfonline.com/doi/abs/10.1080/1367886042000338227

Dreyfus, H., & Dreyfus, S. (1986/88), Mind over Machine: The power of human intuition and expertise in the era of the computer. New York, NY: Free Press

Engineers Australia. (2019). Continuing Professional Development (CPD). Retrieved December 30, 2018, from www.engineersaustralia.org.au/Training-And-Development/Continuing-Professional-Development

Eraut, M. (1994). Developing professional competence. London, UK: Falmer Press

European Society of Veterinary Clinical Ethology. (2017). Code of Ethics and Conduct. Retrieved May 28, from http://www.esvce.org/wp-content/uploads/2017/10/ESCVE-code-of-conduct-and-ethics.pdf

Federal Bar Association. (2018). FBA Mission and Vision. Retrieved November 29, 2018, from http://www.fedbar.org/About-Us/FBA-Mission.aspx

Federation of State Medical Boards. (2018). Vision, Mission and Strategic Goals. Retrieved November 27, 2018, from http://www.fsmb.org/about-fsmb/

Florida Department of Business and Professional Regulation. (2016). General DBPR information. Retrieved January 22, 2019, from http://myfloridalicense.custhelp.com/app/answers/detail/a_id/2218/~/general-dbpr-information%3A

Gonzi, A., Hager, P., & Athanason, J. (1993). The development of competency-based assessment strategies for the professions. National Office for Overseas Skills Research Paper No. 8. Canberra, Australia: Australian Government Publishing Service

Kloosterman, V. (2014). The importance of continuing professional development. Retrieved December 30, 2018, from https://continuingprofessionaldevelopment.org/why-is-cpd-important/

Le Deist, F.D., & Winterton, J. (2005). What Is Competence? Human Resource Development International (8) 1 27-46. Retrieved January 22, 2019, from https://pdfs.semanticscholar.org/4935/1fda77b8c3ac6e376b3ea9299f926628a4d9.pdf

Miller, G.E. (1990). The Assessment of Clinical Skills/Competence/Performance. *Academic Medicine (65)* 9 S63-S67

Murray, M. (2001). Beyond the Myths and Magic of Mentoring: How to Facilitate an Effective Mentoring Process. San Francisco, CA: Jossey-Bass Inc.

Rankin, N. (2002). Raising performance through people: The ninth competency survey. *Competency and Emotional Intelligence 2-21*

Question Mark. (2018). Job Task Analysis (JTA): Rapid Authoring, Comprehensive Reporting for JTA Surveys. Retrieved January 22, 2019, from https://www.questionmark.com/content/job-task-analysis-jta

Reference. (2019). What Is Professional Competence? Retrieved December 30, 2018, from https://www.reference.com/business-finance/professional-competence-a3f8bc9f9f3d3511?aq=professional+competence&qo=cdpArticles

Smith, E.A. (2001). The role of tacit and explicit knowledge in the workplace. *Journal of Knowledge Management (5)* 4 311-321. Retrieved December 30, 2018, from https://www.emeraldinsight.com/doi/abs/10.1108/13673270110411733

The Training Industry. (2018). Performance Management – Competency Model. Retrieved December 30, 2018, from https://trainingindustry.com/wiki/performance-management/competency-model/

Trinder, J.C. (2008). Competency Standards – A Measure of the Quality of a Workforce. The International Archives of the Photogrammetry, Remote Sensing and Spatial Information Sciences (XXXVII) Pt. B6a. (Beijing). Retrieved November 17, 2018, from www.isprs.org/proceedings/XXXVII/congress/6a_pdf/5_WG-VI-5/01.pdf

Tudge, N.J. (2010). Professional Ethics in Dog Training - A Few Thoughts to Ponder! Retrieved November 20, 2018, from https://www.dognosticscareercenter.com/Blogs/6915713

Tudge, N.J. (2015). People Training Skills for Pet Professionals. (n.p.) Lulu Publishing

Tudge, N.J. (2017a). Get Coaching Now. The How, What and Why of Effective Pet Industry Client Consultations. (n.p.) Ingram Spark Self-Publishing

Tudge, N.J. (2017b). Training Big for Small Businesses. (n.p.) Ingram Spark Self-Publishing

Welfel, E.R. (2009). Ethics in Counseling and Psychotherapy. Mason, OH: Cengage Learning, Inc.

Chapter Eight: Ethics in Pet Training and Behavior Consulting

In any business, the individual is constantly faced with ethical challenges. In the pet industry, these ethical challenges are manifested in the choices professionals must make regarding their approach to training and behavior consulting. What will their philosophical approach be, what methods should they use, what tools are acceptable, how should the business be marketed, how does transparency function within this marketing approach and, ultimately, can the business be effective without infringing on the rights of the clients and their pets? (Barry, 2008).

Defining Ethics, Defining Morals

According to the Business Dictionary (2018), ethics speak to "the basic concepts and fundamental principles of decent human conduct." Merriam-Webster (2018) refers to ethics as "the principles of conduct governing an individual or a group." Merriam-Webster (2018) also makes the distinction between ethics and morals: "'Morals' often describes one's particular values concerning what is right and what is wrong…While 'ethics' can refer broadly to moral principles, one often sees it applied to questions of correct behavior within a relatively narrow area of activity." Barry (2008) highlights the importance of not confusing the two, stating that, while they are often regarded as synonyms and many people use the terms interchangeably, when discussing personal matters of one's own individual conscience, people tend to refer to morals while, when discussing external principles of conduct people tend to refer to ethics.

> In any business, the individual is constantly faced with ethical challenges. In the pet industry, these ethical challenges are manifested in the choices professionals must make regarding their approach to training and behavior consulting.

Theories on Ethics

According to Fieser (n.d.), the field of ethics (or moral philosophy) involves "systematizing, defending, and recommending concepts of right and wrong behavior. Philosophers today usually divide ethical theories into three general subject areas:

1. Metaethics: Investigates where our ethical principles come from, and what they mean.

2. Normative Ethics: Defines moral standards that regulate right and wrong conduct. This may involve the consequences of our behavior on others.
3. Applied Ethics: Involves examining specific controversial issues, such as abortion, infanticide, animal rights, environmental concerns, homosexuality, capital punishment, or nuclear war."

Notably, the "lines of distinction between metaethics, normative ethics, and applied ethics are often blurry." (Fieser, n.d.). Indeed, the field of ethics covers a vast range of theories, concepts and categories that are beyond the scope of this publication. In brief, however, we might say that an individual's ethics affect how they make decisions and lead their life on a daily basis. Grim (2005) states that people tend to "think of ethics as a list of dos and don'ts, much in the style of the Ten Commandments." But, in fact, ethics are far more complicated than a system of moral principles or the difference between right and wrong.

According to Grim (2005), there are "cases in which people do the right things for the wrong reasons. There are cases in which people do the wrong thing despite pure motives." Grim (2005) also notes that, as individuals, we "evaluate things ethically at different levels." Each individual has their own sense of right and wrong and their values will vary depending on cultural background, education, life experience, religious beliefs, and influencers. "We are shaped by how we filter stimuli and how we think and act are an output of our own individual experiences, assumptions and perceptions." (Tudge, 2016).

> *The Golden Rule approach to ethics calls for the concept of reversibility, i.e.: "Do unto others, as you would have others do unto you." This is considered the most basic and useful ethical theory.*

The Golden Rule approach to ethics calls for the concept of reversibility, i.e.: "Do unto others, as you would have others do unto you." This is considered the most basic and useful ethical theory and was quoted by Confucius (500 B.C.): "What you do not want done to yourself, do not do to others," Aristotle (325 B.C.): "We should behave to others as we wish them to behave to us," from the Mahabharata (200 B.C.): "Do nothing to thy neighbor which thou wouldst not have him do to thee thereafter," and Jesus Christ (30 A.D.): "As ye would that men should do to you, do ye also to them likewise." (Josephson, 2002). However, the Golden Rule is often said to fall short, as doing unto others what you would have done unto you does

> *The general public benefits from ethical policies through recognition of a professional individual's autonomy and the right to be treated with respect and fairness.*

not take into consideration the needs of the individual, nor does it help with ethical decision-making when dealing with groups of people.

The so-called Silver Rule offers a variation of this focusing on "restraint and non-harm" (Puka, n.d.): "Do not do unto others as you would not have them do unto you." The Silver Rule has its own deficiencies too, however, as it only requires an individual to not harm others and does not ask that person to engage in positive behavior. (Gonen, 2018).

Ethics in the Pet Industry

It is our view that dog trainers, behavior consultants and professional pet care providers are bound to pursue a philosophical approach that blends both the Golden and Silver Rules in that they have an ethical responsibility, a) to do no harm to the animals in their care, and b) to present their qualifications and experience truthfully with full transparency and disclosure (see *Appendix F: The Recommended Corporation Professional Code of Conduct and Ethics Pledge*).

According to Welfel (2012, p.3), professional ethics is about "being confident one has the correct combination of attributes, skills, and character." But how does this apply in the field of animal training or behavior consulting? To answer, we must first address why professional ethics are significant both to the general public as well as to the professional.

According to Tudge (2010), professional ethics "cover the moral issues that can arise from the specialist knowledge that a professional body has. The industry's ethics govern how this knowledge is used when providing a service." The general public benefits from ethical policies through recognition of a professional individual's autonomy and the right to be treated with respect and fairness. The individual professional, meanwhile, whose profession provides ethical guidelines and policies, benefits from the trust earned by being part of said professional body and an appropriate framework to operate within. Furthermore, a professional's membership of a professional body may inspire confidence from their clients, as well as giving said professional the opportunity to continue to improve their skills and expand on their knowledge. Professional ethics bring credibility to the profession itself as the public assumes that those following a specific set of ethical guidelines or policies will act truthfully and competently (Tudge, 2010).

> *Professional ethics bring credibility to the profession itself as the public assumes that those following a specific set of ethical guidelines or policies will act truthfully and competently (Tudge, 2010).*

As such, business ethics are also important, and not just the ethics of how an actual professional's services are planned and delivered. In the article, *Defining 'Business Ethics': Like Nailing Jello to a Wall*, Lewis (1985, p.377) states that: "Business ethics is a topic receiving much attention in the literature. However, the term 'business ethics' is not adequately defined. Typical definitions refer to the rightness or wrongness of behavior, but not everyone agrees on what is morally right or wrong, good or bad, ethical or unethical. To complicate the problem, nearly all available definitions exist at highly abstract levels." However, according to Weinstein (2017), the ethical principles that allow us to solve problems in our daily lives are the same principles that provide guidance not only in business, but also health care, law and education. These principles are:

- Do No Harm.
- Make Things Better.
- Respect Others.
- Be Fair.
- Care.

In its Code of Ethics and Conduct, the European Society of Veterinary Clinical Ethology (ESVCE) reflects these principles, stating that its members "have a responsibility to their patients, clients and to the general public. Welfare of patient and client (including avoiding danger for third parties) are to be considered primarily. Training techniques and advice should not knowingly or deliberately cause avoidable psychological, physical distress or damage to any of the above...When collaborating with people who are not ESVCE Members, they should check that the assistant/collaborator (e.g. dog trainer) also conform to the code of practice."

ESVCE members are also expected to "[p]romote the interests of animal welfare to colleagues and to society at large and, where necessary, promote public education programs and cultural activities, [c]o-operate with colleagues and other professionals for the sake of animal welfare, and [c]o-operate with governments and other appropriate bodies to improve standards of animal welfare and ensure the welfare of all animals in their care."

In the following two sections, we will attempt to summarize the ethical principles currently in place across the professions of medicine and psychology, both of which are pertinent to professionals working in the pet services industry. Professionals who work in the fields of medicine and psychology impact and promote the mental and behavioral well-being of sentient beings, i.e. humans, while pet training and behavior consultants work alongside humans to enhance the mental and behavioral well-being of pets, also sentient beings (see *Chapter Two: Living Property - The Need for a New Legal Definition / The Issue of Sentience*).

Ethics in Medicine

According to Stanford University (n.d.), there are four basic principles of health care ethics:

1. Autonomy: Patients should have autonomy of thought, intention, and action when making decisions regarding health care procedures. The process of decision-making should be free of coercion or coaxing, and patients must understand all benefits and risks associated with a procedure, in order to make a fully informed decision.
2. Justice: Both the burdens and the benefits of new or experimental treatments should be distributed equally among all groups in society and procedures should uphold the spirit of existing laws, while being fair to all involved.
3. Beneficence: Procedures should be provided with the intent of doing good for the patient involved. This demands that health care providers develop and maintain skills and knowledge, continually update training, consider individual circumstances of all patients, and strive for net benefit.
4. Nonmaleficence: This requires that a procedure does not harm the patient involved or others in society.

Ethical Principles of Psychologists

The American Psychological Association's (APA) (2017) Ethical Principles of Psychologists and Code of Conduct (herewith referred to as the Ethics Code) aims to "provide guidance for psychologists and standards of professional conduct that can be applied by the APA and by other bodies that choose to adopt them."

In its Introduction and Preamble, APA (2017) states that the Ethical Standards listed in its Ethics Code are enforceable "rules of conduct for psychologists," and that the Ethics Code intends to "provide specific standards to cover most situations encountered by psychologists. It has as its goals the welfare and protection of the individuals and groups with whom psychologists work and the education of members, students, and the public regarding ethical standards of the discipline." APA (2017) goes on to note that: "The development of a dynamic set of ethical standards for psychologists' work-related conduct requires a personal commitment and lifelong effort to act ethically; to encourage ethical behavior by students, supervisees, employees, and colleagues; and to consult with others concerning ethical problems."

APA (2017) also sets out its five General Principles. These, unlike the Ethical Standards, which are enforceable, are aspirational in nature and should be "considered by psychologists in arriving at an ethical course of action." The intent of the General Principles "is to guide and inspire psychologists toward the very highest ethical ideals of the profession." (APA, 2017). Much could be taken from APA's Ethics Code and General Principles in terms of application and potential adoption by the pet industry and we will set out some examples in this chapter. Meanwhile, we present here a brief outline of APA's (2017) five General Principles paired with, in our view, their relevance to pet industry professionals (in italics):

1. Principle A: Beneficence and Nonmaleficence - Psychologists strive to benefit those with whom they work and take care to do no harm. *Training and behavior professionals must always have the welfare of the pet as their first and foremost priority, not the tools, method or financial gain from the service engagement.*
2. Principle B: Fidelity and Responsibility - Psychologists establish relationships of trust with those with whom they work. *Pet Professionals must be trustworthy and operate with integrity.*

3. Principle C: Integrity - Psychologists seek to promote accuracy, honesty, and truthfulness in the science, teaching, and practice of psychology. *Pet Professionals must be open and honest with clients regarding any methods, tools and approaches they seek to use and/or recommend.*
4. Principle D: Justice - Psychologists recognize that fairness and justice entitle all persons to access to and benefit from the contributions of psychology and to equal quality in the processes, procedures, and services being conducted by psychologists. *Pet Professionals provide fair market value services to all clients in their service areas.*
5. Principle E: Respect for People's Rights and Dignity - Psychologists respect the dignity and worth of all people, and the rights of individuals to privacy, confidentiality, and self-determination. Psychologists are aware that special safeguards may be necessary to protect the rights and welfare of persons or communities whose vulnerabilities impair autonomous decision-making. *Pet Professionals respect the dignity and confidentiality of all clients.*

> *It is essential...that the pet professional's participation is beneficial to the animal. This is a "foundational principle of professional ethics." (Tudge, 2010).*

Striving to benefit those with whom we work and taking care to do no harm (Principle A) should be applicable to both humans and animals, as should establishing relationships of trust with those with whom we work (Principle B). Potential problems associated with the pet industry often involve the non-disclosure of the methods that will be used to train and/or care for a pet (*see also Chapter Nine: Consumer Protection and Transparency / Misrepresentation*.) Honest, accurate discussion about the training methods to be employed would allow pet owners to make reliable decisions regarding informed consent (Principle C).

In any situation where an animal is the "client" (e.g. a training class, a behavior consultation, a trip to the groomer, or a stay in boarding or day care), he rarely has any say in the situation or option to partake in informed consent. Nor is he in the position of being able to direct or take responsibility for his own welfare in such situations, making him extremely vulnerable. It is essential, then, that the pet professional's participation is beneficial to the animal. This is a "foundational principle of professional ethics." (Tudge, 2010).

Principle D references the equal entitlement for all to access and benefit from the same quality of service, stating that: "Psychologists exercise reasonable judgment and take precautions to ensure that their potential biases, the boundaries of their competence, and the limitations of their expertise do not lead to or condone unjust practices." (APA, 2017). Should pets and their owners not also have the right to expect a certain established quality of training not limited by the boundaries of a professional's knowledge and skills, especially when incompetency can lead to unjust and inhumane practices?

Principle E is especially pertinent in terms of protecting "the rights and welfare of persons or communities whose vulnerabilities impair autonomous decision-making." (APA, 2017). It should go without saying that those involved in the care and training of pets treat both owners and their pets with respect and dignity. Pets by their very nature should have their welfare protected, for who is less able to speak for themselves than they? "As pet owners and pet professionals, we are the voice both for our own animals and for those we see in practice. We are the ones that can stand up for them, speak on their behalf, look out for their welfare, and make sure they are treated with kindness and compassion." (Gregory, 2019a).

> *"As pet owners and pet professionals, we are the voice both for our own animals and for those we see in practice. We are the ones that can stand up for them, speak on their behalf, look out for their welfare, and make sure they are treated with kindness and compassion." – Gregory (2019a)*

Breed Bias

The second part of Principle E also states that: "Psychologists are aware of and respect cultural, individual, and role differences, including those based on age, gender, gender identity, race, ethnicity, culture, national origin, religion, sexual orientation, disability, language, and socioeconomic status, and consider these factors when working with members of such groups. Psychologists try to eliminate the effect on their work of biases based on those factors, and they do not knowingly participate in or condone activities of others based upon such prejudices." (APA, 2017).

In the pet industry, prejudice can also be an issue, specifically in the form of Breed Specific Legislation (BSL) (also known as Breed Discriminatory Legislation), a law or legal ordinance that restricts or prohibits the ownership of certain breeds (or types) of dogs. In places where BSL has been implemented it varies from a complete ban of certain types of dogs to regulations imposing restrictions on ownership and special requirements (Pet Professional Guild, 2018).

Under BSL, regulated breeds usually comprise "pit bull" type dogs. However, the breeds targeted vary in different countries and even in different states or counties within the same country. American pit bull terriers, American Staffordshire terriers, American bulldogs, Staffordshire bull terriers and English bull terriers are often included in the "pit bull group," wherein the term "pit bull" is used generically for a number of closely related breeds such as these. In some cases, dogs who are thought to resemble a pit bull are inaccurately labeled, based purely on their appearance. Importantly, a study by Olson et al. (2015), designed to measure agreement among shelter staff in assigning pit bull-type breed designations to shelter dogs and to compare breed assignments with DNA breed signatures, found that visual identification is unreliable.

> While any size or type of dog can bite, breed is not a good predictor. A study by Patronek, Sacks, Delise, Cleary and Marder (2013) concluded that: "Most DBRFs [dog bite-related fatalities] were characterized by coincident, preventable factors; breed was not one of these."

Other breeds that often find themselves the target of BSL include Rottweilers, mastiffs, chow chows, German shepherds and Doberman pinschers. In Europe, the filo Brasileiro, dogo Argentino, presa Canaria and Japanese tosa are included on many of the lists of dogs affected by breed discriminatory laws. The laws usually target any dog that resembles the listed breed so are 'type' specific rather than truly 'breed' specific. (Pet Professional Guild, 2018).

While any size or type of dog can bite, breed is not a good predictor. A study by Patronek, Sacks, Delise, Cleary and Marder (2013) concluded that: "Most DBRFs [dog bite-related fatalities] were characterized by coincident, preventable factors; breed was not one of these. Study results supported previous recommendations for multifactorial approaches, instead of single-factor solutions such as breed-specific legislation, for dog bite prevention." According to Stapleton-Frappell (2016), BSL causes "untold suffering to countless dogs and their families around the world – dogs whose only 'crime' is that they are of a certain breed or type. These dogs are both judged and condemned – often to incarceration and ultimately death –

because of their appearance; with no regard being taken of their positive behavioral history, character traits, socialization, training or home environment." (qtd. in *BARKS from the Guild*).

It may also be the case that some pet dog trainers, either purposely or without due consideration, apply different ethical standards when deciding on the appropriate method of training for an individual dog; and that, based on preconceived, biased beliefs regarding the dog's size and breed, turn to aversive training methods thus potentially causing the animal physical or psychological harm.

Ethical Standards

The specific Ethical Standards, as set out by APA (2017), are broad in order to apply to psychologists in varied roles. Section 2 of APA's Ethical Standards speaks to competence, with Subsection 2.01 Boundaries of Competence stating that services should only be provided "within the boundaries of [a psychologist's] competence, based on their education, training, supervised experience, consultation, study, or professional experience." (2.01 (a)) and should "undertake relevant education, training, supervised experience, consultation, or study." (2.01 (c)). If asked to provide services for which they do not possess the relevant skills, knowledge of level of competency, psychologists should only provide that service if they "make a reasonable effort to obtain the competence required by using relevant research, training, consultation, or study" (2.01 (d)) and that they should always take steps to ensure they protect their clients, students and others from harm (2.01 (e)).

Section 3 of APA's (2017) Ethical Standards specifically speaks to human relations, referencing the importance of taking reasonable steps to avoid harming clients and students. It states that psychologists should never "participate in, facilitate, assist, or otherwise engage in torture, defined as any act by which severe pain or suffering, whether physical or mental, is intentionally inflicted on a person, or in any other cruel, inhuman, or degrading behavior." (3.04 (b) Avoiding Harm). It is our view that pets be given these same priorities and that they, too, should never be subjected to inhumane training tools, practices or methods that risk causing physical and/or psychological pain or suffering. (*See also* Chapter Three: Professionals Should Exemplify and Promote Anti-Cruelty Statutes / Abusive Training Practices *and* Chapter Four: How Pets Learn and the Consequences of Methodology, Equipment and Philosophical Choice / Corporal Punishment.)

Subsection 3.10 of APA's (2017) Ethical Standards speaks to the importance of obtaining informed consent using language that is "understandable" (3.10 (a)) and that, for persons who are "legally incapable of giving informed consent" (*think dogs*), psychologists (*think trainers*) should consider the person's (*think dog and/or owner*) "preferences and best interests" and "take reasonable steps to protect the individual's rights and welfare." (3.10 (b)).

The Place and Critical Need for Ethical Guidelines and Oversight

Animals have the ability "to feel, perceive or be conscious, or to have subjective experiences." (American Animal Hospital Association, 2019). In other words, they are sentient beings with the capacity to experience both positive and negative feelings, which "requires a level of awareness and cognitive ability." (Broom, 2019). "Biological science, as well as common sense, supports the fact that the animals that share our lives are feeling, sensing beings that deserve thoughtful, high-quality care. The care that is offered should provide for the animal's physical and behavioral welfare and strive to minimize pain, distress, and suffering for the animal." (American Animal Hospital Association, 2019). (*See also* Chapter Two: Living Property - The Need for a New Legal Definition / The Issue of Sentience.)

In a training scenario, as a professional becomes confident in a session with a particular animal, they may move too quickly to more complex things, while if they are struggling to master a technique, may elect to remain at a more basic level of teaching (Gregory, 2019b). How does this, however, fit in with the rate at which the animal learns? "Does he improve at the same rate as the person? Possibly, but it is more likely that one or the other will progress more quickly or slowly. How much attention do we actually pay to the animal other than being aware of his response and adjusting for it? If you think about it, we may still be focusing on ourselves and what we are trying to achieve, so if we want a particular behavior and it is not happening, we adjust to try to achieve that goal. Do we stop to think about how the animal is feeling, rather than what he is doing?" (Gregory, 2019b).

> Animals have the ability "to feel, perceive or be conscious, or to have subjective experiences." (American Animal Hospital Association, 2019).

Section 5 of APA's (2017) Ethical Standards speaks to advertising and states that: "Psychologists do not make false, deceptive, or fraudulent statements concerning their training, experience, or competence; their academic degrees; their credentials; their institutional or association affiliations; their services; the scientific or clinical basis for, or results or degree of success of, their services; their fees; their publications or research findings." (5.01 (b)). This is also applicable to the workings of the pet industry in terms of professional transparency and honesty about credentials and education, as well as the

> *Welfel (2012, p.3) presents that ethics encompass five dimensions, and that, when these are all brought together, they represent the "positive ethical ideas and values of behavior counseling professions."*

obligation not to falsely advertise or mislead clients regarding how their pet will be cared for, trained or managed by the professional.

Ethics Across Professional Associations in an Unregulated Profession

Welfel (2012, p.3) presents that ethics encompass five dimensions, and that, when these are all brought together, they represent the "positive ethical ideas and values of behavior counseling professions."

The five dimensions (summarized here by the authors) include:

- Having sufficient knowledge and skills to use effective interventions.
- Respecting the dignity and freedom of clients.
- Using the power of their professional title to act responsibly.
- Behaving in a way that promotes public confidence in the profession.
- Committing to placing the welfare of the client as the highest priority.

As previously stated, pet industry services – which include dog training – are currently unregulated (see *Chapter Three: Professionals Should Exemplify and Promote Anti-Cruelty Statutes / Normative Behavior toward Pets*.) As such, anyone at all can work as a dog trainer, register a business name, put up an attractive website, and set about advertising and marketing their services to potential clients (see also *Chapter Nine: Consumer Protection and Transparency / Misrepresentation*.) Nevertheless, holding membership of a professional body may provide credibility to the trainer, behavior consultant or pet care services provider and imbue a sense of confidence in the general public – not only as to the individual's professional ethics, but also to the credentials of any individual who is a member of that body.

There are many professional organizations worldwide that offer membership and credentials for dog trainers. Few, however, hold their members to a strict code of conduct "which involves the application of their trade through scientific protocols and the objective to cause no harm." (Tudge & Nilson, 2017). Yet how many members of the pet owning public look beyond the membership and examine what those guidelines are, or are even aware of disparities in tools, techniques and philosophies?

Dog trainers, behavior consultants and all those working in the field of pet care services have a duty to do only what is ethical, thereby following APA's (2017) Standard of Ethics 3.04 (b) Avoiding Harm, and should never engage in any act by which pain or suffering, whether physical or psychological, is intentionally inflicted, i.e., as per APA's (2017) General Principle A, they should "take care to do no harm." Trainers interact on a daily basis with their human and canine clients and yet the ethical standards required by the differing professional membership organizations vary substantially. They range from those such as the Pet Professional Guild (PPG) (2012), which, as already stated in *Chapter Five: A Call for an Industry Wide, Professionally Acknowledged Best Practice*, requires its members to sign off on Guiding Principles that clearly depict which training tools may not be used in any circumstances (including shock collars, prong collars, choke chains, startle devices, and any other tool or method that causes pain or fear; PPG states this to be non-negotiable) to organizations who do not prohibit the use of such aversives and support their members' right to use training methods and management protocols based on outdated dominance theory and practices that can result in both mental and physical harm. (See also *Chapter Four: How Pets Learn and the Consequences of Methodology, Equipment and Philosophical Choice / Outdated Approach*.)

> *Holding membership of a professional body may provide credibility to the trainer, behavior consultant or pet care services provider and imbue a sense of confidence in the general public – not only as to the individual's professional ethics, but also to the credentials of any individual who is a member of that body.*

According to Tudge and Nilson (2017), "...professional dog trainers and canine behavior consultants currently have no legal responsibility whatsoever to disclose any information to their clients or the general public regarding the methods they use. At present, the only obligation is an ethical one, which, sadly, not all trainers elect to acknowledge. This can be and, indeed, is very misleading to unsuspecting pet owners who have no knowledge of the pet industry's lack of standards and regulation, or the differences between training methods and equipment. In many cases, pet owners only find out about these differences – and the fallout associated with them – when they find themselves encountering behavior problems caused by the use of outdated aversive techniques and equipment."

> According to Tudge and Nilson (2017), "...professional dog trainers and canine behavior consultants currently have no legal responsibility whatsoever to disclose any information to their clients or the general public regarding the methods they use. At present, the only obligation is an ethical one, which, sadly, not all trainers elect to acknowledge."

The decision as to which membership organization to join should be an important choice for pet professionals for many reasons, but perhaps the most obvious is whether the trainer aligns themselves with the ethical principles of said organization. Do they share the same values? Can they work within the guiding principles of said organization? Only once this is established should other factors such as membership benefits and yearly fees be considered.

As we have outlined in *Chapter Five: A Call for an Industry Wide, Professionally Acknowledged Best Practice / The Humane Hierarchy*, professional animal training and behavior associations often recommend an adherence by their members to a specified humane hierarchy. As we have already explained, under such protocols, the standard is to begin a training and behavior change program using the least invasive and least aversive methods available, then work up to more aversive levels – *as the individual professional deems necessary.*

However, any recommendation to adhere to a humane hierarchy does not take into account the incompetent or the unethical trainer. The professional who lacks either the skills, the knowledge or the desire to correctly implement the least intrusive, yet often most effective training methods, will quickly climb the hierarchy, making use of training and behavior change protocols that will undoubtedly result in fear, anxiety, stress and potential physical harm for the animal. (see *Chapter Four: How Pets Learn and the Consequences of Methodology, Equipment and Philosophical Choice / Where It Begins* and *Chapter Five: A Call for an Industry Wide, Professionally Acknowledged Best Practice / Key Learning Theory*). Simply because something is included as a guideline or an ethical code does not mean that it will either be implemented correctly, nor, indeed, that it will be implemented at all. These very hierarchies argue for why a new Best Practice model is needed to guide, and if necessary, constrain pet professionals. Our proposed model is set out in *Appendix A: The Recommended Best Practice Model for Pet Training and Behavior Consulting Professionals*. When an individual has veiled "permission" to use aversives, either in a legal sense or by a professional body, or even by their own personal standards, it risks leading down a slippery slope whereby those who are struggling to motivate their students may quickly scale the ladder from the use of positive reinforcement to that of aversives.

> Simply because something is included as a guideline or an ethical code does not mean that it will either be implemented correctly, or, indeed, that it will be implemented at all.

Ethics and the Detrimental Effect of Aversives

In the field of animal training and behavior, based on the body of scientific research and study available today, we now know much more about the fallout of aversive techniques and punishment, and we know that pet dogs trained with the use of positive punishment are no more obedient and exhibit increased numbers of potentially problematic behaviors than dogs trained by other means (Hiby, Rooney & Bradshaw, 2004).

There are many more studies of dogs that show the detrimental effects of aversives including, but not limited to:

- Effects of inescapable shock upon subsequent escape and avoidance responding (Overmier & Seligman, 1967).

- Training dogs with help of the shock collar: short- and long-term behavioral effects (Schilder & van der Borg, 2004).
- The relationship between training methods and the occurrence of behavior problems, as reported by owners, in a population of domestic dogs (Blackwell, Twells, Seawright & Casey, 2008).
- Survey of the use and outcome of confrontational and non-confrontational training methods in client-owned dogs showing undesired behaviors (Herron, Shofer & Reisner, 2009).
- Training methods and owner–dog interactions: Links with dog behaviour and learning ability (Rooney & Cowan, 2011).
- The effects of using aversive training methods in dogs—A review (Ziv, 2017).

(*See also* Chapter Four: How Pets Learn and the Consequences of Methodology, Equipment and Philosophical Choice / The Fallout and Chapter Six: Canine Communication and Social Behavior / Canine Warnings *for more on the effects of and fallout from the use of aversives in training*).

Given the research, we are compelled to ask, how can we morally stand by and condone the use of training procedures based on force, fear, pain, threat or intimidation in the name of teaching or training? And how can a professional member association include the use of aversive tools and methods in their codes of ethics and ethical standards?

> *All professionals have an ethical obligation to be competent in their chosen field, meaning they are knowledgeable, schooled in current theory and research pertaining to their industry, and have the necessary skills and education to actually apply that field of knowledge to a working situation with their clients (Tudge, 2010).*

All professionals have an ethical obligation to be competent in their chosen field, meaning they are knowledgeable, schooled in current theory and research pertaining to their industry, and have the necessary skills and education to actually apply that field of knowledge to a working situation with their clients (Tudge, 2010). This is of critical importance. In the case of pet training and behavior consulting, a lack of competency can lead to a professional's inability to effectively and successfully carry out a functional assessment and, thus, to implement an effective behavioral change program based on positive reinforcement, classical and operant conditioning, and management strategies.

The functional assessment is the behavior analytical approach to explaining, describing and controlling behavior. It does not rely on guesswork, trial and error tactics, or anecdotal recommendations, but systematically identifies the functional relationship a behavior has with the environment. When these relationships have been identified, then efficient and effective solutions can be developed. The intended final product of the functional assessment is a contingency statement that the behavior consultant has confidence in. The contingency statement details the antecedents, behaviors and consequences in simple and measurable terms (DogNostics Career Center, 2018). It is also known as the three-term, or ABC contingency (see also Chapter Five: A Call for an Industry Wide, Professionally Acknowledged Best Practice / Key Learning Theory for more on learning; Appendix A: The Recommended Best Practice Model for Pet Training and Behavior Consulting Professionals and Appendix B: The Recommended Model for a Professional's Level of Knowledge and Skill for more discussion on functional assessments).

> *The pet owning public deserves to know whether a service provider will use up-to-date training methods that seek to do no harm, methods that rely on scientifically supported protocols and are based on positive reinforcement, or if the trainer they hire plans to use methods that include pain, fear and potential fallout.*

Ethics within the Framework of Competency

We have already discussed competency in some detail in Chapter Seven: Competency Is Mission Critical and will now examine it in terms of ethics specific to the pet industry. While it is unlikely that a professional can be competent across all of their industry interventions, the important ethical factor is that said professionals recognize any deficit of knowledge and skills and only work within their area of competency.

In the pet industry, professionals should hold themselves accountable and only consult within the range of their competency and, if necessary, refer clients to another professional who can better serve the needs of the client and the case in question. (Tudge, 2016). Professionals should also be diligent and focus their attention on the needs of the client (Welfel, 2009, p.84). As we have already stated, in pet training and behavior, both the animal and the owner are clients. The priority must always be to use successful applied behavior interventions based on the science of positive reinforcement, applied by competent professionals who have an extensive code of ethics (Tudge, 2010).

According to Meine and Dunn (2013), "[e]thical competency is a matter of great importance in the public sector. The search for and promotion of ethical competence has most recently focused on professional organizations and their constituencies." In the meantime, how can pet owners make informed decisions? As we have already outlined in *Chapter Three: Professionals Should Exemplify and Promote Anti-Cruelty Statutes / Truth in Training* and elsewhere, dog trainers are already using multiple terms to advertise and describe their approach to training, including "results based," "positive," "force-free," "balanced," "fear-free," "evidence based," and "compulsion." This assortment of labels reflects both a lack of transparency and much confusion for potential clients. The pet owning public deserves to know whether a service provider will use up-to-date training methods that seek to do no harm, methods that rely on scientifically supported protocols and are based on positive reinforcement, or if the trainer they hire plans to use methods that include pain, fear and potential fallout. As things currently stand, clients will have a difficult time choosing service providers as "so many fear-based training and behavior change methods can be very subtle, or even invisible, in the slick, magical way they are marketed to unsuspecting pet owners." (Pet Professional Guild, 2016). (*See also Chapter Nine: Consumer Protection and Transparency / Misrepresentation*.)

> *Informed consent ensures that all relevant information pertaining to the services the professional will provide and the tools and methods utilized, are understood and agreed to by all parties.*

Informed Consent

Informed consent is a behavioral science concept referring to a professional's acknowledgement that a client has the right and responsibility to ensure they can advance their own welfare, emotional and physical well-being. In the case of animal behavior consulting, a pet owner is required to fulfil this obligation by advocating for their pet. This means that owners – and thus their pets – have freedom of choice in terms of the type of behavioral and training services they venture into, and that they do this voluntarily once they have sufficient information at hand to make informed decisions. Obviously, our pets cannot read and write, so the expectation should always be that both the owner and the professional will do no harm.

> *Irrespective of whether an individual, a membership organization, a professional body, public legislation, or any other source recommends or enforces an ethical code, all individuals have their own moral standards. For pet professionals, the goal should always be to train and care for pets in the most humane and least intrusive manner possible, and to never cause any physical or emotional harm.*

Conversely, the goal must always be to do good, a significant part of which involves not using any method or equipment that may cause physical or psychological harm. As such, informed consent is ethical and in the best interests of both the pet and his owner(s) (Tudge & Nilson, 2017).

Informed consent ensures that all relevant information pertaining to the services the professional will provide and the tools and methods utilized, are understood and agreed to by all parties. A key component of the agreement must be a clear outline of any potential risk from the application and use of the tools, methods and philosophies employed by the professional. This will ensure clients have an appropriate understanding of the circumstances and the expected results that will materialize from the client-service provider relationship, and any pursuing transactions. According to Welfel (2009, p.157), "clients have ethical and legal rights to this information." Indeed, given the full responsibility pet ownership carries both in the home and in public, pet training and behavior professionals should be obligated to fully disclose all aspects of the professional-client relationship in terms of confidentiality, each party's role, methodologies, equipment, systems and individual service provider philosophy (Tudge, 2010).

Summary

It is essential that industry professionals and public service officials are cognizant of a pet's vulnerability and his obvious inability to offer informed consent, as well as the ethical and legal responsibilities pet owners have to their families and local communities, and the umbrella responsibility local governments have in terms of providing for safe public environments. This disclosure process should include statements that address potential conflicts of interest concerned with the animal's welfare and the local and state animal control ordinances and laws. (Tudge & Nilson, 2017).

Irrespective of whether an individual, a membership organization, a professional body, public legislation, or any other source recommends or enforces an ethical code, all individuals have their own moral standards. For pet professionals, the goal should always be to train and care for pets in the most humane and least intrusive manner possible, and to never cause any physical or emotional harm.

Regardless of any ethical guidelines set out by a membership organization or public legislation, it is our opinion that the use of aversives in training or behavior change protocols are not the right choice, either morally or ethically. Nor does their use reflect the current scientific findings.

For individual professionals to act ethically within their own service scope, they must be able to make good moral and ethical choices. They need to be capable of developing a moral vision and hold a set of beliefs, values and ethical principles that apply to their marketing message, their methodology and approach as to how their services are executed, as well as possess the integrity to be honest and transparent with their clients —both two- and four-legged. Essentially, pet professionals must operate within a collection of systems that protects the animals in their care from any intentional – or unintentional – harm through a lack of knowledge and skills. The pet industry also needs an agreed and collective set of principles and ethics to which professionals across all related services are held accountable. (*See also Appendix F: The Recommended Corporation Professional Code of Conduct and Ethics Pledge*).

Bibliography

American Animal Hospital Association. (2019). Sentient beings. Retrieved February 12, 2019, from https://www.aaha.org/professional/resources/sentient_beings.aspx#gsc.tab=0

American Psychological Association. (2017). Ethical Principles of Psychologists and Code of Conduct. Retrieved February 12, 2019, from https://www.apa.org/ethics/code/index

BARKS from the Guild. (2016). Experts United: Breed Specific Legislation Does Not Work. In *BARKS Blog*. Retrieved February 12, 2019, from https://barksfromtheguild.com/2016/09/14/experts-united-breed-specific-legislation-does-not-work/

Barry, J. (2008). The Ethical Dog Trainer: A Practical Guide for Canine Professionals. Wenatchee, WA: Dogwise

Blackwell, E.J., Twells, C., Seawright, A., & Casey, R.A. (2008). The relationship between training methods and the occurrence of behavior problems, as reported by owners, in a population of domestic dogs. *Journal of Veterinary Behavior (3)* 5 207-217. Retrieved January 6, 2019, from https://www.sciencedirect.com/science/article/pii/S1558787807002766

Broom, D.M. (2019). Sentience. In J. C. Choe (Ed.), Encyclopedia of Animal Behavior (2nd edn.) (p.131-133). Amsterdam, Netherlands: Academic Press

DogNostics Career Center. (2018). A Practical Lexicon for Pet Trainers & Behavior Consultants! The Language You Need to Know. (n.p.): Authors

Ethics [Def]. (2019). In Business Dictionary. Retrieved February 12, 2019, from http://www.businessdictionary.com/definition/ethics.html

Ethics [Def]. (2019). In Merriam-Webster. Retrieved February 12, 2019, from https://www.merriam-webster.com/dictionary/ethics

European Society of Veterinary Clinical Ethology. (2017). Code of Ethics and Conduct. Retrieved May 28, from http://www.esvce.org/wp-content/uploads/2017/10/ESCVE-code-of-conduct-and-ethics.pdf

Fieser, J. (n.d.) Ethics. Internet Encyclopedia of Philosophy. Retrieved February 12, 2019, from https://www.iep.utm.edu/ethics/

Gonen, J. (2018). The Golden Rule vs. The Silver Rule. Retrieved February 12, 2019, from https://medium.com/@jordangonen/the-golden-rule-vs-the-silver-rule-2b3aa70291f1

Gregory, K. (2019a, January). Standing Up for Animals. *BARKS from the Guild (34)* 52-54. Retrieved February 12, 2019, from https://issuu.com/petprofessionalguild/docs/bftg_january_2019_online_edition_op/52

Gregory, K. (2019b, March). Finding Your Animal's Voice. *BARKS from the Guild (35)* 58-60. Retrieved February 12, 2019, from https://issuu.com/petprofessionalguild/docs/bftg_mar_2019_online_edition_opt_1/58

Grim, P.P. (2005). Questions of Value Course Guidebook (p.85). Chantilly, VA: The Teaching Company

Herron, M.E., Shofer, F.S., & Reisner, I.R. (2009). Survey of the use and outcome of confrontational and non-confrontational training methods in client-owned dogs showing undesired behaviors. *Applied Animal Behavior Science (117)* 47-54. Retrieved January 6, 2019, from https://vet.osu.edu/assets/pdf/hospital/behavior/trainingArticle.pdf

Hiby, E., Rooney, N.J., & Bradshaw, J.W.S. (2004). Dog training methods: Their use, effectiveness and interaction with behaviour and welfare. *Animal Welfare (13)* 63-69. Retrieved February 12, 2019, from https://www.academia.edu/36255485/Dog_training_methods_their_use_effectiveness_and_interaction_with_behaviour_and_welfare

Josephson, M. (2002). Making Ethical Decisions. Los Angeles, CA: Josephson Institute of Ethics

Lewis, P.V. (1985). Defining 'business ethics': Like nailing Jello to a wall. *Journal of Business Ethics (4)* 5 377–383. Retrieved February 12, 2019, from
https://link.springer.com/article/10.1007%2FBF02388590

Masson, S., La Vega, S., Gazzano, A., Mariti, C., Da Graça Pereira, G., Halsberghe, C.,...Schoening, B. (2018). Electronic training devices: Discussion on the pros and cons of their use in dogs as a basis for the position statement of the European Society of Veterinary Clinical Ethology. *Journal of Veterinary Behavior 25* 71-75. Retrieved May 28, from
https://www.sciencedirect.com/science/article/pii/S1558787818300108?fbclid=IwAR0rsVM-689ZbE2CFDUuMAmatkmEKiIk9id15xbJrTiLac9Nj5UGtPZW9ho

Meine, M.F., & Dunn, T.P. (2013). The Search for Ethical Competency: Do Ethics Codes Matter? *Public Integrity (15)* 2 149-166. Retrieved February 12, 2019, from
https://www.tandfonline.com/doi/abs/10.2753/PIN1099-9922150203

Olson, K.R., Levy, J.K., Norby, B., Crandalla, M.M., Broadhurst, J.E., Jacks, S.,...Zimmerman, M.S. (2015, November). Inconsistent identification of pit bull-type dogs by shelter staff. *The Veterinary Journal (206) 2* 197–202. Retrieved February 12, 2019, from
https://www.sciencedirect.com/science/article/pii/S109002331500310X

Overmier, J. B., & Seligman, M. E. (1967). Effects of inescapable shock upon subsequent escape and avoidance responding. *Journal of Comparative and Physiological Psychology, 63*(1), 28-33. Retrieved February 12, 2019, from
https://www.researchgate.net/publication/17155992_Overmier_JB_Seligman_ME_Effects_of_inescapable_shock_upon_subsequent_escape_and_avoidance_responding_J_Comp_Physiol_Psychol_63_28-33

Patronek, G., Sacks, J., Delise, K., Cleary, D., & Marder, A. (2013, December). Co-occurrence of potentially preventable factors in 256 dog bite–related fatalities in the United States (2000–2009). *Journal of the American Veterinary Medical Association (243)* 121726-1736. Retrieved February 12, 2019, from http://avmajournals.avma.org/doi/abs/10.2460/javma.243.12.1726

Pet Professional Guild. (2012). Guiding Principles. Retrieved February 12, 2019, from
https://petprofessionalguild.com/PPGs-Guiding-Principles

Pet Professional Guild. (2016). Open Letter to Veterinarians on Referrals to Training and Behavior Professionals. Retrieved February 12, 2019, from https://www.petprofessionalguild.com/Open-letter-to-veterinarians-on-referrals-to-training-and-behavior-professionals

Pet Professional Guild. (2017). Pet Professional Guild publishes open letter to pet industry associations on the use of shock. Retrieved February 12, 2019, from https://barksfromtheguild.com/2017/03/06/pet-professional-guild-publishes-open-letter-to-pet-industry-associations-on-the-use-of-shock/

Pet Professional Guild. (2018). Position Statement on Breed Specific Legislation. Retrieved February 12, 2019, from https://petprofessionalguild.com/Breed-Specific-Legislation

Puka, B. (n.d.). The Golden Rule. Internet Encyclopedia of Philosophy. Retrieved February 12, 2019, from https://www.iep.utm.edu/goldrule/

Rooney, N.J., & Cowan, S. (2011). Training methods and owner-dog interactions: links with dog behaviour and learning ability. *Applied Animal Behavior Science 132* 169-177. Retrieved January 6, 2019, from https://www.appliedanimalbehaviour.com/article/S0168-1591(11)00087-6/abstract

Schilder, M., & van der Borg, J. (2004). Training dogs with help of the shock collar: short and long term behavioural effects. *Applied Animal Behaviour Science (85)* 319–334.
http://eldri.ust.is/media/ljosmyndir/dyralif/Trainingdogswithshockcollar.pdf

Stanford University. (n.d.). Medical Ethics 101: What are the Basic Principles of Medical Ethics? Retrieved February 12, 2019, from
https://web.stanford.edu/class/siw198q/websites/reprotech/New%20Ways%20of%20Making%20Babies/EthicVoc.htm

Tudge, N.J. (2010). Professional Ethics in Dog Training - A Few Thoughts to Ponder! Retrieved November 20, 2018, from https://www.dognosticscareercenter.com/Blogs/6915713

Tudge, N.J. (2016, March). Creating Share Meaning. *BARKS from the Guild (17)* 59-61. Retrieved February 12, 2019, from
https://issuu.com/petprofessionalguild/docs/barks_from_the_guild_march_2016/59

Tudge, N.J., & Nilson, S.J. (2017). An Open Letter to County Commissioners re: Consumer Transparency – the Methods Used in Animal Training, Care and Management Will Protect Pets, Their Owners, Local Residents and the Public at Large. Retrieved February 12, 2019, from
https://barksfromtheguild.com/2017/11/13/an-open-letter-to-county-commissioners-re-consumer-transparency-the-methods-used-in-animal-training-care-and-management-will-protect-pets-their-owners-local-residents-and-the-public-at-large/

Weinstein, B. (2017, October 31). What's The Difference Between Ethics And Business Ethics? *Forbes*. Retrieved February 12, 2019, from
https://www.forbes.com/sites/bruceweinstein/2017/10/31/whats-the-difference-between-ethics-and-business-ethics/

Welfel, E.R. (2009). Ethics in Counseling and Psychotherapy (4th edn.). Pacific Grove, CA: Brooks Cole

Welfel, E.R. (2012). Ethics in Counseling & Psychotherapy (5th edn.). Mason, OH: Cengage Learning

Ziv, G. (2017). The Effects of Using Aversive Training Methods in Dogs – A Review. *Journal of Veterinary Behavior: Clinical Applications and Research (19)* 50-60. Retrieved January 4, 2019, from http://www.journalvetbehavior.com/article/S1558-7878(17)30035-7/fulltext

Chapter Nine: Consumer Protection and Transparency

As the pet services industry is currently unregulated (*see also* *Chapter Three: Professionals Should Exemplify and Promote Anti-Cruelty Statutes / Normative Behavior toward Pets* and *Chapter Eight: Ethics in Pet Training and Behavior Consulting / Ethics Across Professional Associations in an Unregulated Profession*) in the United States and many other parts of the world, any one individual can set themselves up to work as a dog trainer – regardless of qualifications, knowledge, skills, or experience.

States Foubert (2016): "Scientific research in animal behavior and canine ethology indicate how to humanely train dogs, but nothing in the law requires that dog trainers apply these proven methods in practice. Dog trainers may use training techniques that bring harm to dogs and deceive consumers as to its efficacy. The onus is on consumers to educate themselves to these dangers when selecting a 'qualified' dog trainer." This strikes us as both unfortunate to say the least (for both dogs and their owners) and incongruous, given that across an overwhelming number of other products, services and industries, consumers are protected by legislation—at both state and federal level.

> *"Scientific research in animal behavior and canine ethology indicate how to humanely train dogs, but nothing in the law requires that dog trainers apply these proven methods in practice." – Foubert (2016)*

In its Statement of Ethics, The American Marketing Association (2019) speaks to "ethical norms" such as the following:

1. Do no harm. This means consciously avoiding harmful actions or omissions by embodying high ethical standards and adhering to all applicable laws and regulations in the choices we make.
2. Foster trust in the marketing system. This means striving for good faith and fair dealing so as to contribute toward the efficacy of the exchange process as well as avoiding deception in product design, pricing, communication, and delivery of distribution.
3. Embrace ethical values. This means building relationships and enhancing consumer confidence in the integrity of marketing by affirming these core

values: honesty, responsibility, fairness, respect, transparency and citizenship.

Ethics in Marketing

The ethics of marketing analysis depends on three components: the intent of the action, the means or methods, and the end or outcome of the strategy or tactic (Murphy, Laczniak, Bowie & Klein, 2012). However, over the last 20 years or so, a number of ethics scandals have plagued the international business environment with fraudulent intent and devastating consequences across the financial sectors of the U.S. economy. Apparently, no industry is exempt from deceptive sales and marketing practices that may run through branding statements, marketing strategies and/or product sales.

> *Over the last 20 years or so, a number of ethics scandals have plagued the international business environment with fraudulent intent and devastating consequences across the financial sectors of the U.S. economy. Apparently, no industry is exempt from deceptive sales and marketing practices that may run through branding statements, marketing strategies and/or product sales.*

What Is Marketing?

It would be remiss to discuss service product transparency and consumer protection without first exploring marketing ethics and strategies. But first, we must ask exactly what is marketing and where does it fit into the realm of ethical business practices?

There are many definitions of marketing available. We only need to consult Johnson and Scholes (2002); Kotler, Bowen and Makens (2003); or Adcock, Halborg and Ross (2001) to understand this extensive topic in terms of corporate strategy and the role it plays on shaping, monitoring and controlling the operations of small and large business operations. In short, marketing is a social process by which individuals and groups obtain what they need and want through creating and exchanging products and value with others. The Chartered Institute of Marketing (2015) defines marketing as the management process that identifies, anticipates and satisfies customer requirements profitably. In other words, marketing is all about the right product, in the right place, at the right time, at the right price.

For small businesses, marketing is essentially about marshalling the resources of an organization, so they meet the changing needs of the customer on whom the organization depends. Regardless of which definition you relate to, the important thing to understand about marketing is that it is a continuous business process through which an organization plans, researches, implements, controls, and evaluates its efforts designed to satisfy both customers' needs and its own objectives. Simply stated, marketing encompasses everything a business does to make its services or products more attractive and available to potential customers and to satisfy customer needs and wants. As such, promotional effectiveness, product maturity and segmentation production are monitored carefully by the business owners and tweaked to enhance profitability in line with the marketing strategies (Lewis & Chambers, 2000).

The majority of businesses operate to generate a profit while nonprofits operate to generate income and ensure they can attain their given and stated mission. When a customer decides to buy a product or service, then an exchange takes place. Normally, this exchange involves money. However crude, most small businesses have marketing strategies that are then developed into operational tactics so they can be allocated to resources within the organization and implemented. The marketing strategy "reflects the company's best opinion as to how it can most profitably apply its skills and resources to the marketplace." (McDonald & Payne, 2001, p.132).

Marketing is an umbrella to the following disciplines: sales, public relations, pricing, packaging, operations, and distribution. According to Adcock, Halborg and Ross (2001, p.31), "…marketing as a function is basically about matching the offerings of the organization to the outside world." As we mentioned earlier, the American Marketing Association (2019) holds its members accountable with a very in-depth and detailed Statement of Ethics. The statement includes a Preamble, a list of Ethical Norms, and a list of Ethical Values, then details how each of these "promises" should be implemented. The preamble concludes: "As marketers, we recognize that we not only serve our organizations but also act as stewards of society in creating, facilitating and executing the transactions that are part of the greater economy. In this role, marketers are expected to embrace the highest professional ethical norms and the ethical values implied by our responsibility toward multiple stakeholders (e.g., customers, employees, investors, peers, channel members, regulators and the host community)." (American Marketing Association, 2019).

Marketing and Conditioning

Professional and seasoned marketers know they can manipulate and influence consumers through the science of associative learning, using both operant and respondent conditioning. We discussed operant and respondent conditioning in more detail in *Chapter Four: How Pets Learn and the Consequences of Methodology, Equipment and Philosophical Choice / A Behavior or an Emotion?* By using respondent, aka Pavlovian, conditioning, marketers attempt to influence the customer through stimulus association. For example, a beautifully groomed dog with an adorable family may be paired with a particular dog food, pet store or piece of training equipment. An image such as this leads to a conditioned response, convincing the pet owner that if they use that specific piece of equipment, shop at that specific store or buy that specific food, they too can be the guardian of a beautifully well-behaved pet living in a gorgeous house with a perfect family, all the while feeling incredibly content. It is not by chance that expensive sports cars are sometimes advertised with beautiful, glamorous women standing next to them or lying across the hood. The conditioning association is that, if you purchase the car, you too can have that life, i.e. that ideal represented by the advertisement and the beautiful, successful people featured in it. Consumers may thus "associate good feelings and having fun with the product and may be more likely to buy the product." (Magloff, 2017).

Marketers use associative conditioning such as this when designing and planning marketing campaigns, whether through digital or print media, online ads, or television or radio commercials. It is the basic conditioning premise of stimulus association, whereby one stimulus is paired with another stimulus that generates a conditioned emotional response (CER), i.e. a feeling or emotion associated with the product. (See *Appendix B: The Recommended Model for the Assessment of a Professional's Knowledge and Skill / Knowledge and Skill Requirements for Training Technicians (Level 1) for more on positive and negative CERs and their role in dog training.*)

Politicians also use this technique when trying to educate or build consensus around party platforms and ideas. Fear tactics may be used to drive buy-in, e.g. the fear of not being well protected in the event of an accident if you do not choose the, allegedly, safest product; the fear of losing your pet if you do not install an electronic boundary system; the fear of becoming more ill if you do not take a specific medication; the fear of being overrun by "the enemy within" if you allow immigration. We can see a real-life example of associative conditioning in the term "pit bull." For a number of years, this term has been sensationally reported in the media and strategically paired with tales of dog fighting and dog bites and now, for some, the term itself brings about an unpleasant emotional response. The associated fear and prejudice, however, drive behavior that is not necessarily thought through in a cognitive sense. In this example, decisions are thus made regarding the so-called bully breeds that are not in any shape or form based on science or current data. (*See Chapter Eight: Ethics in Pet Training and Behavior Consulting / Breed Bias*.)

> *In the pet training industry, some companies offer "lifetime guarantees," yet this is essentially unethical as no behavior can be independently controlled and therefore "guaranteed." By its very nature, behavior is a voluntary or involuntary reaction or action to the individual's environment and is, thus, a variable factor.*

When customers associate a feeling or emotional response with a product or stimulus, they are more likely to want to purchase it. The pairing of a brand with a pleasurable response is very powerful and can be achieved in very few trials or exposures. Conditioning and its influence on consumer behavior is such a wide reaching and important concept that much research has taken place around its effects, specifically in advertising. As Schachtman and Reilly (2011, p.483) explain: "The putative debate between behaviorism and cognition has been discussed by many marketing researchers (e.g. Allen & Janiszewski, 1989; Allen & Shrimp, 1990)." During the exposure of a customer to an advertisement, there are many different stimuli present and types of information flowing. Consequently, a consumer may experience a variety of emotions and changes in emotional state without any actual cognitive awareness. Conversely, a consumer may also feel a change in their emotional reaction to a product or stimulus when exposed to an advertisement and this can certainly be triggered by a cognitive awareness. Baker, Honea and Russell

(2004) present that when brand names appeared at the front of an advertisement, then the effects of the conditioning are more powerful because the exposure to the brand name is longer.

Another application of associative learning in marketing and advertising is the manipulation of buyer behavior through the application of operant conditioning. Here, customers are positively reinforced for making small, entry level buying decisions using discounts, coupons, or free services. In the pet training industry, some companies offer "lifetime guarantees," yet this is essentially unethical as no behavior can be independently controlled and therefore "guaranteed." By its very nature, behavior is a voluntary or involuntary reaction or action to the individual's environment and is, thus, a variable factor. Behavior is considered the dependent because, in applied behavior analysis, to change a behavior you need to control and/or manipulate either of the variable factors, antecedents or consequences (DogNostics, 2018).

Negative reinforcement, or the removal of an aversive (i.e. something the buyer wants to avoid or escape), can also be used to encourage a consumer to purchase a product or service. Using the pet industry as an example, a dog training practice may promise the unsuspecting dog owner that if they use their method, or buy this or that piece of equipment, they will no longer be subjected to whatever is the problematic behavior. Thus, they offer a solution and the problem is, supposedly, magically removed. As we have already examined, however, the consequences of such practices are flawed and can be wide reaching. (See *Chapter Five: A Call for an Industry Wide, Professionally Acknowledged Best Practice / Key Learning Theory*.)

Marketing Ethics

Recognizing the impact marketing can have on the behavior of consumers when they are not necessarily cognitively aware of it inevitably leads to a discussion on the importance of marketing ethics and the need for practitioners to abide by a set of guidelines that promote transparency and consumer protection.

In *Chapter Eight: Ethics in Pet Training and Behavior Consulting / Defining Ethics, Defining Morals*, we discussed how ethics deals with the morality of human conduct. In marketing, ethics refers to the "systematic study of how moral standards are applied to marketing decisions, behaviors and institutions." (Murphy, Laczniak, Bowie & Klein, 2012, p.4). It is an applied field and decisions made regarding these ethics pertain to a range of issues, such as violence, underage sales, price gouging, deception, etc. Murphy et al. (2012, p.4) present that ethical marketing is all about practices that are transparent and trustworthy and that "actions exhibit integrity as well as fairness to consumers." The basic principles of marketing should thus put people first and there are several offered by Murphy et al. (2012) that can be used for evaluating and improving marketing ethics. We present a summary here:

1. Ethical marketing puts people first.
2. Ethical marketers must achieve a standard that is above the law.
3. Marketers are responsible for everything they intend as a means or end.
4. Marketing should cultivate high moral imagination.
5. Marketers should articulate and embrace a core set of principles.
6. Stakeholders must be first and foremost to the ethical marketing decisions.
7. Marketing organizations should determine an ethical decision-making protocol.

Ethics and Law

Ethics and law are certainly connected, but they are not the same. Indeed, some marketing practices are both unethical and illegal, while others are just unethical! According to Murphy et al. (2012), illegal marketing practices can be grouped and stratified (*see below*). We have supplemented these topics with information regarding the current oversight offered by various governing bodies.

Key Categories of Illegal Marketing Practices:

1. Product Safety - Governed by the Consumer Product Safety Commission, charged to protect the public against unreasonable risks associated with a product.
2. Deceptive Advertising – When advertising is deliberately misleading to consumers either by misrepresentation of a product's features or a false claim. Deceptive advertising is regulated by the Federal Trade Commission.
3. Bait and Switch Advertising – Also governed by the Federal Trade Commission, this covers the practice of advertising one product to coerce consumers into a business when there is no intention to actually sell that product but to sell a different, often more expensive product.

Consumer Protection

In 1914, President Woodrow Wilson signed the Federal Trade Commission Act into law and so formed the Federal Trade Commission. The Commission began operation in March 1915 and one of its core missions was to protect consumers. Until this time, consumers had had no protection whatsoever and had to verify for themselves the quality of any goods or services they purchased. Only in situations of gross negligence could a seller be held responsible.

The Federal Trade Commission (2019) identifies its principal mission thus: "Protecting consumers and competition by preventing anticompetitive, deceptive, and unfair business practices through law enforcement, advocacy, and education without unduly burdening legitimate business activity." The first of its Strategic Goals is to "protect consumers from unfair and deceptive practices in the marketplace." Similar wording is used to designate one of three bureaus that fall under the Federal Trade Commission, the Bureau of Consumer Protection, which states (2019) its mandate to "protect consumers against unfair, deceptive and fraudulent business practices." The Bureau extends this, stating that the mandate stops such practices by "collecting complaints and conducting investigations, suing companies and people that break the law, developing rules to maintain a fair marketplace, [and] educating consumers and businesses about their rights and responsibilities." (Bureau of Consumer Protection, 2019).

What, then, are a consumer's rights and responsibilities with regard to pet dog training and behavior consulting, and who is the consumer? The pet industry is somewhat unique in that the consumer is both the pet and the pet's owner. (*See Chapter Eight: Ethics in Pet Training and Behavior Consulting / Ethics within the Framework of Competency*.)

According to Corradi (2015), the United Nations Guidelines for Consumer Protection (1985, revised in 1999), propose a list of objectives described as a consumer's "legitimate needs." Many of these needs seem to have their origin in the Universal Declaration of Human Rights (UDHR), "a milestone document in the history of human rights" that was drafted by representatives from all over the world and proclaimed by the United Nations General Assembly in December 1948 "as a common standard of achievements for all peoples and all nations." (United Nations, 2019).

The needs are:

- The right to be heard.
- The right to information.
- The right to safety.
- The right to choose.
- The right to consumer education.
- The promotion of economic interests of consumers.

According to Butler and Wright (2010, p.1), during the 1960s, there was a "perceived increase in demand from the American public and elected officials for consumer protection legislation." The post-World War II era had left consumers with little power as the marketplace had shifted more favorably toward the merchants. As such, consumers now required more legal protection to correct this shift.

As a result, and by consumer demand, many states developed a diverse collection of legislation commonly called Consumer Protection Acts (CPAs). These CPAs were "designed to supplement the Federal Trade Commission's mission of protecting consumers and are often referred to as 'little-FTC.'" (Butler & Wright, 2010, p.1).

Collectively, then, with the Federal Trade Commission Consumer Protection Bureau and the State Consumer Protection Acts, one might be inclined to think that pet industry consumers are automatically covered and protected from deceptive marketing and fraudulent business practices. But is this actually the case?

Key Definitions

To examine this point, we can start by defining what is meant by "fraudulent" and "deception." According to the Cambridge Dictionary (2019):

- **Fraudulent:** Not what it claims or pretends to be.
    - **Claim:** To state that something is true or is a fact.
    - **Pretends**: To behave as if something is true when you know that it is not, esp. in order to deceive people.
- **Deception**: A statement or action that hides the truth, or the act of hiding the truth.
    - **Truth**: The actual fact or facts about a matter.
    - **Fact**: Something known to have happened or to exist.

Psychology Today (2019), meanwhile, defines deception as "the act—big or small, cruel or kind—of causing someone to believe something that is untrue."

A key question, then, is this: How should dog trainers be marketing and delivering their services so consumers can make informed decisions about their pets' education and care? After all, clients are entitled to be made aware, in a timely, honest, and transparent manner, which methods and equipment a business operator will be using to perform their services.

Misrepresentation

Each year, companies are fined for misrepresenting their services or products. Hiscott (2017) shows how certain large organizations flippantly misrepresent or blatantly lie about their products. In several cases, this has led to them being penalized with multimillion-dollar legal settlements. What follows is a summary of some well-known brands who have lied about their products:

- In 2012, Skechers reached a $40 million settlement with the Federal Trade Commission for making scientifically unfounded claims about its sneakers.
- In 2005, a federal judge forced Listerine to pull ads that claimed the mouthwash was clinically proven to be as effective as floss in fighting tooth and gum decay.
- In 2016, All Natural Juice faced a class action lawsuit for using phrases like "100% Fruit," on their packaging. The company paid $9 million to settle the suit.
- In 2009, Kellogg's made unsubstantiated scientific claims about Rice Krispies, stating that the cereal provided 25% of the daily recommended number of antioxidants and nutrients. The Federal Trade Commission also took Kellogg's to task for claiming its Frosted Mini-Wheats were "clinically shown to improve kids' attentiveness by nearly 20%." The Federal Trade Commission prohibited Kellogg's from making any more claims that were not backed by scientific evidence. (Hiscott, 2017).

In other reports, companies have been identified as being deliberately misleading in their advertisements, not just by pushing the boundaries of truth but by making blatant statements that omit any fact or evidence, scientific or otherwise. In 2017, *Business Insider India* reported the following:

- L'Oréal claimed that two of its skincare products could "boost genes" and generate "visibly younger skin in just seven days."
- Activia brand yogurt landed the company with a class action settlement of $45 million in 2010. The yogurts were marketed as being "clinically" and "scientifically" proven to boost the immune system and able to help to regulate digestion.
- In 2016, the Federal Trade Commission filed a lawsuit against Volkswagen for its advertising campaign promoting its "Clean Diesel."
- Energy drinks company Red Bull was sued in 2014 for its slogan "Red Bull Gives you Wings."
- New Balance was accused of false advertising in 2011 over a sneaker range that it claimed could help wearers burn calories.

In the pet training industry, it is not uncommon to see claims similar to these, which are labels at best and factually inaccurate at worst, given the scientific research now available to us. (*See Chapter Eight: Ethics in Pet Training and Behavior Consulting / Ethics within the Framework of Competency*.) **Each of the following statements is an example of misleading, inaccurate, or blatant mistruth intended to misguide a customer:**

- Bark Busters (2019), an international dog training franchise, claims: "Our dog training is simple, natural and fast."
- Bark Busters (2019) also claims that "[s]eparation anxiety is most often caused by a combination of factors including, a perceived lack of leadership."
- The Sit Means Sit (2019) franchise claims it is "Faster, Smarter, Better."
- Reality television "dog whisperer" Cesar Millan (2015) provides marketing information that is completely unsubstantiated and that has been admonished by the scientific community, e.g.: "Dogs follow balanced energy because it's what their instincts tell them to do. It's up to us to provide that calm, assertive balance."

Articles about how to be "alpha" are a dime a dozen despite being factually inaccurate, outdated and misleading, and can be potentially dangerous to both people and their pets. For example, the most cursory of Google searches will bring up articles such as these:

> *Articles about how to be "alpha" are a dime a dozen despite being factually inaccurate, outdated and misleading, and can be potentially dangerous to both people and their pets.*

- For Paws Corgi Rescue (2000): How to be a Good Alpha (Pack Leader).
- Preston, A. (2004). Secrets to becoming the "Alpha Dog" and be your dog's pack leader.
- Dog Breed Info (2019): Establishing and Keeping Alpha Position - Letting your dog know you are the boss.
- Dog Obedience Training Guides (2012). How to Be the Alpha Dog
- Dog Owner's Guide (n.d.) The alpha factor - Who's the boss around here, anyway?

Indeed, the misrepresentation of methods and fallout from chosen methods is rampant across the worldwide web. At the same time, there are numerous situations where pet owners have reported that dog training professionals have used aversive tools or methods on their pets without prior approval, some of which ended in the death of a family pet:

> *"The alpha myth is everywhere. Google 'alpha dog' on the internet and you get more than 16 million hits. Really. While not all the sites are about dominating your dog, there are literally millions of resources out there – websites, books, blogs, television shows, animal care and training professionals – instructing you to use force and intimidation to overpower your dog into submission. They say that you, the human, must be the alpha. They're all wrong. Every single one of them." - Miller (2018)*

- Midstate woman says kennel used shock collar on her dog: https://www.abc27.com/news/local/midstate-woman-says-kennel-used-shock-collar-on-her-dog/1879524808

- Dog Day Care Put A Shock Collar On My Dog Without Permission, Owner Says: https://www.dnainfo.com/chicago/20170323/mt-greenwood/posh-pet-day-spa-shock-collar-doggie-daycare-luke-mullaney/
- Dog owner finds anti-bark collar on pet after daycare visit: https://abc7chicago.com/pets/dog-owner-finds-anti-bark-collar-on-pet-after-daycare-visit/1821382/
- $60,000 Awarded In Death Of Dog: https://thebark.com/content/60000-awarded-death-dog?fbclid=IwAR2FRsicim5nC_WWZRju58qkRtglEmTaRjkG0BsjR703Paxdfcb08PYLNEM#.XJriO7MpSJg.facebook
- A Dog Died Today. Because of a Trainer: https://positively.com/contributors/a-dog-died-today-because-of-a-trainer/
- "That shock collar had embedded in his neck:" Vet describes dog boarded by Off Leash K9 Training: https://www.wjhl.com/local/-that-shock-collar-had-embedded-in-his-neck-vet-describes-dog-boarded-by-off-leash-k9-training/2009407011

(*See also* Chapter Three: Professionals Should Exemplify and Promote Anti-Cruelty Statutes / Cruelty Cases *and* Chapter Three: Professionals Should Exemplify and Promote Anti-Cruelty Statutes / Truth in Training.)

The Professional Is the Service!

In an article published in *Psychology Today*, Dr. Marc Bekoff (2017), professor emeritus of ecology and evolutionary biology at the University of Colorado, expressed his shock that, "in the United States anyone can call themself [sic] a 'dog trainer.' I went online and did many different searches, and while there are many excellent certification programs, it is the case that anyone can legally hang up a shingle that says 'Dog Trainer' and begin to work with dogs and their humans. I also queried a number of trainers and they also agreed that there really is a 'dirty little secret' about which many, perhaps

> "...anyone can legally hang up a shingle that says 'Dog Trainer' and begin to work with dogs and their humans. I also queried a number of trainers and they also agreed that there really is a 'dirty little secret' about which many, perhaps most, people are unaware, as I was. And, if course, it's not a little secret at all, but rather a huge one, because of the incredible damage that can be done by someone who isn't trained to be a dog trainer..." – Bekoff (2017)

most, people are unaware, as I was. And, if course, it's not a little secret at all, but rather a huge one, because of the incredible damage that can be done by someone who isn't trained to be a dog trainer...Dog training can be abusive, and we must do all we can to make sure it is not."

Service Product Clarity

In the service industry specifically, the service delivery cannot be separated from the service provider or the end user. Rather, it is a continuous process where the consumer meets the person representing the actual product. For example, professional dog trainers cannot deliver their services without interacting directly with their clients throughout the service delivery process. The product the client purchases is the actual service delivery, i.e. the private appointment, the training session or group class, and the professional's ability to deliver on a marketed promise. In the case of dog training, however, the service product is not just the physical product, i.e. the training service that is purchased. It is far more complicated than that (Tudge, 2015).

> *In dog training, customers purchase solutions to their problems and invest in what will – hopefully – become a well-mannered dog. It is here where product misinformation is often used in the marketing message, whereby promises are made and false statements induce customers to make the purchase (Tudge, 2015).*

Unlike retail items or inventory, the services and products offered by a professional trainer or behavior consultant are multilayered. The first layer is the core product. This refers to the user-benefit, problem-solving service the customer is purchasing. In dog training, customers purchase solutions to their problems and invest in what will – hopefully – become a well-mannered dog. It is here where product misinformation is often used in the marketing message, whereby promises are made and false statements induce customers to make the purchase (Tudge, 2015).

The second layer is the actual product. This is the tangible product or service and is the method by which a client receives the core product benefits. For a dog trainer or behavior consultant, this means the consultation or dog training session. The third, and final, layer is known as the augmented product. This contains all the actions taken by the professional to help the customer put the actual product, i.e. the training lesson, to sustained use. These actions can include how the product is delivered, how and what are provided in terms of educational handouts, recommendations of equipment to use, and post-session email and telephone support. This all makes for a very complicated product and it requires strategic thought to determine how the various product layers should be developed, implemented, and managed. Because these service products are multilayered, it also allows for a great deal of confusion, misinformation, or false advertising, which can – and does – hinder clients from making the best purchase decision for their pets (Tudge, 2015). There are a number of resources available to help pet owners make such decisions, including:

- Doggone Safe (2019): Ten Questions to Ask Your Dog Training Professional - Before You Hire Them.
- Companion Animal Psychology (2016): How to Choose a Dog Trainer
- iSpeakDog (n.d.): How to Choose a Dog Trainer.

However, the onus is still on the pet owner to find the right person amongst all the other misinformation available. States Bekoff (2017): "All dogs who need training depend on their humans to make the best choice possible. We owe it to them to do the best we can and to be sure that when we entrust our dogs' well-being and lives to someone who calls themself [sic] a trainer, that they really are qualified to work with these highly sentient beings and their human guardians."

> If a trainer implements aversive methods, then a detailed summary of their philosophical approach and system methodology plus the risks of potential fallout should also be provided, along with an honest account of what a pet may experience in terms of pain, fear and/or punishment during a training session or behavior change program. Today's dog training professionals must rely on science rather than hearsay, myth, misperception and misinformation to lead the charge on how they should be performing their services.

Summary

State Masson et al. (2018): "The importance of ethical issues in engendering client compliance should not be underestimated." The marketing and business practices implemented by pet professionals can significantly impact pet owners and their pets – emotionally, environmentally, physically, and psychologically. As such, it is imperative that pet professionals operate to a high standard of moral code in terms of business transparency and consumer protection. Professional dog trainers and pet industry practitioners should have a specialized knowledge advantage over the ordinary person, their clients. This knowledge should be used honestly and with full transparency. Professionals should avoid clouding a pet owner's decision-making process with inaccuracies, pseudo-science and outdated information. A professional's knowledge and education should be based on current scientific study and not archaic, scientifically unsound methods that enable them to exploit clients and their pets through unfounded and misleading marketing and/or sales information regarding their products and services, not to mention any resulting behavioral fallout from implementing said methods. The consequences can be severely damaging for dogs, and, thus their owners too.

According to The Academy for Dog Trainers (2017), the most important thing to look for in a dog trainer is transparency: "If a dog trainer is not willing to fully disclose, in clear language, exactly what will happen to your dog (in the physical world) during the training process, keep shopping. Look for verbs, not adjectives. Demand to know what specific methods will be employed in what specific situations."

> *A professional's knowledge and education should be based on current scientific study and not archaic, scientifically unsound methods that enable them to exploit clients and their pets through unfounded and misleading marketing and/or sales information regarding their products and services.*

Favre (2011) presents that there are several possible pathways for greater legal protection of animal interests. We have summarized these as follows:

- Adoption of legislation at the state level.
- A change of law through the opinions of judges.
- A change of law at the federal level.
- The market force of consumers.

However, the market force of consumers only comes into play if consumers are aware of the differing approaches to the training and care of pets and the potential fallout of each method. Transparent marketing, sales and business practices are thus imperative. Adoption of legislation at both a State and Federal level needs to be supported by a public who, based on educational awareness, apply political pressure to legislators or bring cases in front of judges who are fully informed. Full transparency and consumer protection will drive each of these processes.

In the pet industry, consumer transparency, supported by honest and truthful marketing and accurate descriptions of how a pet will be trained or cared for, is essential. As it stands, some of the products and services currently on offer (examples of which we have detailed) have already negatively impacted the physical and emotional health of too many sentient beings and will continue to do so. If a trainer implements aversive methods, then a detailed summary of their philosophical approach and system methodology plus the risks of potential fallout should also be provided, along with an honest account of what a pet may experience in terms of pain, fear and/or punishment during a training session or behavior change program. Today's dog training professionals must rely on science rather than hearsay, myth, misperception and misinformation to lead the charge on how they should be performing their services.

Bibliography

Adcock, D., Halborg, A., & Ross, C. (2001). Marketing Principles and Practices. (Fourth Edition). Harrow, UK: Pearson Education

American Marketing Association. (2019). Codes of Conduct: AMA Statement of Ethics. Retrieved March 25, 2019, from http://www.amagvsu.com/statement-of-ethics.html

Baker, W.E., Honea, H., & Russell, C.A. (2004). Do Not Wait to Reveal the Brand Name: The effect of brand name placement on television advertisement effectiveness. *Journal of Advertising (33)* 3 77-85. Retrieved March 25, 2019, from https://tandfonline.com/doi/abs/10.1080/00913367.2004.10639170

Barkbusters. (2019). Dog Training. Retrieved March 25, 2019, from https://www.barkbusters.com/dog-training

Barkbusters. (2019). Does Your Dog Suffer From Separation Anxiety? Retrieved March 25, 2019, from https://www.barkbusters.com/news/separation-anxiety%20in%20dogs

Bekoff, M. (2017). Dog Training's Dirty Little Secret: Anyone Can Legally Do It. Retrieved March 25, 2019, from https://www.psychologytoday.com/us/blog/animal-emotions/201701/dog-trainings-dirty-little-secret-anyone-can-legally-do-it

Business Insider India. (2017). 18 false advertising scandals that cost some brands millions. Retrieved March 25, 2019, from https://www.businessinsider.in/strategy/18-false-advertising-scandals-that-cost-some-brands-millions/slidelist/57380282.cms

Butler, H. N., & Wright, J.D. (2010). Are State Consumer Protection Acts Really Little-FTC Acts? Faculty Working Papers. Paper 41. Retrieved March 25, 2019, from http://scholarlycommons.law.northwestern.edu/facultyworkingpapers/41

Chartered Institute of Marketing. (2015). Marketing and the 7Ps: A brief summary of marketing and how it works. Retrieved March 25, 2019, from https://www.cim.co.uk/media/4772/7ps.pdf

Claim [Def]. (2019). In Cambridge Dictionary. Retrieved March 25, 2019, from https://dictionary.cambridge.org/us/dictionary/english/claim?q=claims

Companion Animal Psychology. (2016). How to Choose a Dog Trainer. Retrieved March 25, 2019, from https://www.companionanimalpsychology.com/2016/12/how-to-choose-dog-trainer.html

Corradi, A. (2015). International Law and Consumer Protection: The history of consumer protection. Hauser Global Law School. Retrieved March 25, 2019, from http://www.nyulawglobal.org/globalex/International_Law_Consumer_Protection.html#_Toc409004451

Crosby, J. (n.d.). A Dog Died Today. Because of a Trainer. Retrieved May 29, 2019, from https://positively.com/contributors/a-dog-died-today-because-of-a-trainer/

Deception [Def]. (2019). In *Psychology Today*. Retrieved March 25, 2019, from https://www.psychologytoday.com/us/basics/deception

Deception [Def]. (2019). In Cambridge Dictionary. Retrieved March 25, 2019, from https://dictionary.cambridge.org/us/dictionary/english/deception

Dog Breed Info. (2019): Establishing and Keeping Alpha Position - Letting your dog know you are the boss. Retrieved March 25, 2019, from https://www.dogbreedinfo.com/topdogrules.htm

Dog Obedience Training Guides. (2012). How To Be The Alpha Dog. Retrieved March 25, 2019, from https://dogobediencetrainingguides.wordpress.com/2012/07/03/how-to-be-the-alpha-dog/

Dog Owner's Guide. (n.d.). The alpha factor - Who's the boss around here, anyway? Retrieved March 25, 2019, from http://www.canismajor.com/dog/alpha1.html

Doggone Safe (n.d.). Ten Questions to Ask Your Dog Training Professional - Before You Hire Them. Retrieved March 25, 2019, from https://doggonesafe.com/Choosing-a-Dog-Trainer

DogNostics Career Center. (2018). A Practical Lexicon for Pet Trainers & Behavior Consultants! The Language You Need to Know. (n.p.): Authors

Fact [Def]. (2019). In Cambridge Dictionary. Retrieved March 25, 2019, from https://dictionary.cambridge.org/us/dictionary/english/fact

Favre, D. (2011). Animal Law, Welfare, Interests, And Rights. New York, NY: Wolters Kluwer Law and Business

Federal Trade Commission. (2018). Strategic Plan for Fiscal Years 2018 to 2022. Retrieved March 25, 2019, from https://www.ftc.gov/system/files/documents/reports/2018-2022-strategic-plan/ftc_fy18-22_strategic_plan.pdf

Federal Trade Commission Bureau of Consumer Protection. (2019). About the Bureau of Consumer Protection. Retrieved March 25, 2019, from https://www.ftc.gov/about-ftc/bureaus-offices/bureau-consumer-protection/about-bureau-consumer-protection

For Paws Corgi Rescue. (2000). How to be a Good Alpha (Pack Leader). Retrieved March 25, 2019, from http://www.forpaws.org/articles/alpha.htm

Foubert, E. (2016). Occupational Licensure or pet Dog Trainers: Dogs are not the only ones who should be licensed. Chicago, IL: The John Marshall Law School

Fraudulent [Def]. (2019). In Cambridge Dictionary. Retrieved March 25, 2019, from https://dictionary.cambridge.org/us/dictionary/english/fraudulent

Fuller, J. (2019, May 20). "That shock collar had embedded in his neck:" Vet describes dog boarded by Off Leash K9 Training. News Channel 11 WJHL Johnson City, TN. Retrieved May 29, from https://www.wjhl.com/local/-that-shock-collar-had-embedded-in-his-neck-vet-describes-dog-boarded-by-off-leash-k9-training/2009407011

Goudie, C. & Weidner, R. (2017, March 27). Dog owner finds anti-bark collar on pet after daycare visit. ABC News 7 WLS Chicago, IL. Retrieved May 29, from https://abc7chicago.com/pets/dog-owner-finds-anti-bark-collar-on-pet-after-daycare-visit/1821382/

Hiscott, R. (2017). 8 Companies That Sold You Lies. Huffington Post. Retrieved March 25, 2019, from https://www.huffingtonpost.com/2014/05/16/companies-lied-to-you_n_5318940.html

iSpeakDog (n.d.). How to Choose a Dog Trainer. Retrieved March 25, 2019, from http://www.ispeakdog.org/how-to-choose-a-dog-trainer.html

Johnson, G., & Scholes, K. (2002). Exploring Corporate Strategy. Upper Saddle River, NJ: Prentice Hall

Kotler, P., Bowen, J., & Makens, J. (2003). Marketing for Hospitality and Tourism. (Third Edition). Upper Saddle River, NJ: Pearson Education

Lewis, R., & Chambers, R. (2000). Marketing Leaderships in Hospitality (3rd edn.). New York, NY: John Wiley & Sons Inc.

London, K. (2019, March). $60,000 Awarded In Death Of Dog. Retrieved May 29, 2019, from https://thebark.com/content/60000-awarded-death-dog

Ludwig, H. (2017, March 23). Dog Day Care Put A Shock Collar on My Dog Without Permission, Owner Says. DNA Info Chicago. Retrieved May 14, 2019, from https://www.dnainfo.com/chicago/20170323/mt-greenwood/posh-pet-day-spa-shock-collar-doggie-daycare-luke-mullaney

Magloff, L. (2017). Operant Conditioning vs. Classical Conditioning in Advertising. Retrieved March 25, 2019, from https://bizfluent.com/info-12030739-operant-conditioning-vs-classical-conditioning-advertising.html

McDonald, M., & Payne, A. (2001). Marketing Planning for Services. Oxford, UK: Reed Educational and Professional Publishing

Millan, C. (2015). Natural Dog Law 2: To Dogs, Energy Is Everything. Retrieved March 25, 2019, from https://www.cesarsway.com/natural-dog-law-2-to-dogs-energy-is-everything/

Miller, P. (2018). Danger! Dominance Theory! Why Every Mention of "Alpha Dogs" or "Dominant Dogs" is Dangerous to All Dogs. Retrieved March 25, 2019, from https://dogbizsuccess.com/danger-dominance-theory/

Murphy, P.E, Laczniak, G.R., Bowie, N.E., & Klein, T.A. (2012). Ethical Marketing. Oxon, UK: Routledge

Preston, A. (2004). Secrets to becoming the "Alpha Dog" & be your dog's pack leader. Retrieved March 25, 2019, from https://foreverhusky.org/images/guides/9AphaDogSecretsSiberian.pdf

Pretend [Def]. (2019). In Cambridge Dictionary. Retrieved March 25, 2019, from https://dictionary.cambridge.org/us/dictionary/english/pretend

Schachtman, T., & Reilly, S. (Eds.). (2011). Associative Learning and Conditioning Theory: Human and Non-Human Applications. Oxford, UK: Oxford University Press

Sit Means Sit. (2019). Franchise Information for Sit Means Sit. Retrieved March 25, 2019, from https://www.franchiseclique.com/franchise/Sit-Means-Sit

The Academy for Dog Trainers. (2017, June 16). Transparency in Dog Training [Video File]. Retrieved March 25, 2019, from https://www.youtube.com/watch?v=XKyLqv4Q5kl

Truth [Def]. (2019). In Cambridge Dictionary. Retrieved March 25, 2019, from https://dictionary.cambridge.org/us/dictionary/english/truth

Tudge, N.J. (2015). People Training Skills for Pet Professionals: Your Essential Guide to Engaging, Educating and Empowering Your Human Clients. (n.p.): Lulu Publishing Services

United Nations. (2016). Guidelines for Consumer Protection. Retrieved March 25, 2019, from https://unctad.org/en/PublicationsLibrary/ditccplpmisc2016d1_en.pdf

Wilson, L. (2019, March 27). Midstate woman says kennel used shock collar on her dog. ABC7 News. Retrieved May 29, 2019, from https://www.abc27.com/news/local/midstate-woman-says-kennel-used-shock-collar-on-her-dog/1879524808

Chapter Ten: Pet Industry Oversight Recommended Implementation Model

In this final chapter, we present our recommended model for how to establish a State or Regional "Pet Industry Executive Oversight Committee" (known hereafter as "The Committee"). The Committee will act as a liaison between the State Government and the Pet Industry to initiate industry oversight. The Committee will also monitor the industry's continual evolution in the ongoing effort to bring about professionalization by increasing the standards of required education and service delivery while ensuring consumer transparency and protection. (*Note: Recommendations outlined in this chapter apply specifically to the United States. Consult the relevant local legislation for other regions/countries.*)

1. Register a 501c6 Not for Profit Corporation

The Committee should be registered as a Nonprofit Corporation (known hereafter as "The Corporation") in your State. Please consult your local State legislation with regard to how to complete this process accurately.

As detailed above, the purpose of The Corporation is the registry, oversight and monitoring of Pet Industry standards and procedures across the State. The Corporation also seeks to ensure the professionalization of the Pet Industry based on current scientific literature, as well as the protection of the consumer (i.e. the pet and the pet owner) by the implementation of industry transparency.

2. Develop the Corporate Bylaws

The Corporate Bylaws are a detailed set of rules adopted by The Corporation's Board of Directors. The Corporate Bylaws are a very important legal document to have in place as they specifically detail how The Corporation will be managed and run. They contain provisions for how The Corporation will conduct its affairs and detail the duties of its directors and the responsibilities of its officers and employees. The Corporate Bylaws need to be completed so The Corporation can include them in its application for a Tax Exempt Status with the Internal Revenue Service (IRS). The link for the relevant forms can be found at https://www.irs.gov/charities-non-profits.

3. Apply for Federal IRS Nonprofit Status

For detailed and up-to-date information on applying for a Tax Exemption Status with the IRS, see https://www.irs.gov/charities-non-profits/other-non-profits/business-leagues.

4. Corporate Structure

The Corporation membership will be comprised of individual State Registered Pet Trainers and/or Behavior Consultants as well as pet training organizations who agree to abide by the ethics and registration criteria (see *Appendix A: The Recommended Best Practice Model for Pet Training and Behavior Consulting Professionals* and *Appendix F: The Recommended Corporation Professional Code of Conduct and Ethics Pledge*.) The name of The Corporation should be "[State Name] Pet Industry Executive Oversight Committee."

a. Board Members

The Board of Directors will consist of 12 members who will serve for limited terms. Board Members will be appointed to meet the following criteria:

- Two representing Professional Pet Trainers that meet the requirements of the State Registered parameters (3-year term).
- A representing Pet Behavior Consultant that meet the requirements of the State Registered parameters (3-year term).
- One Veterinary Behaviorist or State Licensed Veterinarian (3-year term).
- Two State Bar Lawyers (4-year term).
- A representative from the State Senate Committee on Business, Professions and Economic Development or their Assigned Delegate (2-year term).
- A Representative from the State Senate Committee on Consumer Transparency and Protection or their Assigned Delegate (2-year term).
- Two Local Business Owners from within the Pet Industry (2-year term).
- Representatives from the Management Teams of two separate Animal Rescue Organizations (3-year term).

b. Company Officers

- Officers will be appointed from and by the Board of Directors. They will fulfil the roles of President, Vice President, Treasurer and Secretary.

- Officers shall be elected by the Board of Directors at the Board's first meeting of the calendar year or as soon as practical thereafter.
- Officers shall remain in office until their successor has been selected.
- The Board of Directors may elect a single person to any two or more offices simultaneously, except that the offices of Treasurer and Secretary must be held by separate individuals.
- The Secretary will keep minutes of all meetings of the Board of Directors, will be the custodian of the corporate records, will give all notices as are required by law or the Corporate Bylaws, and, generally, will perform all duties incident to the office of Secretary and such other duties as may be required by law, by the Articles of Incorporation, or by these Corporate Bylaws.
- The Treasurer will have charge and custody of all funds of The Corporation, will oversee and supervise the financial business of The Corporation, will render reports and accountings to the Directors as required by the Board of Directors, and will perform in general all duties incident to the office of Treasurer and such other duties as may be required by law, by the Articles of Incorporation, or by these Corporate Bylaws or which may be assigned from time to time by the Board of Directors.
- Any Officer elected or appointed to office may be removed by the Board of Directors whenever, in their judgment, the best interests of The Corporation will be served. Such removal, however, will be without prejudice to any contract rights of the Officer.

c. Executive Director

An Executive Director will be appointed by the Board of Directors. The Executive Director will act as the key liaison between The Committee and its affiliate members.

d. Board Meetings

The Board of Directors will meet in person a minimum of three (3) times each year with monthly meetings being conducted virtually. Additional or urgent board meetings may be called by the Secretary upon the written request of three (3) Directors. Notice of all board meetings should be given to each board member no less than two (2) days nor more than ten (10) days prior to the meeting. A majority of the incumbent Directors (not counting vacancies) shall constitute a Quorum for the conduct of business. At board meetings where a Quorum is present, a majority vote of the Directors attending shall constitute an act of the Board unless a greater number is required by the Articles of Incorporation or any provision of these Corporate Bylaws.

5. Key Operational Policies and Procedures
    a. Implement and manage a professional ethical Code of Conduct procedure inclusive of reporting and infringement procedures (*see* *Appendix F: The Recommended Corporation Professional Code of Conduct and Ethics Pledge*).
    b. Implement a Best Practice Model for Applied Behavior Interventions (see *Appendix A: The Recommended Best Practice Model for Pet Training and Behavior Consulting Professionals*).
    c. Implement a minimum competency requirement for the key pet training and behavior consulting roles in terms of skills, knowledge and experience (*see* *Appendix B: The Recommended Model for the Assessment of a Professional's Knowledge and Skill*).
    d. Implement a policy on marketing transparency to protect consumers (*see* *Appendix D: The Recommended Consumer Acknowledgement Form for Transparency in Dog Training/Behavior Consulting Services*).
    e. Implement a biennial registration renewal process that includes a Continued Education Units (CEU) component (*see* *Appendix G: The Recommended Policy for Registration Renewal via Continuing Education*.)
    f. Manage a public directory of State Registered Professionals with complete transparency of skills, credentials and experience.

6. Key Policy Advisory Roles
    a. Review, comment and advise on any loopholes found in the current State Animal Cruelty Statutes that impede the accountability of points (a) and (b) in Section 5, above.
    b. Advise on ethics complaints that infringe on Animal Cruelty Statutes.
    c. Review, comment and advise on any necessary additions to the State Consumer Transparency and Protection Statutes regarding industry marketing, equipment, tools and procedures.

7. Membership
   a. Members register through a reasonable biennial fee, to be determined by The Corporation, and are approved based on acknowledgement of the Code of Ethics and meeting the minimum competency requirements (*see* *Appendix F: The Recommended Corporation Professional Code of Conduct and Ethics Pledge*).
   b. Members conform to the minimum competency requirements set by The Corporation (*see* *Appendix B: The Recommended Model for the Assessment of a Professional's Knowledge and Skill*).
   c. Members adhere to the Best Practice Model for Applied Behavior Interventions in line with point a) in Section 5, above (*see* *Appendix A: The Recommended Best Practice Model for Pet Training and Behavior Consulting Professionals*).
   d. Members agree to the continued consistent use of *Appendix D: The Recommended Consumer Acknowledgement Form for Transparency in Dog Training/Behavior Consulting Services*.

Appendix A: The Recommended Best Practice Model for Pet Training and Behavior Consulting Professionals

Part One: Prior to the First Consultation – Decision Chart

1. Has the client completed a Background Information Questionnaire prior to you meeting them (*see Part Two: The Initial Consultation – Background Information Checklist 2 (b)*)?
    a. Yes, proceed to #2.
    b. No, have the client complete a Background Information Questionnaire, then review it and proceed to #2.
2. Do you need to ask the client for any additional clarification(s) prior to contacting them regarding the suitability of you taking the case?
    a. Yes, then schedule a call with the client. Proceed to #3.
    b. No, then proceed to #3.
3. Do you have the required level of competency to be working with the individual training/behavior case?
    a. Yes, proceed to arranging the initial consultation.
    b. No, then proceed to question #4.
4. Can you work on this case with support from a peer?
    a. Yes, then secure a peer to support you and proceed to the initial consultation.
    b. No, a peer is not available or does not have the level of expertise required. Refer to #5.
5. Should the case be worked under the supervision of a more experienced behavior consultant?
    a. Yes, secure a behavior consultant as a supervisor and proceed to arranging the initial consultation.
    b. No, an experienced behavior consultant is not available or does not have the level of expertise required for this case. Refer to #6.
6. Does this case require a veterinary behaviorist and, if so, is one available to you and your client?
    a. Yes, refer the case to a veterinary behaviorist in person or via online support.

b. No, refer the case to a veterinary behaviorist via remote consult.

Part Two: The Initial Consultation – Background Information Checklist

1. Have you scheduled the appointment in a suitable location taking into consideration safety for all involved?
    a. Yes, then proceed to #2.
    b. No, then schedule the appointment and proceed to #2.
2. Have you obtained the necessary clarification and/or additional details and data from the pet's guardian with reference to Sections I-VII?
    a. Yes, proceed to Part Three: The Initial Consultation - Lifestyle Guide Checklist.
    b. No, then conduct a more detailed in person interview while on site to secure the necessary and relevant information from sections I-VII.
        I. **Pet Information**
            a. Age, breed, entire/desexed. If desexed, at what age (if known)?
        II. **The Pet's History**
            a. Where was the pet obtained from and at what age (if known)?
            b. What training has the pet undertaken?
            c. Does the pet have any history of aggression, reactivity, anxiety or fear towards people?
            d. Does the pet have any history of aggression, reactivity, anxiety or fear towards other pets or animals?
        III. **Living Conditions**
            a. Where does the pet spend most of the day?
            b. Where does the pet sleep?
            c. What is the configuration of humans versus pets in the home?
            d. How many pets live in the home, for how long and where do they sleep?
        IV. **Feeding Protocols**
            a. What time of day does the pet eat?

       b. What does the pet eat?
       c. Does the pet eat alone or with other pets?
       d. How does the pet eat, from a bowl or an interactive toy?
       e. What supplements does the pet receive?
       f. What treats does the pet eat?

V. **Mental and Physical Enrichment**
       a. What daily exercise does the pet get?
       b. Who else does the pet play with (canine and/or human), what play experience does the pet have and when?
       c. How does the pet play and with what type of toys?

VI. **Health and Wellness**
       a. Does the pet suffer from a current illness?
       b. Does the pet have any chronic illnesses?
       c. What is the pet's vaccination history?
       d. Has the pet been seen in the last three months by a veterinarian?

VII. **How Does the Pet Behave Around?**
       a. Children.
       b. Adults.
       c. Other pets.
       d. Strangers.

Part Three: The Initial Consultation - Lifestyle Guide Checklist

Have you considered the following?

1. Has the pet's recent behavior changed drastically and does the behavior indicate a level of pain, discomfort, fear, anxiety or a phobia?
    a. Yes, then defer your program until the pet is given a medical "all clear" by a veterinarian.
    b. No, if the pet's behavior has not changed drastically and does not indicate pain, discomfort, fear, anxiety or a phobia and the pet has been seen by a veterinarian within the last three months, then continue with your program.
2. Have you educated the owners regarding overt and covert behaviors and canine body language?

3. Have you baselined the pet's communication topography?
4. Does the owner understand how their pet communicates?
5. Have you recommended play and games to help strengthen the guardian-pet reinforcement history and increase mental enrichment?
6. Has the guardian been educated on how to limit exposure to any problematic stimuli?
7. Has the guardian been educated on how to help create and strengthen positive conditioned emotional responses (+CER) using play and fun?
8. Have you coached the guardians on avoiding aversive and invasive stimuli in the environment and as a by-product to their interactions with their pet?

Part Four: Functionally Assessing the Problem Behavior – ABC Matrix

Have you determined the following?

1. The actual behavior in terms of its duration, intensity and frequency, based on what is observable, using applied behavior analysis terminology and not labels.
2. The problematic stimulus – either the discriminative stimulus and/or the conditioned stimulus.
3. What is currently reinforcing the behavior (+R or –R).
4. The setting events that reliably create the backdrop to the behavior.
5. Any motivating operations including conditioned emotional responses that impact the value of the reinforcement.
6. A baseline measure of the problematic behavior.
7. Are you able to reliably describe the two- or three-term contingency and develop a hypothesis regarding the behavior in question?
    a. The behavior is elicited or evoked by...
    b. The behavior is maintained by...
8. Do you have a reliable contingency statement regarding the ABC?

Part Five: The Behavior Change and/or Training Program – Checklist

1. Have you built into your plan the teaching of incompatible and alternative behaviors to the problematic one?
2. Have you built into your plan the utilization of current +CER opportunities to counter problematic ones (-CER) such as leash walks, eating, guardians arriving home etc.?
3. Have you built into your plan a measurement criterion to ensure any interventions are positively impacting the problematic behavior(s)?
4. Have you built into your plan a process for introducing desensitization and counterconditioning programs to enhance the development of appropriate +CERs?
5. Have you provided your client with a copy of your training plan?

Part Six: Informed Consent and Transparency – Checklist

1. Have you reviewed with your client all aspects of the problematic behavior, including any required management approaches and changes to the pet's living conditions that will be required to ensure antecedent control?
2. Have you coached the pet guardian on changes required to feeding protocols, mental enrichment activities and physical stimulation?
3. Have you outlined to the client how the training plan will proceed, including scheduled meeting requirements, training philosophy, equipment and tools that will be used, and the level of support you will provide in person, via email, telephone or electronic link up?
4. Has the client agreed to proceed with the recommended program overview given the conditions outlined in #2?
5. Have you agreed reasonable and achievable goals with the client based on their pet and his living environment?
6. Has the client agreed to your terms and conditions and signed off on your proposed training/behavior change plan?

Part Seven: Weekly Ongoing Assessment and Measurement Decision Chart

1. Do you have a system to review and revise, where necessary, the level of success the pet owner is experiencing with your recommended program?
2. Are you seeing progression in terms of the problematic behavior decreasing in frequency, duration or intensity (dependent on the dimension best chosen to measure)?
    a. Yes, then continue.
    b. No, then revisit your original hypothesis regarding the behavior and its antecedent/reinforcement contingencies.
3. Having revisited your hypothesis and made any necessary changes to the plan, is the problematic behavior improving?
    a. No, then reach out to a peer for support revising the functional assessment.
    b. Yes, then continue.
4. Having revisited your hypothesis and made any necessary changes to the plan after seeking peer support, is the problematic behavior improving?
    a. No, then secure supervision from a more experienced and qualified consultant.
    b. Yes, then continue.
5. Having revisited your hypothesis and made any necessary changes to the plan after seeking supervision, is the problematic behavior improving?
    a. No, then refer the case to a more experienced consultant and/or seek a veterinary behaviorist.
    b. Yes, then continue.

Part Eight: Wrapping Up and Professional Sign-Off

1. Have you officially recognized and acknowledged with your client the success of the training/behavior program in writing, including the following?
    I. Any ongoing management concerns with recommended environmental antecedent control, necessary training equipment and safety measures.

II. The required maintenance schedule of reinforcement to maintain new and appropriate behaviors.

   a. Yes, congratulations!
   b. No, then craft an official notification for your client.

Appendix B: The Recommended Model for the Assessment of a Professional's Knowledge and Skill

Knowledge and Skill Requirements for Training Technicians (Level 1)

Training Technician – A Definition

The word Technician may be defined in a number of ways, such as: "A person skilled in the technique of an art or craft," or "An expert in the practical application of science." For the purposes of this model, a Canine Training Technician is defined as an individual "skilled in the application of science and artistic endeavor who delivers results through the development of mutually respectful, caring relationships." Canine Training Technicians work primarily on teaching pet dog manners and work alongside a Professional Canine Trainer or a Professional Canine Behavior Consultant.

Eligibility

- All applicants must be able to demonstrate their training experience in at least one of the following ways:
    - Over a period of 12 months, a minimum of 50 hours' experience of group training classes or 50 hours of private training of pet dog manners. One training hour unit is defined as 1 x 45-60 minutes of one group class or 1 x 45-60 minutes of private training.
  Or,
    - Over a period of 24 months, a minimum of 70 hours' experience of group training classes or 70 hours of private training of pet dog manners to be eligible to apply. One training hour unit is defined as 1 x 45-60 minutes of one group class or 1 x 45-60 minutes of private training.
- Applicants must have completed 10 continuing education credit hours at professional seminars, workshops and/or webinars during the previous two years or less.
- Applicants can be either full-time or part-time professionals or volunteers in a training environment; eligibility is determined by the number of hours of experience and acquisition of Continuing Education Units (CEU).
- Applicants must provide one written reference from a colleague who can confirm their date of entry into the industry and confirm their logged hours of

training. A second reference must be provided from a client of the applicant or a veterinarian.
- Applicants must provide proof of business insurance (applies to North America, Australia and any other country that provides professional insurance) or insurance cover for the organization where they are working or volunteering.
- Renewal eligibility occurs every 24 months. Training Technicians must provide proof of 10 continuing education units (CEU).

Assessment Process

The Training Technician assessment is divided into four sections:

Section I	Knowledge base assessment exam
Section II	Basic training skills videos or live demonstrations
Section III	Creating a positive conditioned emotional response video or live demonstration
Section IV	Running training classes videos or live demonstrations

I. **Knowledge Base Requirements**

An 85% pass mark is recommended to ensure knowledge competency.

Canine Communication/Body Language/Social Behavior

Distance increasing signals	Stress signs
Distance decreasing signals	Modal (fixed) action patterns
Conflicted body language	Nature and nurture
Posture	Threat displays
Pupil dilatation	Freezing
Facial muscles	Sweating paws
Displacement behaviors	Trembling/shaking
Tail positions	Tongue flick
Ear positions	Whale eye
Play bow	Piloerection
Appeasement gestures	Happy/relaxed body language

Teaching Relaxing Strategies

Recognizing the need for relaxation in the context of:

| Overstimulation | Play | Digging |
| Jumping up | Barking | Puppy mouthing |

General Training and Management

House training	Bite inhibition
Socialization	Resource guarding
Managing and preventing problem behaviors	Developmental periods (critical periods)
Environmental cues	

Emotional Well-Being Managed through Adequate Mental and Physical Stimulation

Teaching appropriate physical stimulation activities	Teaching appropriate mental stimulation activities

Ethics (Components That May Be Assessed)

Ensuring safety in all interactions	Understanding professional competency
Use of humane and ethical positive reinforcement-based procedures	

The Science of Learning

Nonassociative learning: • Habituation • Sensitization	Understanding operant conditioning: • Three-term contingency: stimulus-response-stimulus • Cues, overshadowing, blocking, salience • Superstitious behaviors
Understanding respondent conditioning: • Stimulus-stimulus-response • Extinction	Use and application of reinforcers: • Primary • Secondary • Schedules of reinforcement

Behavior chaining: • Forwards • Backwards	

Equipment

Management equipment	Training toys
Safety equipment	Training equipment

II. Basic Training Skills Provided in Person or by Video

The applicant must be proficient at each of the following 10 skills. They can each be tested, or a select number can be randomly selected via an independent database for candidate testing.

1. Conditioning the Bridge (A bridge is a training tool, e.g. clicker, verbal, flashlight, thumbs up, that links the animal's current behavior to the reinforcer received. It is a tool that is faded once the behavior has been learned.)
   - Candidate must demonstrate how to condition a bridge (word, clicker, whistle, tongue click, thumbs up or flashlight).
2. Name Recognition and Giving Attention
   - Candidate must demonstrate how to condition the dog's name so he looks at them when they say his name.
   - Candidate must demonstrate that they can ask the dog to look at them using a verbal and/or visual cue other than the dog's name.
3. Sit
   - Candidate must demonstrate teaching the dog to sit.
   - Candidate must appropriately add a verbal and/or visual cue.
   - Candidate must demonstrate that the dog can respond to the verbal/visual cue, giving only one cue with a 2-3 second latency.
   - Candidate must demonstrate using and fading the bridge.
   - If using the luring method, the candidate must demonstrate fading the lure.
4. Drop/Down
   - Candidate must demonstrate two different ways of teaching the dog to lie down.
   - Candidate must appropriately add a verbal and/or visual cue.

- Candidate must then demonstrate that the dog can perform the down behavior on a single cue when standing 6 feet away from the dog with a 2-3 second latency.
- If using the luring method, the candidate must demonstrate fading the lure.

5. Stand
    - Candidate must demonstrate teaching the dog to stand.
    - Candidate must appropriately add a verbal and/or visual cue.
    - Candidate must demonstrate that the dog can respond to the verbal/visual cue, giving only one cue with a 2-3 second latency.
    - If using the luring method, the candidate must demonstrate fading the lure.

6. Stay
    - Candidate may choose the position in which to demonstrate teaching the dog to stay (i.e. sit, drop, stand).
    - Candidate must demonstrate how to teach the dog to stay.
    - Candidate must build duration on the stay and demonstrate 10 seconds of stay.
    - Candidate must introduce distance to the stay and demonstrate the dog staying in position for 10 seconds with the candidate 6 feet away from the dog.
    - Candidate must demonstrate this occurring on two occasions in different venues (e.g. indoors and outdoors, in different rooms of the house, in different outside settings).
    - Candidate must discuss the role that distraction and diversity play in teaching the stay.

7. Loose Leash Walking
    - Candidate must demonstrate at least two methods of teaching a dog to walk on a loose leash.
    - Candidate must demonstrate that the dog trained can loose leash walk at least 65 feet, reinforcing only at the end of the 65 feet:
        - The leash should not become tight at any stage during the walk and the dog should be no more than 2 feet away from the candidate.

8. Recall
    - Candidate must demonstrate how to teach the dog to recall (i.e. come back when called).
    - Candidate must twice demonstrate the dog performing an off-leash recall from a distance of 20 feet in a distracting environment (e.g. outdoors, people walking past, noise). Although it is preferred that the dog is off leash

for this demonstration, a light line may be used for the sake of safety if necessary.
- Candidate must discuss the reasons behind teaching this exercise to pet dog guardians.

9. On the Mat
   - Candidate must demonstrate how to teach the dog to go to his bed/mat/crate.
   - Candidate must demonstrate progressing this to the point where the dog can be asked to drop on the mat and stay for 5 seconds.
   - If using the luring method, the candidate must demonstrate fading the lure and changing to a verbal or visual cue.
   - Candidate must discuss the advantages for the pet dog guardian of teaching this exercise.

10. Tricks
    - Candidate must demonstrate teaching the dog a simple trick. Teach <u>one</u> of the following:
        - Give paw (shake or high five)
        - Bow
        - Speak (bark)
        - Spin/Twist
        - Sit pretty (say please)
        - Roll over
    - The dog must repeat this trick three times in succession, responding with a 2-3 second latency.
    - If using the luring method, the candidate must demonstrate fading the lure and changing to a verbal or visual cue.
    - The candidate must discuss the importance of teaching tricks in pet dog training.

The following supplementary requirements must also be met:

- The candidate must discuss the role that distraction and diversity play in teaching a "stay" during one of the 10 skills videos.
- The candidate may choose to train behaviors using either:
    - *Targeting* (a training aid whereby an animal touches one of his body parts to an object) - include how to fade the target and transition to a verbal/visual cue.

- Discuss other methods that could be used to acquire the behavior if more suitable to the application.
    o *Luring* (a type of training that involves using a reinforcer to guide the animal into the desired position or to undertake the desired behavior) - include how to fade the lure and transition to a verbal/visual cue.
        - Discuss other methods that could be used to gain the behavior should this method fail.
- The candidate must give a brief verbal or caption explanation of what they intend to teach and how it will be taught at the beginning of the film clip or live demonstration:
    o E.g. I am going to demonstrate how to train a "sit" using a lure.
    o E.g. A caption box with the text "sit – using lure" displayed before the film clip begins.
- The candidate must ensure that the evidence of training methods presented in each video complies with the least invasive, scientifically advised techniques.
- The candidate must be aware of behavioral signals being offered by the dog used for the demonstration.
- The candidate must make allowances for behavioral issues and demonstrate how to handle those issues should they occur:
    o This assessment will be considered not satisfactory if the training does not reflect appropriate action in the face of canine stress, discomfort or confusion.

Assessment Factors

- The candidate will be assessed on how any untoward behavioral issue(s) that arise are handled.
- The candidate will be assessed on their handling of the environment to enable optimal learning for the dog.
- The candidate must take into account the dog's breed, age, individual idiosyncrasies and needs.
- The candidate must justify their choice of method for the behavior being taught. The candidate need only <u>justify each method once</u>.
- The candidate must discuss and demonstrate how to generalize behaviors during at least one of the skills exercises and incorporate the following:

- Latency: This is the time interval between a stimulus and the response to that stimulus once trained. Each skill must be performed within 2-3 seconds of the cue being given. When the candidate is demonstrating a completed behavior, the dog must consistently respond within 2-3 seconds of being cued.
- When asked to discuss a part of an exercise, the candidate must briefly discuss (1 minute maximum) the manner and the reasons for using the nominated technique.
- Although the majority of the skills videos may be filmed in the same location, at least one video must demonstrate training in alternative place.
  - Likewise, in a live demonstration, at least one alternative venue must be used.

III. Conditioned Emotional Response (CER)

Note: Given that this procedure can take a considerable amount of time to train, it is recommended that a video submission rather than a live presentation be used for expediency.

In this demonstration, the candidate must explain what a conditioned emotional response is and how to achieve it. The candidate must demonstrate how to change the dog's experience of an object or procedure from being either neutral, annoying or frightening to a happy emotional response or an alternative positive response. The video may show segments of the candidate's progression. The candidate must show the baseline behavior of the dog, parts of the training procedure and the training outcome, together with their explanation of a CER. Evidence of training methods presented scientifically informed techniques.

The candidate must be aware of the behavioral signals being offered by the dog in the demonstration:

- The candidate must make allowances for any behavioral issues and demonstrate how to handle those issues should they occur.

- o This assessment will be considered not satisfactory if the training does not reflect appropriate action in the face of the dog's stress, discomfort or confusion.
  - The candidate will be assessed on how any untoward behavioral issue(s) that arise are handled.
  - The candidate will be assessed on their handling of the environment to enable optimal learning for the dog.
- The candidate must consider the dog's breed, age, personality, individual idiosyncrasies and needs.

IV. Running Training Classes

Note: A class is considered to be 3+ dogs (see notes below).

Two videos or live presentations are required. The candidate may choose one (1) from Group A and one (1) from Group B

Group A
- An Adult Beginners Class – Dogs must be over 12 months of age (video length: 15 minutes).
- A Juvenile Beginners Class – Dogs must be between 6-12 months of age (video length: 15 minutes).

Group B
- A Baby Puppy Class – Dogs must be between 8-12 weeks of age (video length: 15 minutes).
A Senior Puppy Class – Dogs must be between 13-24 weeks of age (video length: 15 minutes).

1. Candidate must be the sole instructor in these videos but is permitted to have an assistant.
    a. Assistant is just that, they will assist and not teach any of the class.
    b. Candidate must ensure the assistant is given clear instructions regarding expectations of their duties before the class begins.
        i. If, due to circumstance, the candidate needs to direct the assistant to help, the candidate must ensure this is done appropriately with due consideration to the assistant and the class.

2. The class must comprise beginner dogs and handlers (i.e. owners) in each of these demonstrations.
    a. The assessor does not want to see experienced handlers with beginner dogs or experienced dogs with beginner handlers.
        i. The assessor needs to be able to assess the candidate's ability with completely novice dogs and handlers.
3. The candidate needs to submit the names, ages and breeds of the dogs that are in each demonstration.
    a. There must be a minimum of three dogs in the class and a maximum of six dogs (unless the candidate has an assistant, and then the class may contain eight dogs).
    b. The candidate must submit a media release form if video is being used. This form contains the signatures of the human students in the class, allowing the candidate to use the video of them for the assessment.
    c. Without submission of the appropriate paperwork, videos will not be assessed.
        i. This component of the assessment is necessary for the candidate to understand privacy ethics and the need to seek written consent.
4. The video must be a basic pet dog manners class; not an agility class, a competition obedience class, a tracking class or any other dog sport class.
5. The video must not be of a dog-free lesson.
6. The complete lesson plan for the chosen week for each demonstration must be submitted with the video or to the assessor if a live presentation.
    a. Usually a program is run over several weeks. It is not necessary to see the plan for the whole program, but the candidate is required to submit a simple lesson plan for the full lesson for each demonstration.
    b. Without submission of the lesson plan, videos and demonstrations will not be assessed.
    c. It must be clear to the assessor who is the candidate, who is the assistant, which class is being taught and which week in the program is being demonstrated.
7. During each demonstration the candidate must demonstrate appropriate (suitable and proper for the circumstances i.e. polite, all-inclusive, etc.) interpersonal skills.
8. During each demonstration the candidate must demonstrate appropriate, effective, humane dog training skills.

9. During each demonstration the candidate must teach behaviors relevant to the age and level status of the class being taught for both human and canine clients.
10. During each demonstration the candidate must explain to the learners why they are teaching them the new exercise.
11. Each video demonstration must be filmed in one session. The candidate must not edit any 15-minute training videos.
    a. The candidate may begin the presentation at any time throughout the lesson, but the video must not stop and start, cutting out parts of the lesson.
12. Each video must show the candidate teaching a new exercise.
    a. The candidate is not expected to spend the entire 15 minutes on the one exercise. The candidate may show some revision of previous exercises or evidence of games played in class.
13. The candidate must also include a one (1) paragraph description of the suitability of their class training area including safety aspects (no more than 250 words).

The assessor will be looking for the following skills:

1. An understanding of human student learning styles:
    a. Visual – watching a demonstration.
    b. Auditory – listening to an explanation.
    c. Kinesthetic – practical application ("hands on").
2. The candidate's appropriate interaction with children or disabled people if they are in present in the class.
3. The candidate's appropriate interaction if there are cultural differences present in the class.
4. Class choreography:
    a. Instructor position in relation to students.
    b. Position and organization of dogs/guardians to minimize disruption and distress.
    c. The candidate has accurately assessed the suitability of the canine students in the class with regards to age, level of experience, temperament for working in a group class, i.e. nonaggressive and non- or minimally reactive.
    d. The use of barriers and environmental/management features where necessary.
    e. Appropriate choice of demonstration dog if used.

5. Lesson structure/content – should be designed to maximize and engage dogs and students.
6. The candidate's subject knowledge.
7. The candidate's handling skills – both dogs and people.
8. The candidate's sense of humor, if appropriate.
9. The candidate's patience.
10. The candidate's attending skills (to both dogs and handlers).
    a. Inclusive of all interactive communication skills.
11. The candidate's diplomacy, where needed.
12. The candidate's ability to correctly handle every aspect of the training class including safety, appropriate training skills, appropriate curriculum for the nominated class and the candidate's ability to keep order within the class.

Knowledge and Skill Requirements for Professional Trainers (Level 2)

Professional Canine Trainer - A Definition

The word Trainer may be defined in a number of ways. For the purposes of this model, we define a Canine Trainer as a professional who teaches obedience classes, day training, private training sessions, and board and train programs and who focuses primarily on pet dog skills and manners. A Canine Trainer is "a training professional skilled in the application of science and artistic endeavor who delivers results through the development of mutually respectful, caring relationships."

Eligibility

- All applicants must be able to demonstrate their training experience in at least one of the following ways:
    - 170 hours over the past 12 months of group training classes and/or private training of pet dog manners. One training hour unit is defined as 1 x 45-60 minutes of one group class or 1 x 45-60 minutes of private training.

  Or,

    - Over a period of 24 months, a minimum of 200 hours' experience of group training classes and/or private training of pet dog manners. One training hour unit is defined as 1 x 45-60 minutes of one group class or 1 x 45-60 minutes of private training.

- Applicants must have completed 20 continuing education credit hours at professional seminars, workshops and/or webinars during the previous two years or less.
- Applicants can be either full-time or part-time professionals or volunteers in a training environment; eligibility is determined by the number of hours of experience and acquisition of Continuing Education Units (CEU).
- Applicants must provide one written reference from a colleague who can confirm their date of entry into the industry and confirm their logged hours of training. A second reference must be provided from a client of the applicant or a veterinarian.
- Applicants must provide proof of business insurance (applies to North America, Australia and any other country that provides professional insurance) or insurance cover for the organization where they are working or volunteering.
- Renewal eligibility occurs every 24 months. Professional Trainers must provide proof of 20 CEUs.
- If the applicant is applying to undertake the Professional Trainer credential and has passed the Training Technician credential within the previous 12 months, permission may be given for some of the assessments to be waived. The assessments that may be waived are:
    - The conditioned emotional response.
    - Basic skills completed in the Training Technician assessments.
    - Running a class demonstration.

Assessment Process

The Professional Trainer assessment is divided into four sections:

Section I	Knowledge base assessment exam
Section II	Basic training skills videos or live demonstrations
Section III	Creating a positive conditioned emotional response video or live demonstration
Section IV	Running training classes videos or live demonstrations

Section I must be successfully completed before the other Sections can be undertaken.

I. Knowledge Base Requirements

Although many of the knowledge base requirements for Level Two are similar to Level One, the examination is more difficult and must ensure that the candidate has the required knowledge to undertake the job description above. An 85% pass mark is recommended to ensure knowledge competency.

Learning, Behavior and Training Skills:

Operant conditioning	Respondent conditioning
Bridging stimuli	Antecedents and antecedent control including setting events, motivating operations, discriminative stimuli
Applied Behavior Analysis terms (the ABCs)	Results of coercion
Adding cues	Learned helplessness
Stimulus control	Transferring stimulus control
Impulse control	Reinforcement schedules
Reinforcement ratios	Toys as reinforcers
Primary and secondary reinforcers	Intrinsic motivation and intrinsic reinforcers
Fluency	Latency
Forward and backward chaining i.e. the linking of the various components of a behavior from first to last, or last to first	Successive approximations
Luring, targeting, shaping	Extinction
Spontaneous recovery	Matching Law
Premack Principle	Law of Effect
Desensitization and counterconditioning	Sensitization
Habituation	

Biology, Anatomy, Health and Development:

Thermoregulation	Canine vital signs

General health and well-being	Anatomy
Body systems	Canine senses
Parasites	Fungal infections

Business Consulting and Best Practice:

Analogies and metaphors	Logical fallacies
Guarantees in dog training	Best practice procedures
Ethics	Humane hierarchies
People skills for dog trainers	Human learning styles

Ethology and Social Behavior:

Canine body language	Distance increasing signals
Distance decreasing signals	Cutoff signals
Canine vocalization	Ontogenetic behavior
Canine aggression	Canine evolution
Survival instincts	Critical periods
Separation anxiety	Predation

II. Basic Training Skills Provided in Person or by Video

As described under **Eligibility**, if the candidate has already successfully undertaken the Training Technician credential then it is only necessary for them to demonstrate those skills on the list not yet allocated for assessment.

If a candidate is entering at this level, rather than undertaking the Training Technician credential first, it will be necessary for all basic skills to be demonstrated, as described in _Knowledge and Skill Requirements for Training Technicians (Level 1)_.

III. Conditioned Emotional Response (CER)

As described under **Eligibility**, if the candidate has already successfully undertaken the Training Technician credential within the required timeframe, then it is not necessary for the Professional Trainer candidate to undertake this assessment.

If a candidate is entering at this level, rather than undertaking the Training Technician credential first, it will be necessary for the candidate to undertake the CER assessment, as described in _Knowledge and Skill Requirements for Training Technicians (Level 1)_.

IV. Running Training Classes

As described under **Eligibility**, if the candidate has already successfully undertaken the Training Technician credential within the required timeframe, then it is not necessary for the Professional Trainer candidate to undertake this assessment.

If a candidate is entering at this level, rather than undertaking the Training Technician credential first, it will be necessary for the candidate to undertake the training class assessment, as described in *Knowledge and Skill Requirements for Training Technicians (Level 1)*.

Knowledge and Skill Requirements for Professional Behavior Consultants (Level 3)

Professional Canine Behavior Consultant - A Definition

The word Consultant may be defined in a number of ways. The Pet Professional Accreditation Board (PPAB) defines a Consultant as a professional who undertakes consultations and focuses primarily on modifying pet behavior problems that are elicited by emotions. Consultants are also professional dog trainers who can competently teach obedience classes, day training, private training sessions, and board and train programs that focus on pet dog skills and manners. For the purposes of this model, a Consultant is a behavior and training professional skilled in the application of science and artistic endeavor, who delivers results through the development of mutually respectful, caring relationships.

Eligibility

- All applicants must be able to demonstrate their training experience in at least one of the following ways:
    - 300 hours over the past 12 months of group training classes and/or 150 hours of private training consultations. One training hour unit is defined as 1 x 45-60 minutes of one group class or 1 x 45-60 minutes of private training.
- Applicants must have completed 30 continuing education credit hours at professional seminars, workshops and/or webinars during the previous two years or less.
- Applicants can be either full-time or part-time professionals or volunteers in a training environment; eligibility is determined by the number of hours of experience and acquisition of Continuing Education Units (CEU).
- Applicants must provide one written reference from a colleague confirming their date of entry into the industry and confirming their logged hours of training. A second reference must be provided from a client of the applicant and a third from a veterinarian.
- Applicants must provide proof of business insurance (this applies to North America, Australia and any other countries that provide professional insurance) or insurance cover for the organization where they are working or volunteering.

- Renewal eligibility occurs every 24 months. Professional Canine Behavior Consultants must provide proof of 30 CEUs.
- If the applicant is applying to undertake the Professional Behavior Consultant credential and has passed the Professional Trainer credential within the last 12 months, permission may be given for some of the assessments to be waived. The assessments that may be waived are:
    - The conditioned emotional response.
    - Basic skills completed in the Training Technician assessments.
    - Running a class demonstration.

Assessment Process

The Professional Behavior Consultant assessment is divided into five sections:

Section I	Knowledge base assessment exam
Section II	Basic training skills videos or live demonstrations
Section III	Creating a positive conditioned emotional response video or live demonstration
Section IV	Running training classes videos or live demonstrations
Section V	Case studies

Section I must be successfully completed before the candidate can undertake Sections II – IV. Sections II-IV must be successfully completed before the candidate can undertake Section V.

I. **Knowledge Base Exam**

Although many of the knowledge base requirements for Level Three are similar to Level Two, the examination is far more difficult and must ensure that the candidate has the required knowledge to undertake the job description of Behavior Consultant. The pass mark for this examination would depend on the calculations determined by the professional body running the examination, but at no time should that pass mark be less than 85%.

The following are subjects about which a Professional Canine Behavior Consultant possess in their knowledge base:

Part 1: Learning and Behavior Modules

Module 1 - Operant Conditioning

- Explain in theory what operant conditioning is and its application
- Explain in theory how operant extinction works.
- Identify the potential strengths and weaknesses of each quadrant in behavior change procedures.
- Understand when, during behavior change, it is applicable to use respondent conditioning protocols and/or operant conditioning protocols.
- Define and differentiate between antecedent and postcedent training protocols and their effect on behavior.

Module 2 - Respondent Conditioning and Nonassociative Learning

- Explain in theory what respondent conditioning is and its application.
- The roles of reflexes, unconditioned and conditioned stimuli, and the conditioning process.
- Explain in theory how respondent extinction works.
- Explain the difference between counterconditioning and desensitization.
- Explain habituation and sensitization.
- Explain what high order conditioning is and how it occurs.
- Be able to implement a behavior change plan that accounts for the problematic stimulus and includes the reinforcement strategy, a counterconditioning plan, a desensitization hierarchy, and relaxation protocols.
- Know how to implement basic counterconditioning procedures to develop positive conditioned emotional responses for key training tools and equipment, and behavioral problems.
- Have a strong understanding of nonassociative learning, associative learning and social/observational learning and be able to contrast and compare the behavioral perspective on behavior with the ethological and medical model

orientation.

Module 3 - Aversives and Punishments: Differential Reinforcement as Alternatives to Using Punishment

- Compare and contrast positive punishment with negative punishment.
- Know how to manage clients' interactions with their pets to avoid further use of aversives.
- Understand what aversives are and their potential to create unwanted fallout behavior.
- Understand the various types of differential reinforcement schedules and their use (i.e. DRI, DRO and DRA).

Module 4 - Training Techniques and Theory

- Theory and application of luring, prompting, shaping, capturing, and targeting.
- How to put behaviors under stimulus control, transfer and maintain stimulus control.
- Primary and secondary reinforcement, which to use and when.
- Reinforcement schedules (fixed, variable, etc.).
- Understand how differential reinforcement can/should be used as a substitute for punishment
- Matching Law, Premack Principle, and differential outcome effect.

Module 5 - Applied Behavior Analysis

- Canine social heritage and adaptive significance of complex behavior patterns in the language of Applied Behavior Analysis (ABA).
- ABA terms and definitions.

Module 6 - Functional Assessments

- Possess an applied knowledge of behavior measurement systems including baseline, goal and behavior dimensions.
- Understand dimensions of behavior that can be measured, including latency.

- Understand the three-term ABC contingency, including direct and distant antecedents, discriminative stimuli, setting events, and motivating operations.
- Understand how setting events and motivating operations impact behavior.
- When conducting a functional assessment that comprises an informant interview, direct observation and functional analysis, the candidate must be able to explain when and why, given the risks, they would embark on the third component, the functional analysis.
- Functionally analyze behavior and the relationships in the three-term or two-term contingencies.

Part 2: Biology and Anatomy Modules

Module 1 - Basic Anatomy of the Dog

- Canine anatomy and physiology.
- Prevention of illness or injury through care and management.

Module 2 - Canine Genetics and the Canine Sensory System

- Natural and artificial selection.
- How genetics affect behavior.
- How breed development and function affect sensory systems.

Module 3 - Nervous and Endocrine Systems

- Central and peripheral nervous system; autonomic nervous system.
- Neuronal function and communication.
- Sensory exposure and synaptic growth during key developmental stages.
- Roles of key neurotransmitters – dopamine, serotonin, glutamate, GABA.
- The brain and limbic system (canine emotions and memory).
- Learning processes.
- Reflexes – primary and secondary effects on behavior.
- The major endocrine glands and role in behavior.
- Hormones – their function and effect on behavior.

Module 4 - Integumentary, Cardiovascular, Respiratory, Digestive, and Urinary Systems

- The integument system and prevention of illness/injury.
- Role of exocrine sweat glands/thermoregulation.
- Heart rate variations across the lifespan – normal heart rate of puppies/dogs.
- Heart rate across structural sizes.
- Normal respiratory rate for dogs.
- Respiration and thermoregulation.
- Protein, carbohydrates, fats, vitamins, and supplements.
- Kidney function, excretion, and homeostasis.

Part 3: Ethology and Social Behavior Modules

Module One - Canine Communication and Social Behavior

- Species typical behaviors.
- Body language.
- Facial expression.
- Rituals and their roles (e.g. play, aggression); meta signals.
- Affiliative/agonistic/mixed/ambivalent signals and contexts in which they may occur.
- Auditory, visual, olfactory and vocal communication.
- How vocalization reflects the emotional state.

Module Two - Negative Emotional States: Cause and Manifestation

- Superstitious behavior.
- Fear, anger, aggression, and anxiety.
- The impact of fear on a dog's ability to communicate.
- How fear is conditioned.
- Contexts in which active/passive appeasement and/or aggression may occur plus physical and vocal manifestations thereof.
- How external factors/stress/context affects communication.
- Stress and distress.

Module Three - Physiology, Behavior and Evolution

- Fight or flight response.
- Elements affecting behavior (learned/genetic); how they occur; why they develop.
- Effect of operant and respondent conditioning on behavior and how these are influenced by external stimuli.
- Key figures in behavioral science (Pavlov, Skinner, etc.).
- Differences between feral/stray/tame dogs and how this status may affect behavior.
- Biological evolution and speciation of the domestic dog.
- Evolution of the wolf.
- How wolves are different to dogs.
- Breed characteristics/differences; risk of generalization.
- How different breeds display different components of motor action patterns.

Part 4: Health and Development Modules

Module One - Working with Veterinarians and Diseases in Dogs

- Understand when physical and behavioral signs may be indicative/suggest that a veterinary behaviorist referral is required.
- Be proficient in recognizing behavioral and physical indicators that deem it necessary for a dog to be referred to a veterinarian.
- Be able to outline own role and roles of the veterinarian and client as a cooperative relationship established to achieve the behavioral objectives.
- Recognize and be able to describe the prodrome, ictal and postictal stages of a canine seizure.
- Describe common cognitive dysfunctional behavior in canines and be able to recognize nonspecific signs that are extremely variable.
- Describe household management changes that will be helpful to supporting a veterinary behaviorist's treatment plan.
- Explain the process for remaining in one's field of expertise and knowing when not to dispense advice across lines of competence, such nutrition, medical procedures and pharmacological intervention.
- Be familiar with and be able to describe the key diseases a domesticated dog is at risk of contracting throughout his life cycle.

Module Two - Understanding Canine Development

- Recognize the difficulty in guiding pet owners on the subtle changes in canine behavior that may be developmental versus behavioral.
- Discuss the sensitive periods of development of the dog, including the process of socialization and its importance on canine development.
- Understand the history and development of canine temperament tests and the propositions for and against them regarding the welfare of dogs.
- Understand and be able to compare the learning ability of canines at different stages of their lives.
- Understand at what time and for how long puppies experience a sensitive period in their development.
- Explain how a lack of critical and timely exposure and socialization impacts a canine's neurological development and the resulting effect on healthy mental development.
- Understand how appropriate amounts of physical activity and mental enrichment programs can contribute toward the normal development of canines.
- Possess a comprehensive understanding of all the necessary puppy development skills and key behaviors required to provide for a mentally and physically well-developed dog acclimatized to sharing a home with his human family.

Module Three - Understanding and Recognizing Mental Health

- Understand and recognize when a behavioral problem may already be or may become pathological and/or is rooted in anxiety, as well as the neurochemical response to that anxiety.
- Understand the differences between nonaffective and affective aggression in canines or operant versus respondent aggression.
- Understand and recognize abnormal canine behavior with or without aggression and the necessary role of a veterinary behaviorist in diagnostics criteria and description.
- Understand what factors should be taken into consideration when working with a breeder to ensure a puppy is provided adequate and sufficient exercise, enrichment and handling.
- Understand the role of play in canine behavior and its place in behavior change programs given that it is mutually incompatible with stress or fear.
- Identify the different types of play and how these can impact a dog's natural

drives and sensory/motor systems.
- Discuss the specific positive reinforcement training procedures and protocols that can be implemented to decrease the likelihood that a dog will inflict physical damage on another dog or person.
- Explain how humane, effective, positive reinforcement training contributes to the feeling of empowerment for a canine and how this impacts problem solving and reduces the propensity for problematic behaviors.
- Explain how allowing the dog to choose his involvement in training impacts empowerment.

Part 5: Business and Consulting Skills and Best Practices

Module 1 - Managing Risk and Liability

- Explain the liability risks open to pet guardians and pet industry professionals and how these can be mitigated by conducting sound consultations and refraining from dispensing advice in the absence of the necessary and relevant information.
- Thoroughly define the ethics of topics such as competence, confidentiality, informed consent, ethics of assessment and diagnosis.
- Compare and contrast the individual roles of each person involved in a behavior change program and the individual responsibilities for liability, informed consent and confidentiality.
- Explain and discuss the merits of the different models of ethical decision-making and how the candidate will provide a safe working environment for both people and their dogs.
- Explain using ABA terms and the science of behavior why it is considered unethical to make specific guarantees on one's training and behavior consulting services.
- Define methods of moral reasoning and ethical challenges versus dilemmas.
- Act professionally and diligently when functionally analyzing behavior, taking into consideration all aspects of safety, ethics and informed consent.

Module 2 - Managing Clients

- Understand the individual and unique learning opportunities presented by working with different clients and which supportive people skills can enhance client learning.

- Understand how an individual's learning style may impact one's ability to teach an individual or a group, and how to best manage an interaction to ensure a win-win outcome.
- Recognize that behavior consulting takes place in an emotionally charged situation; the candidate must show they can make recommendations for dealing with argumentative, contrary and challenging clients so they can be an effective consultant.
- Explain how candidate will "negotiate" realistic goals and a means of achieving them in a manner that empowers the client and promotes success of one's recommended programs.
- Be proficient in making recommendations to clients on how they can practice their mechanical skills.
- Recognize and be able to implement good client coaching tactics to ensure the necessary transfer of knowledge.

Module 3 - Program Development (High Level Theory)

- Describe the intended final product of the functional assessment and how a contingency statement is developed.
- In each behavior change program, be able to accurately define the components the candidate will use to determine gauge the success of the plan.
- Be familiar with the procedures for developing a behavior change program to address the key and most prevalent problematic behaviors experienced by professional dog trainers and behavior consultants.
- Understand why engaging a dog's mind in active enjoyment is beneficial to his well-being.
- Understand the appropriateness and application of different training protocols.
- Be proactive and creative in solving problem behaviors and finding substitute behaviors.
- When developing behavior change programs as a best practice, utilize the development of contingency statements and applied behavior analysis.
- Explain the concept of critical thinking and the various types of logical fallacies.
- Understand as a best practice the practical applications and necessity of use

of functional assessments and the means to understand and analyze behavior.

Module 4 - Program Development (Mechanics and Practice)

- Demonstrate an understanding of the humane hierarchy model and discuss its limitations.
- Be able to recognize training equipment and management aids that work through the application of aversives and be able to discuss the merits of different equipment that, if conditioned correctly, can be used safely and without discomfort to the dog.
- Explain why differential reinforcement an acceptable replacement for punishment is and how its protocols work without using escape or avoidance contingencies.
- Recognize as a best practice when to train individual behaviors versus the appropriate use of sequencing or forward and back chaining.
- Practice competent implementation of desensitization programs for client application.
- Know when to use cold trials as a best practice in behavior change programs.
- Recognize when to make use of postcedent protocols given the behavior reinforcement history.
- Be competent in the training mechanics of bridges, placement of reinforcement and latency of reinforcement.
- Understand the appropriateness of using demonstration dogs in class and which dogs are most suitable.

Part 6: Scientific and Practical Method
Module 1 - Creating Protocols/Data

- Demonstrate an understanding of scientific method when creating a protocol for behavior modification.
- Explain how reliability and validity are measured when working with continuous and discrete data.
- Compare and contrast experimental and anecdotal evidence, from where these types of data are gathered, and how they are best used by the trainer or consultant.
- Explain why empirical data does not prove causation, and the limitations of using empirical data when developing a contingency statement.

- Understand the relationship and difference between a dependent and independent variable when measuring and interpreting data.

II. Basic Training Skills Provided in Person or by Video

As described under **Eligibility**, if the candidate has already successfully undertaken the Professional Trainer credential then it is only necessary for them to demonstrate those skills on the list not yet allocated for assessment.

If a candidate is entering at this level, rather than undertaking the Training Technician and/or Professional Trainer credentials first, it will be necessary for all basic skills to be demonstrated, as described in *Knowledge and Skill Requirements for Training Technicians (Level 1)*.

III. Conditioned Emotional Response (CER)

As described under **Eligibility**, if the candidate has already successfully undertaken the Professional Trainer credential within the required timeframe, then it is not necessary for the Professional Behavior Consultant candidate to undertake this assessment.

If a candidate is entering at this level, rather than undertaking the Professional Trainer credential first, it will be necessary for the candidate to undertake the CER assessment, as described in *Knowledge and Skill Requirements for Professional Trainer (Level 2)*.

IV. Running Training Classes

As described under **Eligibility**, if the candidate has already successfully undertaken the Professional Trainer credential within the required timeframe, then it is not necessary for the Professional Behavior Consultant candidate to undertake this assessment.

If a candidate is entering at this level, rather than undertaking the Training Technician and/or Professional Trainer credentials first, it will be necessary for the candidate to undertake the training class assessment, as described in *Knowledge and Skill Requirements for Professional Trainer (Level 2)*.

V. Case Studies

Case studies show the ability for a professional to systematically work through a behavior consulting case using applied behavior analysis. The behavior analytical approach does not rely on guesswork, trial and error tactics or anecdotal recommendations, but systematically identifies the functional relationship the behavior has with the environment. When these relationships have been identified, then efficient and effective solutions can be developed and implemented. A recommended template for the development of professional Case Studies can be found in *Appendix E: The Recommended Case Study Template for Behavior Consultants*.

Appendix C: The Recommended Career Stage Mentoring Model

Career Stage Mentoring. Where are you now? What is your goal?

Competency demands that a professional trainer working with pets must have the required knowledge, education, skill development, and experience necessary to meet best practice. (*See also* [Chapter Seven: Competency Is Mission Critical](#).)

Pre-Level 1 to Level 1: Technician

Mentoring for Pre-Level 1 to Level 1: Technician

Definition Pre-Level 1: **No formally assessed knowledge or skills, no years of experience, someone starting out in the industry.**

Definition Level 1: Technician: **The Technician is capable of teaching pet manners classes with the knowledge of their own limitations in resolving behavior problems and with the ability to understand when referral to a more qualified professional is necessary.**

Who should mentor Pre-Level 1: Technician? **Optimal would be a Level 2: Trainer, but a Level 1: Technician with 5+ years' experience, together with required continuing education units (CEU) would be acceptable.**

Mentor's Role
1. Assist mentee in determining education that meets the requirements for the desired goals of scientifically based, positive reinforcement training:
    a. Discuss objectives:
        i. What are the mentee's goals; short- and long-term?
        ii. Suggest appropriate educational facilities for gaining and testing knowledge.
        iii. Assist mentee with application for educational facility.
        iv. If needed, be available to advise and guide during educational period.
    b. Who will be involved?
        i. Mentor, mentee, educational facility and staff.
    c. Make time:
        i. Mentor to create regular, agreed upon meeting times with mentee, to encourage and discuss mentee's progress.

ii. A minimum of weekly meetings should be scheduled.
   d. Mentor and mentee must feel comfortable with each other to gain the most from the relationship:
      i. Ensure clear pathways should either mentor or mentee seek a change (i.e. if either mentor or mentee feel uncomfortable with each other, there should be an avenue for an alternative pairing).
   e. Be a support base in times of mentee insecurity or struggle with education.
2. Practical skills can be learned by mentee at the same time as knowledge is being gained:
   a. Mentor to assist in acquisition of required practical skills for Level 1: Technician. This can be taught directly by the mentor, or the mentor can assist in arranging for the mentee's training of practical skills:
      i. Mentee needs practical training skills and coaching (people) skills for undertaking group class work.
      ii. Mentor helps arrange practical skills training, trains those skills themselves, or supports the mentee if the skills form part of the knowledge assessment from the educational facility.
      iii. Mentee needs to be assessed on their ability to apply practical training and coaching skills.
3. While undertaking formal learning, the mentee can gain experience by taking on assistant duties with the mentor or with a facility the mentor helps the mentee to find:
   a. If experience is gained with the mentor, time should be allowed to discuss the mentee's progress:
      i. This could be done daily, weekly or as demanded by the mentoring objectives previously agreed between mentor and mentee.
   b. An agreed feedback format should be adhered to:
      i. Necessary for feedback are the following:
         1. The mentor should listen to the perspective of the mentee.
         2. The mentor should then share their perspective of the performance.
         3. Based on the points of the discussion, together, mentor and mentee should develop a plan for the progression of skills learning and assessment.

4. To attain Level 1: Technician competency, the mentor helps the mentee to achieve the following competencies:
    a. Correct knowledge level, as assessed by formal examination.
    b. Practical skills and coaching ability by direct observation, discussion and assessment of required skills.
    c. Experience in the field over the period of learning and formal testing.
    d. Should the mentee not meet the requirements for Level 1: Technician, then ongoing assistance from the mentor will be required to build on the mentee's knowledge and skills:
        i. Under these circumstances, the mentor should help the mentee to fully understand where they are not yet competent and help or assist in finding help, so the mentee can strengthen the knowledge and/or skills required.

Level 1: Technician to Level 2: Trainer

Mentoring for Level 1: Technician to Level 2: Trainer

Definition Level 1: Technician: **The Level 1: Technician is capable of teaching pet manners classes with the knowledge of their own limitations in resolving behavior problems and with the ability to understand when referral to a more qualified professional is necessary.**

Definition Level 2: Trainer: **This level of service offers similar abilities as the technician but with a deeper understanding of the scientific principles involved in training, as well as the ability to better understand and assist with minor behavioral problems and the knowledge of appropriate referral to an animal behavior consultant when necessary.**

Who should mentor Level 2: Trainer? **Optimal would be Level 3: Behavior Consultant, but Level 2: Trainer with 5+ years' experience together with required continuing education units would be acceptable.**

Mentor's Role:

1. Assist mentee in determining education that meets the requirements for the desired goals of scientifically based, positive reinforcement training:
    a. Discuss objectives:
        i. What are the mentee's goals; short- and long-term?

ii. Suggest appropriate educational facilities for gaining and testing knowledge:
    1. Mentees who have long-term experience with some formally assessed education may not need to undertake more formal study in order to achieve Level 2: Trainer. However, the required knowledge and skills must still be formally assessed as competent at this level before a Level 2: Trainer qualification can be recognized.
iii. Assist mentee with application for educational facility if required.
iv. If needed, be available to advise and guide during educational period.

b. Who will be involved?
    i. Mentor, mentee, educational facility and staff.
c. Make time:
    i. Mentor to create regular, agreed upon meeting times with mentee to encourage and discuss mentee's progress.
    ii. A minimum of weekly meetings should be scheduled.
d. Mentor and mentee must feel comfortable with each other to gain the most from the relationship:
    i. Ensure clear pathways should either mentor or mentee seek a change (i.e. if either mentor or mentee feel uncomfortable with each other, there should be an avenue for an alternative pairing).
e. Be a support base in times of mentee insecurity or struggle with education.

2. Practical skills can be learned by mentee at the same time as knowledge is being gained:
    a. A mentee who has at least two years of service with a minimum of 200 hours of group class training or private training of pet manners over the two years as a Level 1: Technician may only need minimal guidance for attaining Level 2: Trainer qualification.
    b. Irrespective of years of service, to attain the Level 2: Trainer qualification, both knowledge and practical skills must be assessed as competent at this higher level and the mentor should be able to assist with seeking appropriate, formal testing facilities:
        i. Should the mentee have attained the Level 1: Technician status within a 12-month period before undertaking assessment for

Level 2: Trainer, some credit transfer of acquired basic and coaching skills may be possible. The mentor should discuss with the mentee the points relative to this and be able to inform them of their suitability for this transfer.
  c. Mentor to assist in acquisition of required practical skills for Level 2: Trainer either directly or by assisting in arranging for mentee's training of practical skills:
     ii. Mentee needs practical training skills and coaching (people) skills for undertaking group class work together with a broader knowledge of minor behavior problems and an understanding of the limitations of a Level 2: Trainer when faced with more complex behavior issues.
     iii. Mentee needs to be assessed on their ability to apply practical training and coaching skills.
3. While undertaking formal learning, the mentee can gain experience by taking on assistant duties with the mentor, or with a facility the mentor helps the mentee to find:
  a. If experience is gained with the mentor, time should be allowed to discuss the mentee's progress:
     i. This could be done daily, weekly, or as demanded by the mentoring objectives previously agreed between mentor and mentee.
  b. If the mentee has at least three–five years' experience with at least 250 hours of group class training or private training of pet manners over the time and does not undertake formal study to ensure suitability for Level 2: Trainer qualifications, the mentor should observe the knowledge and skills of the mentee and discuss strengths and shortfalls with the mentee before formal assessment.
  c. An agreed feedback format should be adhered to:
     i. Necessary for feedback are the following:
        1. The mentor should listen to the perspective of the mentee.
        2. The mentor should then share their perspective of the performance.
        3. Based on the points of the discussion, together, mentor and mentee should develop a plan for the progression of skills learning and assessment.

4. To attain Level 2: Trainer competency, the mentor helps the mentee to achieve the following competencies:
    a. Correct knowledge level, as assessed by formal examination.
    b. Practical skills and coaching ability by direct observation, discussion and assessment of required skills.
    c. Experience in the field over the period of learning and formal testing.
    d. Should the mentee not meet the requirements for Level 2: Trainer, then ongoing assistance from the mentor will be required to build on the mentee's knowledge and skills:
        i. Under these circumstances the mentor should help the mentee to fully understand where they are not yet competent and help or assist in finding help, so the mentee can strengthen the knowledge and/or skills required to reach Level 2: Trainer.

Level 2: Trainer to Level 3: Behavior Consultant

Mentoring for Level 2: Trainer to Level 3: Behavior Consultant

Definition Level 2: Trainer: **This level of service offers similar abilities as the Level 2: Trainer, but with a deeper understanding of the scientific principles involved in training, as well as the ability to better understand and assist with minor behavioral problems and the knowledge of appropriate referral to a veterinarian or board certified veterinary behaviorist when necessary.**

Definition Level 3: Behavior Consultant: **A Behavior Consultant is a professional who undertakes private consultations and focuses primarily on behavior change programs rather than the delivery of training skills. Level 3: Behavior Consultants are also professional dog trainers who can competently undertake the Level 1: Technician and Level 2: Trainer requirements.**

The Level 3: Behavior Consultant delivers results through empathy and mutual respect for both client and pet, paired with a full understanding of behavioral science.

The Level 3: Behavior Consultant is aware of their limitations in the ability to prescribe and diagnose and can refer to a veterinarian or board certified veterinary behaviorist with more academic and expansive knowledge. *Note: Any person wishing to become a Level 3: Behavior Consultant MUST first show proof of formal testing of skills and knowledge equal to Level 2: Trainer.*

Who should mentor Level 3: Behavior Consultant? **Optimal would be a Veterinarian or Board Certified Veterinary Behaviorist, but a Level 3: Behavior Consultant with 5+ years' experience together with required continuing education units would be acceptable.**

Mentor's Role

1. Assist mentee in determining an educational facility that meets the requirements for the desired goals of scientifically based, positive reinforcement behavior modification.
    a. Discuss objectives:
        i. What are the mentee's goals; short- and long-term?
        ii. Suggest appropriate educational facilities for gaining and testing knowledge:
            1. A mentee who has undertaken study only to the Level 2: Trainer stage is not yet ready to be assessed on the knowledge or skills required of a Level 3: Behavior Consultant credential.
            2. The mentor needs to ensure that the mentee understands the much greater responsibilities undertaken by a Level 3: Behavior Consultant and the need for appropriate education in this field.
        iii. Assist mentee with application for educational facility if required.
        iv. If needed, be available to advise and guide during educational period.
    b. Who will be involved?
        i. Mentor, mentee, educational facility and staff, consenting clients of mentor or an appropriate consultant who allows the mentee access to their cases.
    c. Make time:
        i. Mentor to create regular, agreed upon meeting times with mentee to encourage and discuss mentee's progress.
        ii. A minimum of weekly meetings should be scheduled.
    d. Mentor and mentee must feel comfortable with each other to gain the most from the relationship:

i. Ensure clear pathways should either mentor or mentee seek a change (i.e. if either mentor or mentee feel uncomfortable with each other, there should be an avenue for an alternative pairing).
    e. Be a support base in times of mentee insecurity or struggle with education.
2. Practical skills can be learned by mentee at the same time as knowledge is being gained:
    a. The mentor should take the mentee under their guidance or assist the mentee in gaining opportunities to understudy current appropriately qualified behavior consultants.
    b. A mentee who has long years of service as a Level 2: Trainer may be familiar with many behavior modification techniques:
        i. Irrespective of years of service, to attain a Level 3: Behavior Consultant qualification, both knowledge and practical skills must be assessed as competent at this higher level and the mentor should be able to assist with seeking appropriate, formal testing facilities.
        ii. Should the mentee have attained the Level 2: Trainer status within a 12-month period before undertaking assessment for Level 3: Behavior Consultant, some credit transfer of acquired basic and coaching skills may be possible. The mentor should discuss with the mentee the points relative to this and be able to inform the mentee of their suitability for this transfer.
    c. Mentor to assist in acquisition of required practical skills for Level 3: Behavior Consultant either directly or by assisting in arranging for mentee's training of practical skills:
        i. Together with the basic skills and coaching abilities acquired through Level 1: Technician and Level 2 Trainer, a Level 3: Behavior Consultant needs to demonstrate specific skills related to Applied Behavior Analysis. It is the mentor's duty to ensure that together with formal education regarding these skills, the mentee is exposed to seeing these methods appropriately performed in the field. If the mentor is not able to have the mentee observe their own clients, then the mentor needs to assist the mentee to find appropriate consultants who are able to assist.

3. While undertaking formal learning, the mentee can gain experience by taking on assistant duties with the mentor or with a suitable facility the mentor helps the mentee to find.
    a. If experience is gained with the mentor, time should be allowed to discuss the mentee's progress:
        i. This could be done daily, weekly, or as demanded by the mentoring objectives previously agreed between mentor and mentee.
        ii. If experience is gained elsewhere, the mentor must still consult with the mentee about progress and, with permission of the mentee, the mentor should also be able to seek information from the organization/person the mentee is working with.
    b. An agreed feedback format should be adhered to:
        i. Necessary for feedback are the following:
            1. The mentor should listen to the perspective of the mentee.
            2. The mentor should then share their perspective of the performance.
            3. Based on the points of the discussion, together mentor and mentee should develop a plan for the progression of skills learning and assessment.
4. To attain Level 3: Behavior Consultant competency, the mentor helps the mentee to achieve the following:
    a. Correct knowledge level, as assessed by formal examination.
    b. Practical skills, coaching ability and Applied Behavior Analysis skills by direct observation, discussion and assessment of required skills.
    c. Experience in the field over the period of learning and formal testing.
    d. Should the mentee not meet the requirements for Level 3: Behavior Consultant, then ongoing assistance from the mentor will be required to build on the mentee's knowledge and skills:
        i. Under these circumstances, the mentor should help the mentee to fully understand where they are not yet competent and help or assist in finding help, so the mentee can strengthen the knowledge and/or skills required to reach Level 3: Behavior Consultant.

Appendix D: The Recommended Consumer Acknowledgement Form for Transparency in Dog Training/Behavior Consulting Services

Before engaging a dog trainer, dog behavior consultant or other dog training service, consumers have the right to transparency in terms of the risks and benefits associated with the services provided. Consumers are entitled to the knowledge of whether the selected professional uses a predominantly positive reinforcement training philosophy or whether they use alternative methods that, according to the growing body of scientific research, can cause physical and/or psychological damage to the dog. The consumer's rights should also include a knowledge of the professional's choice of tools and how they are used.

Before undertaking the training/behavior change plan of their selected professional, the consumer must be comfortable that the following information has been received and any questions answered to their satisfaction.

The professional discussed with me or showed me their: 1. Formal training/behavior consulting credentials gained 2. Letters of reference and/or client testimonials 3. Detailed information regarding their training philosophy and practices 4. A list of tools that may be used during the training/behavior change program and provided education on how they would be used	Yes Yes Yes Yes	No No No No
The professional has undertaken recent (within 12 months) continuing education seminars/workshops or courses and has provided relevant documentation	Yes	No
The professional named and explained the relevant professional organizations with which they are associated	Yes	No
The professional allowed me to view some of their training in either a class situation or via video	Yes	No
After time spent with my dog the professional has provided me with a written training/behavior change plan specific to my dog and his circumstances and based on mutually agreeable goals	Yes	No

Pet Training and Behavior Consulting: A Model for Raising the Bar to Protect Professionals, Pets and Their People

The professional answered my questions regarding the training/behavior change plan in a proficient and transparent manner	Yes	No
The professional allowed me the opportunity to provide input into my dog's training/behavior change plan	Yes	No
In relation to the training philosophy used, the professional explained to me what happens when my dog gets it right and what happens when he makes a mistake, as well as the precise consequences that would be orchestrated by the professional in each case	Yes	No
Based on my dog's size, age, health and breed as well as his training plan/behavior change plan, the professional explained which training techniques and equipment will be used with my dog	Yes	No
The professional explained any risks or dangers related to the techniques and tools that will be used on my dog and outlined any potential physical or emotional fallout	Yes	No
The professional explained to me that I have the right to refuse their use of certain techniques/equipment on my dog	Yes	No
The professional explained to me my right to terminate my dog's training/behavior change plan at any time	Yes	No
The professional explained to me that the training/behavior change plan may need to be amended, based on my dog's reactions to the techniques and equipment used	Yes	No
The professional explained to me that before undertaking any techniques or using any training tools not discussed in the training/behavior change plan, they will place the changes in writing and that I will need to sign off on them before they are implemented	Yes	No
Prior to any punishment or corrections being used in my dog's training/behavior change plan, I will be advised of exactly what the professional plans or may plan to do or use and will be afforded the time to question this and offer my informed consent	Yes	No
The professional confirmed that they will use only the training methods/equipment nominated in the signed training/behavior change plan or in any altered training plans on which we concur and that I have signed	Yes	No

The professional confirmed that the dog training/behavior consulting business they represent is insured, and that the insurance covers my dog in case of illness, injury, loss or death in the care of the professional or the professional's business	Yes	No
It was agreed that, should my dog require medical care and/or treatment while in the care of the professional, I have been able to nominate my preferred veterinary provider to whom my dog should be taken	Yes	No
I agree to the professional using the minimal amount of physical force possible to restrain my dog to ensure safety in an on-the-spot emergency that places my dog in danger or if a person or another dog's life is in danger.	Yes	No
Both parties agree that, if my dog's training/behavior change plan includes training while I am not present, the professional may use only those techniques, methods or pieces of equipment nominated in the original plan	Yes	No
The professional agrees that in the event of any training services taking place in my absence then a minimum of 2 minutes of video will be provided by them for each skill trained	Yes	No
By signing this document, the professional has confirmed their commitment to using our agreed training/behavior change plan and to confirm any changes in writing before using any alternatives not included in the original plan	Yes	No

We certify that we have discussed all items above regarding the training/behavior consulting of the dog belonging to his legal owner and certify that all conditions above will be met.

Name of Dog:	
Signature of Legal Dog Owner:	
Printed Name of Legal Dog Owner:	
Signature of Professional:	
Printed Name of Professional:	

Name of Employer/ Business (if applicable):	
Date:	

Appendix E: The Recommended Case Study Template for Behavior Consultants

Section 1: Client

a) Do you have permission from your client to use their dog as a case study?
b) How long has the client had the dog?
c) Has the client owned dogs before?
d) If so, which breed(s)?
e) How busy is the client's home?
f) Give details of all other pets (name, age, breed) and people (name, age, occupation) in the household.

Section 2: Dog(s) Presenting with the Behavior Problem

a. Name of dog.
b. Breed or composition.
c. Age of dog.
d. Sex of dog.
e. Is the dog spayed/neutered?
f. If yes, at what age?
g. How long has the client had the dog?
h. Has the dog had other owners?
i. If yes, how many?
j. If yes, why was the dog given up (state unknown if the owner has no information on this)?
k. What is the dog's reinforcement history with primary care taker?
l. What is the dog's reinforcement history with other individuals in the household?

Section 3: Dog's Health

a. Has the dog had a recent veterinary checkup?
b. Did the vet have a special interest in behavior?
c. Was the dog also seen by a veterinary behaviorist?
d. If yes, provide details.
e. Did you notice any limping or "lopsided" physical behaviors or any other unusual physical characteristics?
f. If yes, provide details.
g. Does the dog have any current medical conditions?
h. If yes, please indicate the nature of the problem.
i. Does this dog have functional structure, free of twisted limbs or free of poor structure that may be in need of medical attention?
j. If the dog has a medical condition, is he/she taking medication or require other specific treatment (give details)?
k. Is the dog up-to-date on vaccinations?
l. When did the dog last have a fecal test?
m. Is the dog on heartworm prevention/dewormer?

Section 4: Dog's Diet

a. What is the dog fed?
b. If the dog eats manufactured pet food, what is the brand(s)?
c. How is the dog fed (feeding schedule/free feeding)?
d. What type of treats/snacks?

Section 5: Dog's Housing

a. Where does the dog sleep?
b. How many hours a night does the dog sleep?
c. Is the sleep interrupted?
d. How well does the dog relax in the home when there is no activity?
e. Where does the dog stay if left home alone?
f. How long is the dog left home alone?
g. How frequently is the dog left home alone?

Section 6: Dog's Exercise and Mental Stimulation

a. How does the client exercise the dog?
b. How long does the exercise last?
c. Is the dog responsive to toys?
d. If yes, which toys?
e. Does the dog have regular access to dog chews/chew toys?
f. Does the dog have access to play time with other dogs?
g. Does the dog enjoy the company of other dogs?
h. If no, give details.
i. Does the client take the dog out with them on errands/to work/visit friends and family etc.?
j. If yes, give details/frequency.

Section 7: Dog's Training History

a. Did the dog attend a puppy socialization class?
b. Has the client attended any training classes with the dog?
c. If yes, give details.
d. Does the client spend any time training the dog at home?
e. If yes, give details (i.e. what type of training, how often does it occur).
f. What is the training equipment currently being used and what equipment has been used in the past?
g. Assessment of known cues.
h. Recommendation of needed cues.

Section 8: Initial Assessment - Behavior Problem(s)

a. Give details of the problem behavior(s) as reported by the client, anecdotal data.
b. Has the dog had a veterinary checkup regarding this specific behavior problem?
c. If yes, what was the outcome?

d. How does the dog behave during the consult (general observations)?
   e. Prior to your intervention, was the behavior getting worse, staying the same or improving?

Section 9: Functional Assessment

   a. Add your detailed functional assessment here (use behavior analytic language where applicable and include details of multiple contingencies).
   b. Detail the behavior in measurable terms.
   c. Explain the antecedent package and postcedent package identifying the relevant components.
   d. Assess the dog's emotional state prior, during and after the problem behavior and his overall mood state when not engaging in the problem behavior, and how your behavior change recommendations will address this.
   e. Did you conduct a functional analysis?
   f. If no, explain why not.
   g. If yes, give details.
   h. Detail your contingency statement regarding the behavior?

Section 10: Behavior Modification Plan

   a. Detail your suggestions for the behavior modification plan (include details of any equipment or management protocols you recommend the client use/implement as well as given time scales, if any).
   b. Did you recommend involvement of a vet for pharmacological intervention? If yes, give details (which drug(s) the vet prescribed and why).
   c. Explain how many sessions were planned and how components of the behavior change plan were broken down across the sessions.

Section 11: Owner Compliance

   a. How many sessions did you see the client for?

b. What were your perceptions of the owner in terms of owner compliance?
c. Do you feel the entire household is onboard with working with the dog?
d. What are the client's goals in dealing with the behavior problem(s)?

Section 12: Follow-Up

a. Did you conduct any follow-up visits regarding this case?
b. If yes, how many?
c. If no, state why not.
d. Did you conduct any follow-up by phone, text or email (state which ones and how often)?
e. What was the outcome of this case?
f. Were you and/or clients satisfied with the outcome of this case?
g. If no, what do you feel you or the client (or both) could have done differently to change the outcome?

Appendix F: The Recommended Corporation Professional Code of Conduct and Ethics Pledge

Preamble

The survival and enhancement of the pet industry depends upon recognition that the numerous professions found within the industry must be based on respect for the dignity of the animals in our care, the people we serve, and the colleagues with whom we work. We must seek to establish the highest ethical standards, abiding by the codes of this registering body, and to satisfy the needs of our clients in a professional, proficient and ethically appropriate way. We must work together to ensure that the industry is not brought into disrepute. Acceptance of and adherence to this Code of Ethics is implicit for members of this registering body.

Application of the Code

The Code of Ethics applies to all members of this registering body, irrespective of grade of membership, and commits members to complying with the standards, codes, rules and procedures of the Pet Industry Executive Oversight Committee (known hereafter as The Corporation).

Please note that a lack of knowledge about or misunderstanding of this code is not in itself a defense against an allegation of unethical conduct.

Personal Code of Conduct

Professionals recognize and accept that:

1. The professional's role is one that is beneficial to the pet.
    a. Professionals always hold the pet's welfare as their top priority.
2. Professionals recognize that the pet is the vulnerable party in the consultation process as he/she cannot offer informed consent.
    a. As pets are unable to give informed consent, it is incumbent upon the professional to act for the animal's benefit and to be their voice.
3. Professionals ensure that consent from a pet's owner/guardian for working with their pet is informed by clear explanation of the nature and purpose of the procedures they intend to use. This includes:

      a. Making clear the frequency, expected duration and the client's financial commitment for the work carried out by the member for the client.
      b. Fully explaining the training philosophy that will be used for working with the pet.
      c. Answering questions from the owner with regards to the training plan.
      d. Explaining any risks or dangers related to techniques and/or tools that will be used and any consequent physical or emotional fallout that may occur.
      e. Informing the owner of the right to refuse certain equipment, methods or techniques.
      f. Informing the client that, based on developments or progress, the training plan may need to be modified.
      g. Informing the owner that no guarantee shall be offered as to the resolution of the training or behavior problem.
      h. Informing the owner that any change in methods or equipment will not be undertaken before discussion with them.
      i. Informing the owner of his/her right to terminate the contract at any time.
4. Professionals take into consideration the emotional, physical and environmental well-being of each client, i.e. both the pet and the owner/guardian of the pet.
5. Professionals do not condone or endorse any treatment by a pet's owner that in any way compromises the pet's physical or mental well-being. The professional will not be party to any such acts.
      a. If an owner insists on any treatment that in any way compromises the pet's physical or mental well-being, it is incumbent on the professional, after discussion with the owner, to terminate the relationship if agreement cannot be reached.
      b. Professionals must opt out of a consulting agreement rather than attempt to manage an unethical course of action.
6. Professionals consult within the boundaries of their own competence.
      a. Professionals will refer to other professionals whose knowledge and/or skill level is appropriate to the needs of the individual training or behavior case.
7. Professionals do not attempt or speak to or diagnose any illness or make any references to a diagnosis or medical treatment.

a. The professional will ensure that any problem related to illness or in possible need of diagnosis will be referred to an appropriate veterinary professional.
8. Professionals only use procedures, protocols and training tools that are empirically based and have a proven track record.
   a. To this end, it is incumbent upon the professional to ensure ongoing education to be fully cognizant of current best practice.
9. Professionals recognize that the pet owners are responsible for their pets and the owner has the right to make decisions about the professional treatment of their pets.
   a. The professional is bound to honor the owner's wishes or may choose to withdraw from the consultation should opinions be in conflict.
10. Professionals ensure that all communications are professional and based on fact.
    a. Professionals ensure that all communications are clear to the client by using plain language or by ensuring adequate explanation of terms used.
    b. Professionals also ensure that all communications are considered confidential unless required by law to share with appropriate authorities.
    c. Professionals seek clients' written permission if information is to be shared with other professionals:
       I. Client anonymity is essential if client case studies are to be used for educational purposes.
11. Professionals discuss, disagree with or recommend industry practices and trends based on best practice and current scientific literature.
    a. Professionals may disagree with other professionals' methods and/or their practices, but they must refrain from ad hominem attacks.
12. Professional communication with colleagues and with clients remains informed, skilled and civil.
13. Professionals apply the following ethical principles to each situation they encounter:
    - Respect for the freedom and dignity of others.
    - Do no harm.
    - Do good.
    - Act fairly.

- Be faithful to promises made.

Business Practices

1. Professionals must not lay claim, directly or indirectly, to qualifications, competencies or affiliations they do not possess.
    a. Professionals will not use the name or lay claim to membership of the registering body for financial and/or commercial gain, unless directly permitted to do so by The Corporation.
2. Professionals agree to carry professional liability insurance and care, custody and control coverage where available and mandated by local legislation.
3. Professionals act according to local and state laws in terms of reporting animal cruelty.
4. Professional adhere to all local and state laws in terms of all public and business practices.
5. Professionals consider communications with their clients to be privileged.
    a. Confidentiality is only breached if animal cruelty or welfare laws are contravened and the client cannot be dissuaded from using their current approach with immediate effect.
6. Professionals will be honest and transparent in their business marketing. This includes:
    a. Only making statements regarding their service philosophy and methods that are factually accurate.
    b. Openly stating the professional philosophy, method, and choice of operational equipment used and recommended to the client.
    c. Displaying all up-to-date and valid credentials and industry affiliations in a transparent manner.
7. Professionals will deal fairly with each other in the dissemination of professional information and advice.
8. Professionals agree to the use of the Recommended Consumer Acknowledgement Form for Transparency in Dog Training/Behavior Consulting Services (see *Appendix D: The Recommended Consumer Acknowledgement Form for Transparency in Dog Training/Behavior Consulting Services*) with each client.
9. Professionals will ensure that for each membership renewal period they are up-to-date on the requisite continuing education units (CEU).

Ethics Pledge

Professionals pledge to:

1. Use their knowledge and skills for the benefit of pets and their owners.
2. Practice their profession conscientiously, with dignity, and in keeping with this document.
3. Accept, as a lifelong obligation, the continual improvement of professional knowledge and competence.
4. Commit to the highest professional and ethical standards in any business practices and in the approach to pet training and pet care.
5. Always treat clients, i.e. both pets and their owners, with respect, kindness and caring.
6. Always respect client confidentiality.
7. Work openly and honestly with clients.
8. Work openly and honestly with industry colleagues.

Becoming a member of this registering body is an agreement to the standards, codes of practice, education and training philosophy of this corporation. Failure to abide by the Code of Ethics may result in termination of membership.

Ethics Review Process

The establishment of an Ethics Committee (known hereafter as "The Committee") will require the appointment of a Committee Chair plus a select group of other individuals comprised of the members of the registering body administration, members of the registering body and/or impartial professionals. The number of individuals needs to be adequate to allow for differing opinions; this document recommends a minimum of the Committee Chair plus three others. The key role of The Committee is to investigate any reported ethics violations (*see next section*).

Under these guidelines, the registering body will consider two types of ethics inquiries:

1. Membership Qualification Inquiries.

    - To instigate a Type 1 inquiry, the initial evidence submitted must indicate why the member may be in breach of the membership qualifications, based on the registering body's Code of Conduct. In the first instance, The Committee will refer the inquiry to the registering body's appointed Executive Director to review the member's details re: membership acceptability.

2. Alleged Ethics Violations.

- To instigate a Type 2 inquiry, the initial evidence submitted must indicate why the member's conduct is alleged to be unethical and/or is in violation of the registering body's professional ethics. In the first instance, appointed members of The Committee will review the documented evidence independently and submit their findings, along with their recommendations for any proposed action(s). The Committee Chair will make the final decision, based on the collective findings and advisories.

The Committee may choose to deal with an inquiry according to Type 1 or Type 2 or may convert an inquiry from one type to another, as appropriate.

How to Report an Ethics Violation

Reports of alleged membership violations will be handled according to the Ethics Review Policy as outlined above. Inquiries must be limited to alleged violations of the registering body's pledge, key values and professional ethics. The responsibility for the investigation of alleged membership violations is designated to the Committee Chair and members of The Committee. In addition:

- Inquiries must be made in a timely fashion; allegations of violations occurring more than thirty (30) days prior will be considered only under special circumstance, as determined by The Committee.
- Any person who feels they have been treated in a fashion that violates the ethics of the registering body may file an inquiry; The Committee will only consider inquiries filed on behalf of a third party if the inquiry is accompanied by verifiable independent evidence such as publicly available records, reports, business records, including those of a public agency, judgments of a court, marketing advertisements, commercial documents and reports, commercial publications, and the like.

- All ethics inquiries will be investigated and handled to an appropriate timeline.

Filing a Report of an Alleged Membership Violation
   a. For an inquiry to be considered, the inquirer must send the inquiry about the alleged violation, in writing, to the Committee Chair.
   b. The report must remain confidential.
   c. All violation reports must contain the following:
      I. The name of the inquirer.
      II. The name of the alleged violator.
      III. Reference to specific parts of the regulatory body's codes.
      IV. Actual text from the violated code.
      V. Details of when and where the violation was alleged to have occurred.
      VI. Details of who was involved.
      VII. Details of exactly what happened and how this relates to a breach of the Code of Ethics.

Report Receipt
   a. The Committee Chair must acknowledge receipt of the alleged violation, without comment, within 48 hours of receipt.
   b. The individual filing the report will be notified to keep the inquiry confidential.
      I. This means no information about the inquiry will be discussed with any other party.
      II. If confidentiality is breached, it may be considered a breach of the Code of Ethics.
   c. The Committee Chair will forward the inquiry to relevant parties representing The Committee within 48 hours and notify the registering body administration that an inquiry has been filed.
      I. The details of the inquiry will be kept confidential in order to preserve the registering body administration's ability to fairly and objectively interact with the member.

Investigation
   a. The Committee will review the inquiry.

I. If necessary, The Committee will gather more information and schedule an interview with the inquirer.
   b. If the initial review indicates that the alleged infraction is not a violation of the registering body's codes, then the inquirer will be notified in writing.
      I. No investigation will be pursued unless further facts or evidence are proffered.
   c. If it appears that a violation of the codes has occurred, based on preponderance of evidence (i.e. is more likely to be true than not), then the Committee Chair will notify the individual or group that are the subjects of the inquiry and provide seven (7) calendar days for a reply.
      I. If there is no reply to the inquiry notification, then The Committee will make a decision based on all available information.
   d. Once all the information has been gathered, the Committee Chair and The Committee will decide on any sanctions.
      I. These may include:
         i. The need for further education and/or mentoring.
         ii. Membership suspension.
            o From one week up to six months.
            o This may be combined with education.
         iii. Exclusion.
            o Termination of membership.

Appeal

   a. Should an individual wish to appeal The Committee's decision, ten (10) calendar days will be allocated to do so.
   b. All currently held materials plus any appeal documentation considered by The Committee will be forwarded to the Chairman of the Board and/or a Board Member.
   c. The final decision will be made by the Board of Directors within five (5) calendar days and the individual will be notified of this in writing.

Confidentiality

   a. Total confidentiality must be maintained by all involved parties throughout the entire ethics review process.
   b. A violation of confidentiality by any party involved in the matter will be considered a violation of the registering body's codes and will be dealt with accordingly.
   c. All parties involved will be notified that a determination has been made.

d. Details of the determination will remain private.

Resources

Australian Psychological Society. (2007). Code of Ethics. Melbourne, Vic: Author. Retrieved June 11, 2019, from https://www.psychology.org.au/getmedia/d873e0db-7490-46de-bb57-c31bb1553025/18APS-Code-of-Ethics.pdf

European Society of Veterinary Clinical Ethology. (2017). ESVCE Code of Ethics and Conduct. Retrieved June 11, 2019, from http://www.esvce.org/wp-content/uploads/2017/10/ESCVE-code-of-conduct-and-ethics.pdf

Pet Professional Guild. (2018). The PPG Ethics Review Process. Retrieved June 11, 2019, from http://www.petprofessionalguild.com/ThePPGEthicsCommittee

Appendix G: The Recommended Policy for Registration Renewal via Continuing Education

Continuing Education Units (CEUs) are required every 24 months to maintain a State or Regional Registered Professional designation. In order to assure a consistent, clear guideline that can be applied to all Registered Professionals, the directions set out below apply.

Eligibility and Calculation of CEUs

CEUs may be granted to the following types of educational events, herein referred to as "course/seminar" and event content **must** be based on current, scientifically valid principles.

- Academic classes.
    - Offered by an accredited academic institution, usually a college or university.
- Teleclasses.
    - Both live and recorded.
- Online classes.
- Seminars.
    - Live, live steamed and video recorded.
- Learning courses.
- Workshops.
- Educational videos.

1. CEUs will only be granted for courses/seminars where the content covers one or more of the current knowledge or skill competencies.
2. Additionally, professional development courses/seminars that fall outside the core competencies but meet all other CEU requirements are allowed. (*See Appendix B: The Recommended Model for the Assessment of a Professional's Knowledge and Skill for more on required competencies.*)

Valid Units for Attendee/Participants

- Attendees/participants will receive 1 CEU per one hour of in-class lecture time.

- Attendees/participants will receive an additional 0.5 CEU per hour of "active workshop" participation at an educational event.
    - "Active workshop" is defined as a small group of attendees working together, under the immediate direction and supervision of the event presenter or their designated assistant, with set goals to be achieved and approved by the presenter.
    - This type of registration is usually referred to as a "working" spot versus an "auditor" spot (where attendees do not participate but observe and listen).

As a Presenter

- Presenters can earn 1.5 CEUs per hour of presentation/lecture, when the course/seminar meets the subject matter and scientific qualifications. There is a maximum of eight (8) hours given for presenter CEUs.
- Animal training classes regularly offered to the general public as part of a Member's animal training and/or behavior consulting business do not qualify for CEUs.

Publications

Authoring Articles

An "article" is defined as a researched piece of work, approximately 1,000 words or more, and including references, quotes and citations. An animal industry publication is defined by the State or Regional Registering Body as the distribution of printed or electronic publications by an industry organization that may be available to the general public or as a benefit of paid membership.

- Authoring an article published in an animal industry or peer-reviewed publication which meets the subject matter and scientific criteria described above in **Eligibility and Calculation of CEUs** may qualify for 2 CEUs.
- An author may only request CEUs once per article regardless of the number of publications in which it appears.

Authoring Books

A "book" is defined as a researched piece of work, of approximately 40 pages or more, and including references, quotes and citations.

- Authoring a published book which meets the subject matter and scientific criteria described above in **Eligibility and Calculation of CEUs** may qualify for 12 CEUs.
    - 8 CEUs may be earned for a book whose target audience is the general public.
- An author may only request CEUs once per book.

Webinars

- Presenters can earn 1.5 CEUs per hour of presentation/lecture, when the course/seminar meets the subject matter and scientific qualifications outlined above in **Eligibility and Calculation of CEUs**.
- Webinars will be allocated CEUs based on the length of the webinar.

Limitations on CEU Credits

- For each full day of a course or seminar there will be a maximum of 8 CEUs per day.
- Multi-speaker courses/seminars lasting more than three days in length will not be granted more than 36 CEUs.
- Single-speaker courses/seminars, regardless of length, will not be granted more than 25 CEUs.
- Members may use no more than 25 CEUs per presenter, per recertification period, unless as part of a multi-speaker course or seminar.
- Presenters may apply and receive CEUs only once per presentation, per certification period, regardless of the number of times they deliver the same presentation within that certification period.

Application for CEU Credit

- Anyone requesting CEUs must submit their request using the appropriate application form**.

    ** *Details required for form:*

- Name and contact details of applicant
- Applying as:
    - Sponsor
    - Presenter
    - Participant
- Title of Event
- Name(s) of Presenter(s)
- Event Description
- Event Objectives
- Date(s) of Event
- Commencement and closing time of daily events:
    - Including time zone
- Address of event (if in physical location)
- List of participant hours:
    - Lecture
    - Hands on
    - Homework
- Signature of applicant

- All ongoing or on demand courses will be approved for a term of one year, from January 1 to December 31 of the same calendar year, to facilitate recertification.

Verification of Attendance

- For course/seminar events, the Host (i.e. the individual or organization hosting a course/seminar) should maintain an attendance log for all those attending.

- For webinars, teleclasses, or online courses/seminars (whether live or previously recorded), attendees should be issued with an attendance certificate listing the approved CEUs.
- For webinars, teleclasses or online courses/seminars that are live, Hosts may take attendance during the first and last 15 minutes of the course/seminar to verify attendance.

Applying for CEUs as a Host of a Program or Course

- The Host may request CEUs prior to the date of the course/seminar. The online form must be completed by the host organization.
    - Details required for application form are as ** above.

Appeal for Denied CEUs

If a CEU application is denied, the applicant may appeal to the State or Regional Registering Body. The applicant must submit evidence and information in support of the application in writing to support the appeal.

The State or Regional Registering Body may, at its sole discretion, request additional information prior to ruling on the appeal. Approval of an appeal requires a two-thirds majority of selected committee participants to pass. If the appeal is not granted by the Registering Body, the applicant may not reapply for CEUs for the same course/seminar unless the course/seminar content has been significantly altered.

Approved Educational Providers

The State or Regional Registering Body will approve institutions, courses, and third party education providers as "approved educational providers." These parties will be provided an approved "Educational Provider" badge for their website.

www.ingramcontent.com/pod-product-compliance
Lightning Source LLC
Chambersburg PA
CBHW081152290426
44108CB00018B/2519